Making Meaning®

SECOND EDITION

Funding for Developmental Studies Center has been generously provided by:

The Annenberg Foundation, Inc.

The Atlantic Philanthropies (USA) Inc.

Booth Ferris Foundation

The Robert Bowne Foundation, Inc.

The Annie E. Casey Foundation

Center for Substance Abuse Prevention
   U.S. Department of Health and Human Services

The Danforth Foundation

The DuBarry Foundation

The Ford Foundation

Google Inc.

William T. Grant Foundation

Evelyn and Walter Haas, Jr. Fund

Walter and Elise Haas Fund

The Horace Hagedorn Foundation

J. David and Pamela Hakman Family Foundation

Hasbro Children's Foundation

Charles Hayden Foundation

The William Randolph Hearst Foundations

Clarence E. Heller Charitable Foundation

The William and Flora Hewlett Foundation

The James Irvine Foundation

The Robert Wood Johnson Foundation

Walter S. Johnson Foundation

Ewing Marion Kauffman Foundation

W.K. Kellogg Foundation

John S. and James L. Knight Foundation

Lilly Endowment, Inc.

Longview Foundation

Louis R. Lurie Foundation

The John D. and Catherine T. MacArthur Foundation

A.L. Mailman Family Foundation, Inc.

The MBK Foundation

Mr. and Mrs. Sanford N. McDonnell

Mendelson Family Fund

MetLife Foundation

Charles Stewart Mott Foundation

National Institute on Drug Abuse,
   National Institutes of Health

National Science Foundation

New York Life Foundation

Nippon Life Insurance Foundation

NoVo Foundation

Karen and Christopher Payne Foundation

The Pew Charitable Trusts

The Pinkerton Foundation

The Rockefeller Foundation

Louise and Claude Rosenberg, Jr. Family Foundation

The San Francisco Foundation

Shinnyo-en Foundation

Silver Giving Foundation

The Spencer Foundation

Spunk Fund, Inc.

Stephen Bechtel Fund

W. Clement and Jessie V. Stone Foundation

Stuart Foundation

The Stupski Family Foundation

The Sulzberger Foundation, Inc.

Surdna Foundation, Inc.

John Templeton Foundation

U.S. Department of Education

The Wallace Foundation

Wells Fargo Bank

Making Meaning®

SECOND EDITION

DEVELOPMENTAL
STUDIES CENTER™

Strategies That Build
Comprehension and Community

Second edition published 2008.

Making Meaning is a registered trademark of Developmental Studies Center.

Developmental Studies Center wishes to thank the following authors, agents, and publishers for their permission to reprint materials included in this program. Many people went out of their way to help us secure these rights and we are very grateful for their support. Every effort has been made to trace the ownership of copyrighted material and to make full acknowledgment of its use. If errors or omissions have occurred, they will be corrected in subsequent editions, provided that notification is submitted in writing to the publisher.

"The Balloon Man" from *Here, There, and Everywhere* by Dorothy Aldis, copyright 1927, 1928, copyright renewed © 1955, 1956 by Dorothy Aldis. Used by permission of G.P. Putnam's Sons, a division of Penguin Young Readers Group, a member of Penguin Group (USA) Inc., 345 Hudson Street, New York, NY 10014. All rights reserved. Index from *Planet Reader: Raptors!* by Lisa McCourt. Scholastic Inc./Troll Communications. Copyright © 1997 by Lisa McCourt. Reprinted by permission. Excerpt from *A Day in the Life of a Garbage Collector* by Nate LeBoutillier. Text copyright © 2005 by Nate LeBoutillier. Reprinted by permission of Capstone Press. All rights reserved.

Developmental Studies Center
2000 Embarcadero, Suite 305
Oakland, CA 94606-5300
(800) 666-7270, fax: (510) 464-3670
devstu.org

ISBN: 978-1-59892-703-0

Printed in the United States of America

3 4 5 6 7 8 9 10 MLY 17 16 15 14 13 12

Table of Contents

continues

Acknowledgments

Many people were involved in the development and production of the *Making Meaning* program. We are grateful for their time, expertise, suggestions, and encouragement.

We wish to thank the members of our Teacher Advisory Board, who piloted the lessons and gave us expert feedback that helped shape the format and content of the program and who collaborated with us in numerous invaluable ways:

Albany Unified School District
Hannelore Kaussen
Christiane Zmich

Emeryville Unified School District
Shawna Smith
Gabrielle Thurmond

Moraga Elementary School District
Dot Cooper

Newark Unified School District
KelLee Cannis
Elizabeth Chavez
Hemawatie Dindial
Midge Fuller
Lynn Gurnee
Kara Holthe
Krissy Jensen
Joshua Reed

West Contra Costa Unified School District
Betty Buganis
Molly Curley
Simon Ellis
Sally Feldman
Nina Morita

Acknowledgments

We also wish to thank the teachers and administrators of Newark Unified School District in Newark, California, and Frayser Elementary School in the Jefferson County Public School District in Louisville, Kentucky, who field-tested the program, allowing us to observe lessons in their classrooms and providing us with feedback to help us refine the program. We particularly wish to acknowledge the following individuals:

Bunker Elementary School
Pam Abbot
Debbie Fujikawa
Katherine Jones
Judy Pino
Lisa Serra
Bob Chamberlain, *Principal*

Graham Elementary School
Shannon Carter-Steger
Pam Hughes
Belen Magers, *Principal*

Kennedy Elementary School
Jennifer Balaian
Elizabeth Chavez
Hemawatie Dindial
Midge Fuller
Lynn Gurnee
Sarah Roberts
Carol Viegelmann, *Principal*

Lincoln Elementary School
Robert Foley, *Principal*

Milani Elementary School
Jennifer Boyd
Paula Clevenger
Gail Fay
Michelle Leipelt
Karen Wetzell
Susan Guerrero, *Principal*

Musick Elementary School
Chris Scheving
Wendy Stacy
Cary Bossi, *Principal*

Schilling Elementary School
George Mathiesen, *Principal*

Snow Elementary School
Kathryn Keleher, *Principal*

Special thanks to the following individuals for their advice, feedback, writing, classroom collaboration, and many significant contributions to the program:

John Thomas, *Assessment Consultant*
Hemawatie Dindial, *Teacher, grade K*
Gail Fay, *Teacher, grade 6*
Midge Fuller, *Teacher, grade 3*

Hannelore Kaussen, *Teacher, grade 2*
Nina Morita, *Teacher, grade 1*
Karen Wetzell, *Teacher, grade 5*
Christiane Zmich, *Teacher, grade 4*

Finally, we wish to thank the many children's book publishers that assisted us during the development of this program and upon whose books these lessons are based.

Annick Press Ltd.

Barron's Educational Series, Inc.

Boyds Mills Press

Candlewick Press

Capstone Press

Charlesbridge Publishing

Child's Play USA

Chronicle Books

The Communication Project

Crabtree Publishing Company

Dawn Publications

EDC Publishing

Farrar, Straus & Giroux

Firefly Books

Grolier Publishing Company

HarperCollins Children's Books

Heinemann

Henry Holt & Company
    Books for Young Readers

Holiday House

Houghton Mifflin Harcourt
    Publishing Company

Hyperion Books for Children

Kids Can Press

Lee & Low Books

Lerner Publishers Group

Little, Brown & Company

National Book Network

Penguin Putnam
    Books for Young Readers

Persea Books

Random House Children's Books

Scholastic Inc.

Simon & Schuster

Square Fish Books

Star Bright Books

Sterling Publications

Tom Doherty Associates, LLC

Walker & Co.

Acknowledgments

This program was developed at Developmental Studies Center by:

Shaila Regan, *Senior Program Advisor*

Grady Carson, *Program Manager*

Kenni Alden, *Curriculum Developer*

Dennis Binkley, *Assistant Director of Program Development*

Susie Alldredge, *Director of Program Development*

Julie Contestable, *Contributing Writer*

Sarah Rosenthal, *Curriculum Developer*

Jackie Jacobs, *Curriculum Developer*

Laurel Robertson, *Curriculum Developer*

Mollii Khangsengsing, *Program Development Coordinator*

Charlotte MacLennan, *Manager of Libraries*

Peter Brunn, *Director of Professional Development*

Thuy Do, *Manager of Professional Development*

Neal Davis, *Curriculum Developer/ Media Specialist*

Learning Media, New Zealand, *Contributing Writer*

Annie Alcott, *Contributing Writer*

Abigayil Koss, *Contributing Writer*

Darien Meyer, *Contributing Writer*

Maddie Ruud, *Contributing Writer*

Robyn Raymer, *Contributing Writer*

Alexa Stuart, *Contributing Writer*

Nancy Johnson, *Teacher Consultant*

Lisa Alden, *Consultant*

Lori Birnbaum Galante, *Book Consultant*

Erica Hruby, *Editor/Project Manager*

Valerie Ruud, *Managing Editor*

Lisa Kent Bandini, *Director of Editorial and Design*

Ellen Toomey, *Designer*

Roberta Morris, *Art Director*

Joslyn Hidalgo, *Production Manager*

Jennie McDonald, *Manager of Publisher Relations and Rights*

Kimo Yancey, *Editorial and Rights Associate*

Scott Benoit, *Production Designer*

Garry Williams, *Designer*

Renee Benoit, *Media Production Manager*

Introduction

You hold in your hands a brand new tool for elementary school teachers. The *Making Meaning*® program is a reading comprehension curriculum for kindergarten through grade eight, and the first program of its kind to bring together the very latest research in reading comprehension with support for fostering your students' growth as caring, collaborative, and principled people.

We are well aware of the demands that elementary school teachers face in the teaching of reading today. Among those demands are the many activities that must be squeezed into the school day, the pressure of increased standardized testing, and a student population with increasingly diverse needs. The *Making Meaning* program offers maximum support for teaching reading comprehension in this environment. It is not another loosely defined program that adds hours of preparation to an already crammed to-do list. Rather, it is a fully fleshed-out curriculum that integrates easily into what you already do, incorporates an understanding of how real classrooms function, and teaches the specific strategies students need to become effective readers, at a level and pace that is accessible to everyone.

You'll notice that in this, the second edition of the *Making Meaning* program, we've added new units and lessons designed to help your students read and make sense of expository nonfiction, including science and social studies books, articles, and functional texts. In addition, we have provided you with more support for helping your English Language Learners grow as readers. (See page xxviii for more information about supporting your English Language Learners.) To enhance the home-school connection, we have included after each unit samples of letters you can send home to parents offering suggestions for supporting students' independent reading at home.

Research-based, Classroom-tested

Research documents what many teachers have known all along, that the fact that a child can read a page aloud does not mean he or she can understand it. Teaching children to make sense of what they read has been an enduring challenge in school. To address this challenge, the creators of the *Making Meaning* program drew on 20 years of research by people like P. David Pearson and Michael Pressley, who described the strategies that proficient readers naturally use and the conditions that foster those strategies in children. The *Making Meaning* program also draws on portraits from many classrooms in which reading comprehension is successfully taught, such as those described by Lucy Calkins in her work with the Reader's Workshop and by Ellin Keene and Susan Zimmerman in their book *Mosaic of Thought*. The *Making Meaning* program brings this research together in a unique yearlong curriculum of easy-to-implement daily lessons. Reading comprehension strategies are taught directly through read-aloud experiences, and the students learn to use these strategies to make sense of their own reading through guided and independent strategy practice.

The *Making Meaning* program is also unique in its focus on teaching the whole child. There is ample evidence in our society of the need to help children develop their minds in a context of caring for others, personal responsibility, empathy, and humane values. Years of research in child development reveal that children grow intellectually, socially, ethically, and emotionally in environments where their basic psychological needs are met. To this end, the *Making Meaning* program helps you create a classroom climate in which your students feel a strong sense of belonging, psychological safety, autonomy, and responsibility to themselves and the group. Teachers know that such an environment doesn't just happen; it must be deliberately created through setting up purposeful interactions among students, teaching them social and problem-solving skills, and helping them to integrate prosocial values into their lives. As you teach the *Making Meaning* lessons, you will see that the children's ability to learn reading comprehension is inextricably linked to their ability to work together and to bring democratic values like responsibility, respect, fairness, caring, and helpfulness to bear on their own behavior and interactions.

In addition to a solid research base, the *Making Meaning* program has been shaped by discussions with, and pilot testing by, a wide range of classroom teachers, to assure that it is effective and fits into the normal classroom day. It can replace an existing reading comprehension program or supplement other widely used programs, such as basal instruction, literature circles, or guided reading. It is designed to be accessible to all students, whatever their reading levels, and includes support for English Language Learners.

Please refer to the bibliography on page 343 for sources of research on reading and social and ethical development.

An Overview

The pages that follow provide a detailed scope and sequence for teaching reading comprehension at your grade level. The daily lessons revolve around clearly defined teaching objectives and build in complexity as students move through the program.

A week of lessons typically begins with a read-aloud of an engaging piece of text, followed by a whole-class discussion of what the text is about. This same read-aloud book is used on subsequent days to teach the students a comprehension strategy and to give them guided practice with the strategy. The week usually ends with the students practicing the strategy independently by using classroom library books and discussing their thinking. Each lesson typically requires 20–30 minutes of classroom time, depending on the grade level. In addition to the lessons, the students participate in Individualized Daily Reading, during which they read texts at their appropriate reading levels independently for up to 30 minutes each day.

The following comprehension strategies are taught in the *Making Meaning* program:

- Retelling
- Using schema/Making connections
- Visualizing
- Wondering/Questioning
- Making inferences
- Determining important ideas
- Understanding text structure
- Summarizing
- Synthesizing

These strategies reflect the most up-to-date research, state standards, and the standards of the National Council of Teachers of English.

Not all strategies appear at each grade level. The program begins with the most developmentally appropriate strategies in the primary grades, and additional strategies are introduced in the intermediate and upper grades.

Strategy Development in the *Making Meaning* Program

	K	1	2	3	4	5	6	7	8
Retelling	■	■	❑						
Using Schema/Making Connections	■	■	■	❑	❑	❑	❑	❑	❑
Visualizing	■	■	■	■	■	■	■	■	■
Wondering/Questioning	■	■	■	■	■	■	■	■	■
Making Inferences	❑	❑	■	■	■	■	■	■	■
Determining Important Ideas		❑	■	■	■	■	■	■	■
Understanding Text Structure		❑	■	■	■	■	■	■	■
Summarizing			❑	❑	■	■	■	■	■
Synthesizing					❑	■	■	■	■

■ formally taught   ❑ informally experienced

Putting the Program into Practice

The *Making Meaning* program includes:

- The *Teacher's Manual*, which describes the lessons in detail and provides a sequence of instruction for the academic year

- 20–30 children's trade books to use as read-alouds

- An *Assessment Resource Book* (grades 1–6) to help you regularly monitor the progress and needs of your students and class

- A *Student Response Book* for each student (grades 2–6), which coordinates with specific lessons and provides pages for response to text, recording thinking about text, journal writing, and an independent reading log

We created the *Making Meaning* program to meet the needs of a broad spectrum of classroom teachers. Both beginning and experienced teachers who piloted the program reported that it is a powerful tool that they were able to quickly and easily bring into their classrooms. Students improved not only in their reading comprehension, but also in their critical thinking and their ability to work together, regardless of setting.

Focus on Comprehension

THE GRADE 1 COMPREHENSION STRATEGIES

The strategies that follow are taught in the grade 1 level of the program.

Using Schema/Making Connections

Schema is the prior knowledge a reader brings to a text. Readers construct meaning by making connections between their prior knowledge and new information in a text. In *Making Meaning* grade 1, the students learn to connect what they know from their own experience to stories before, during, and after a read-aloud.

Retelling

Readers use retelling to identify and remember key information in a text. They focus on the important ideas or sequence of events as a way of identifying what they need to know or recall. In *Making Meaning* grade 1, the students learn to retell stories, using characters and plot to organize their thinking.

Wondering/Questioning

Proficient readers wonder and ask questions to focus their reading, clarify meaning, and delve deeper into text. They wonder what a text is about before they read, speculate about what is happening while they read, and ask questions after they read to gauge their understanding. In *Making Meaning* grade 1, the students wonder and ask questions before, during, and after a read-aloud to make sense of the text.

Visualizing

Visualizing is the process of creating mental images while reading. Mental images can include sights, sounds, smells, tastes, sensations, and emotions. Good readers form mental images to help them understand, remember, and enjoy texts. In *Making Meaning* grade 1, the students visualize to make sense of figurative language and deepen their understanding and enjoyment of poems and stories.

Making Inferences

Not everything communicated by a text is directly stated. Good readers use their prior knowledge and the information in a text to understand implied meanings. Making inferences helps readers move beyond the literal to a deeper understanding of texts. In *Making Meaning* grade 1, the students informally make inferences to think more deeply about both narrative and expository texts.

Understanding Text Structure

Proficient readers use their knowledge of narrative and expository text structure to approach and comprehend texts. For example, readers who understand that stories have common elements, such as setting, characters, and plot, have a framework for thinking about stories. Readers who understand that expository texts have common features, such as headings and subheadings, use those features to help them unlock the text's meaning. In *Making Meaning* grade 1, the students informally use story elements to help them think about stories. They also identify features of expository texts and use those features to help them understand the texts.

Determining Important Ideas

Determining the important ideas in texts helps readers identify information that is essential to know and remember. What is identified as important in a text will vary from reader to reader, depending on the purpose for reading and prior knowledge. In *Making Meaning* grade 1, the students informally explore which ideas in texts are important and support their thinking with evidence from the texts.

THINKING TOOLS

"Thinking Tools" help the students implement the strategies they are learning and delve more deeply into texts. In grades K–2, the students informally use "Stop and Wonder" as preparation for "Stop and Ask Questions," a thinking tool they learn and use in grades 3–6.

Stop and Wonder

The teacher stops at various places during a read-aloud, and the students discuss what they are hearing and wondering. When the teacher resumes reading, the students listen to hear whether what they wonder about is addressed in the text.

Focus on Social Development

Helping students to develop socially and ethically, as well as academically, is part of the educator's role and, we believe, should be integrated into every aspect of the curriculum. Social and academic learning flourish when they are integrated naturally, rather than pursued separately. During *Making Meaning* lessons, the students listen to and discuss literature in pairs, groups of four, and as a class, and through their interactions come to recognize that talking about books is a way to understand them. As they work together, they develop caring and respectful relationships, creating a safe and supportive classroom environment conducive to sharing their thinking. They are encouraged to take responsibility for their learning, be aware of the effect of their behavior on others and on their work, and relate the values of respect, fairness, caring, helpfulness, and responsibility to their behavior.

Social development objectives for each week's lessons are listed in the Overview of the week. The week's lessons provide activities, questions, and cooperative structures that target these objectives. (For a list of the cooperative structures in grade 1, see page xix.) The lessons also provide opportunities for the students to decide such things as how they will divide the work and how they will report their ideas. Learning how to make these decisions helps them become responsible group members.

Social skills chosen for emphasis at each grade level are developmentally appropriate. Within a grade, the skills vary from unit to unit, depending on the comprehension strategy being taught, the activities, and the literature used for the read-alouds. Social skills emphasized in grade 1 include talking and listening to one another, speaking clearly, sharing ideas, and respecting other people's ideas.

The lessons at the grade 1 level are designed for pair work. In Unit 1 we recommend randomly pairing the students and changing pairs frequently so that each student gets to work with a variety of partners. In Units 2–9, we suggest pairs stay together for an entire unit, which helps them develop and expand their interpersonal skills. (See "Considerations for Pairing ELLs" on page xxx.) Working with the same partner over time helps students work through and learn from problems, build successful methods of interaction, and develop their comprehension skills together.

Random pairing sends several positive messages to the students: there is no hidden agenda behind how you paired students (such as choosing pairs based on achievement); every student is considered a valuable partner; and everyone is expected to learn to work with everyone else. Random pairing also results in heterogeneous groupings over time, even though some pairs may be homogeneous in some way during any given unit (for example, both partners may be female). The box below suggests some methods for randomly pairing the students.

Some Random Pairing Methods

- Distribute playing cards and have the students pair up with someone with the same number or suit color.

- Place identical pairs of number or letter cards in a bag. Have each student pull a card out of a bag and find someone with the same number or letter.

- Cut magazine pictures in half. Give each student a picture half. Have each student pair up with the person who has the other half of the picture.

Building caring classroom relationships is the key to creating a successful learning community. Research has shown that students thrive in classroom communities that meet their basic psychological needs for autonomy, belonging, and competence. When such classrooms emphasize the importance of cooperation, collaboration, kindness, and personal responsibility, students are more likely to treat one another with respect. As a result, they feel safer and more secure in school and are more willing to take risks to share their thinking. They are better able to stand up for what they believe and be sensitive to others' feelings and opinions. Students are more likely to be motivated to learn for the sake of learning, rather than for good grades or other extrinsic rewards. They can work out problems, and they are more likely to take responsibility for their behavior and their learning.

Class meetings are an effective way to foster cooperation among students and build and strengthen community. Class meeting lessons occur regularly throughout the year. Their purposes include helping the students get to know one another, solving problems students are having working together, and checking in to follow up. (For more about class meetings, see "Class Meeting Lessons" on page xxv.)

Cooperative Structures

Cooperative structures are taught and used at every grade level to increase the students' engagement and accountability for participation. The structures help the students learn to work together, develop social skills, and take responsibility for their learning. Students talk about their thinking and hear about the thinking of others. Suggested uses of cooperative structures in the lessons are highlighted with an icon. In addition, you can use cooperative structures whenever you feel that not enough students are participating in a discussion, or, conversely, when many students want to talk at the same time.

Cooperative Structures in the Program

- **Turn to Your Partner.** The students turn to a partner sitting next to them to discuss a question.

- **Think, Pair, Share.** The students think individually about a question before discussing their thoughts with a partner. Pairs then report their thinking to another pair or to the class. This strategy is especially appropriate when the students are asked to respond to complex questions.

- **Think, Pair, Write.** As in "Think, Pair, Share," the students think individually before discussing their thoughts with a partner. The students then write what they are thinking. They might share their writing with another pair or with the class.

- **Heads Together.** Groups of four students discuss a question among themselves. Groups then might share their thoughts with the class.

- **Group Brainstorming.** Groups of four generate as many ideas as they can about a question as a group member records. These lists are then shared with the class.

In grade 1, the students learn "Turn to Your Partner" and "Think, Pair, Share." Other structures are added as developmentally appropriate.

Managing the Program

The *Making Meaning* program for grade 1 consists of nine units. The units vary in length from one to four weeks. In Units 1–3, each week has two days of instruction. In Units 4–9, each week has three days of instruction and practice. During some weeks, a class meeting replaces a day of practice. The chart below provides an overview of the year.

Grade 1

Unit / Read-aloud	Length	Focus
1 ▶ The Reading Life: Fiction and Narrative Nonfiction • *Quick as a Cricket* by Audrey Wood • *When I Was Little* by Jamie Lee Curtis • *Where Do I Live?* by Neil Chesanow • *It's Mine!* by Leo Lionni	4 weeks	• Building a reading community • Listening to and discussing stories • Learning the procedure for listening to read-alouds • Learning "Turn to Your Partner"
2 ▶ Making Connections: Fiction • *Matthew and Tilly* by Rebecca C. Jones • *McDuff and the Baby* by Rosemary Wells • *Chrysanthemum* by Kevin Henkes	3 weeks	• Making text-to-self connections to enjoy and understand stories
3 ▶ Retelling: Fiction • *Caps for Sale* by Esphyr Slobodkina • *Curious George Goes to an Ice Cream Shop* edited by Margret Rey and Alan J. Shalleck • *Peter's Chair* by Ezra Jack Keats	3 weeks	• Using the sequence of events to retell stories
4 ▶ Visualizing: Poetry and Fiction • *Did You See What I Saw? Poems about School* by Kay Winters • "The Balloon Man" by Dorothy Aldis • *In the Tall, Tall Grass* by Denise Fleming • *Sheep Out to Eat* by Nancy Shaw • *The Snowy Day* by Ezra Jack Keats	4 weeks	• Visualizing and describing images that a text brings to mind • Learning "Think, Pair, Share"
5 ▶ Wondering: Fiction and Narrative Nonfiction • *An Extraordinary Egg* by Leo Lionni • *George Washington and the General's Dog* by Frank Murphy • *Down the Road* by Alice Schertle	3 weeks	• Using wondering to understand fiction and nonfiction texts

Grade 1 *(continued)*

Unit / Read-aloud	Length	Focus
6 ▶ Making Connections: Expository Nonfiction • *Hearing* by Sharon Gordon • *A Good Night's Sleep* by Allan Fowler • *Dinosaur Babies* by Lucille Recht Penner	3 weeks	• Using background knowledge and making text-to-self connections to understand nonfiction texts
7 ▶ Wondering: Expository Nonfiction • *A Kangaroo Joey Grows Up* by Joan Hewett • *A Harbor Seal Pup Grows Up* by Joan Hewett • *Throw Your Tooth on the Roof* by Selby B. Beeler • *A Look at Teeth* by Allan Fowler	3 weeks	• Using background knowledge, retelling, and wondering to understand nonfiction texts
8 ▶ Exploring Text Features: Expository Nonfiction • *Raptors!* by Lisa McCourt • *A Day in the Life of a Garbage Collector* by Nate LeBoutillier • *An Elephant Grows Up* by Anastasia Suen	3 weeks	• Exploring expository text features
9 ▶ Revisiting the Reading Life • *Julius* by Angela Johnson	1 week	• Reflecting on the students' growth as readers

USING THE UNIT AND WEEK OVERVIEWS

To prepare for a *Making Meaning* unit, begin by reading the unit Overview. It will acquaint you with the goals of the unit and the literature used during each week of the unit. It will also alert you to the social skills and values that will be emphasized, based on the type of student interaction likely to occur in the lessons.

Prepare for each week by reading the week Overview and previewing the week. This will help you see how instruction flows from lesson to lesson and alert you to any advance preparations or special requirements for the week.

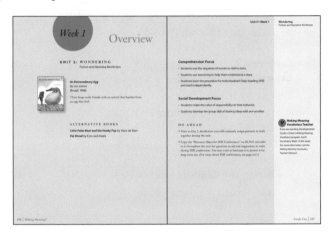

PREPARING THE LESSONS

The two- or three-day weeks in *Making Meaning* grade 1 generally follow this pattern:

Day 1	Day 2	Day 3
Read-aloud & (beginning in Unit 5) **Individualized Daily Reading (IDR)**	**Strategy Lesson &** (beginning in Unit 5) **IDR**	(beginning in Unit 4) **Strategy Practice &** (beginning in Unit 5) **IDR**

Some weeks may vary from this pattern, and periodically a class meeting lesson will substitute for one of the days. Each of the lesson types is described below.

Read-aloud Lessons

Students' listening comprehension typically exceeds their reading comprehension. Listening to and discussing texts together enables them to build background knowledge and vocabulary, enjoy a common experience, build community, share ideas, and collaborate to construct meaning. Every week begins with a read-aloud lesson. After the reading, discussion questions check the students' surface-level understanding of the text in preparation for exploring a comprehension strategy with the text on the following day.

To Prepare for a Read-aloud:

- Read the entire lesson and anticipate how your students will respond.

- Collect materials and anticipate room arrangement needs.

- Practice reading the text aloud. Focus on reading slowly.

- Review the Suggested Vocabulary and the ELL (English Language Learner) Vocabulary lists and locate these words in the text. To better define these words smoothly while reading aloud, write each definition on a self-stick note and place the note next to the word in the read-aloud. Notice if there are any additional words you will need to define for your students.

- Locate any suggested stopping points in the text. Again, you might use a self-stick note to mark each stopping point.

- Decide what level of support your English Language Learners will need. You might need to read the story aloud to your ELLs prior to the whole-class read-aloud or summarize the story for them. (For a list of *Making Meaning* read-aloud titles available in Spanish, visit devstu.org/downloads.) Also, review any ELL Notes in the lesson and provide extra support for your students as appropriate. (See page xxviii for more information about supporting your English Language Learners.)

- Extensions appear at the end of some lessons. Review and decide on any extensions you want to do with your class. Some may require additional materials or preparation.

Alternative Books

You may want to substitute another book for the provided read-aloud text. In the Overview of the week, you will find some suggestions for books that are suitable for teaching the comprehension focus of the week. You can also use an alternative book if you decide to repeat a week of instruction.

The alternative books suggested in the *Making Meaning* program are offered in Developmental Studies Center's Comprehension Strategies Libraries. These grade-level libraries (grades K–8) of 20–26 trade books are designed to support instruction in the specific strategies used in the lessons. Visit Developmental Studies Center's website at devstu.org for more information.

Strategy Lessons

The strategy lesson introduces the strategy that is the comprehension focus for the week. Typically, you will reread the read-aloud book from Day 1 and ask questions that help your students move beyond the surface meaning to a deeper exploration of the text. You will then guide the students to develop their understanding through carefully structured activities. This approach encourages the students to explore and develop a strategy before you explicitly label it.

To Prepare for a Strategy Lesson:

- Read the entire lesson and anticipate how your students will respond.

- Collect materials and anticipate room arrangement needs.

- Practice using the strategy at least once in your own reading to help you anticipate difficulties the students might have.

- Plan how you will pace the lesson to keep it moving. A lesson is designed to take 20–30 minutes on average.

- Review suggested discussion questions and decide which ones you will ask.

- Always remember that making meaning of text—not using a particular strategy—is the primary goal of the program. Keep discussions focused on the text and remind the students that strategies serve readers by helping them understand what they read.

- Review and plan any extensions you want to do with your class.

Strategy Practice Lessons

In the latter part of grade 1, the strategy lesson is followed by a strategy practice lesson, with teacher support gradually reducing as the students become more comfortable with the strategy. The students practice using the strategy with a text they have heard you read aloud, and you facilitate and support their work by asking focused questions and guiding discussion. You monitor the students and provide individual help as needed.

To Prepare for a Strategy Practice Lesson:

- Read the entire lesson and collect materials.

- Practice any teacher modeling required in the lesson.

- Plan how you will pace the lesson to keep it moving.

- Review suggested discussion questions and decide which ones you will ask.

- Review and plan any extensions you want to do with your class.

Class Meeting Lessons

Class meeting lessons happen periodically throughout the year and are designed to help build the reading community, a critical element in the success of the *Making Meaning* program. Class meetings usually occur on the last day of a week, although sometimes they are suggested on other days. Early in the year, class meetings focus on helping you and your students establish a caring, collaborative reading community. Subsequent class meetings focus on checking in to see how the students are doing and on solving problems with working together.

To Prepare for a Class Meeting Lesson:

- Read the entire lesson and collect materials.

- Anticipate room arrangement needs for the class meeting.

- Plan how you will introduce the topic of the class meeting.

- Plan how you will facilitate the discussion so it feels safe to discuss problems (for example, reminding the students to say "people" instead of using names).

- Plan where you might use a cooperative structure to increase participation and accountability.

INDIVIDUALIZED DAILY READING (IDR)

Making Meaning includes an Individualized Daily Reading (IDR) component, which is introduced in the second half of grade 1. During IDR, the students spend up to 20 minutes a day independently reading books at their appropriate reading levels.

The Teacher's Role

Individualized Daily Reading in the *Making Meaning* program is different from other types of independent reading, such as free reading, SSR (Sustained Silent Reading), and DEAR (Drop Everything and Read). In those programs, students select their own books, which may or may not be at their appropriate reading levels, and the teacher plays a largely neutral role. In IDR, the students read texts at their appropriate reading levels for a specified period of time. You, the teacher, are actively involved, conferring with individual students, helping them select appropriate books, and assessing and supporting their reading as they read.

IDR Conferences

In grade 1, the students begin informal independent reading early in the year. When the formal IDR program is introduced to the students in Unit 5, you will teach the students your expectations for IDR and for using the classroom library. Early in the year, your IDR conferences will focus on ensuring that the students are reading appropriately leveled books and on getting to know the students as readers. As the year progresses, your conferences will focus more on assessing the students' comprehension, and supporting struggling readers.

In Unit 5, you will begin using the "Resource Sheet for IDR Conferences" (BLM13). This is a list of questions and suggestions to help you probe the students' thinking. Also in Unit 5, you will begin to document some of your IDR conferences using the "IDR Conference Notes" record sheet (BLM14). We recommend that you document at least one IDR conference per student per unit. Over time, these notes will become an important source of information about each student's growth as a reader (see "Assessment" on page xxxv). Blackline masters for the resource sheet and conference notes can also be found at the end of the *Assessment Resource Book*.

Reading Appropriately Leveled Books

For IDR to succeed, the students must be reading books they can comprehend and read fluently with few miscues (accuracy errors). Early in the year, you can match students to books by informally assessing their reading ability. One procedure you might use is to have the students select books that interest them, and then listen to each student read aloud. Note whether the student is reading with accuracy (reading most of the words without miscues) and understanding. To gauge a student's surface understanding, you can use prompts and questions such as "Tell me what you just read" or "What does that mean?" If a student is reading a book that is too difficult or easy, help her select a more suitable book.

Another technique for evaluating the appropriateness of a book is the "five finger rule." As a student reads a page aloud, count any words he doesn't know. More than five unknown words on a page usually indicates that the book is too difficult. When your students become familiar with the five finger rule, you can encourage them to use the technique on their own, making them responsible for checking the appropriateness of the books they choose for IDR.

It is very important for the students to build reading fluency as a foundation for comprehension. If you have students who are reading far below grade level, make sure they have time every day to practice reading decodable texts, and check in regularly to monitor their rate and accuracy.

Setting Up a Leveled Classroom Library

For IDR the students will require access to a wide range of narrative and expository texts at various levels. For easy browsing, you might display books in boxes or baskets labeled with the name of the book category. Categories can include:

- Genres (e.g., mystery, science fiction, folktale, biography)
- Subjects or topics (e.g., presidents, animals, weather, school)
- Themes (e.g., faraway places, friendship, growing up)
- Favorite authors or illustrators
- Popular series
- Student favorites

A classroom library ideally consists of 300–400 titles, although many teachers start with a smaller collection and add to it over time. The library should include a balance of fiction and nonfiction books. To address various reading levels, at least 25 percent of the library should be books one to two grades below grade level, and at least 25 percent should be books one to two grades above grade level.

Sources of texts include book clubs, bookstores, your school or community library, donated books, basal readers, textbooks, and children's magazines and newspapers. You can purchase a leveled classroom library, or you can level the books in your current classroom library.

Developmental Studies Center's Individualized Daily Reading Libraries can be used to start an excellent independent reading classroom library or to round out an existing library. The libraries are organized by grade level (K–8) and readability to enable teachers to provide "just right" fiction and nonfiction books for their students. Visit Developmental Studies Center's website at devstu.org for more information.

Leveling Books

Following is information on two leveling systems that can help you with the sometimes difficult and time-consuming process of leveling books. (More information about leveling can be found in Brenda M. Weaver's *Leveling Books K–6: Matching Readers to Text*.)

- **The Pinnell and Fountas Leveling System**

  Educators Gay Su Pinnell and Irene C. Fountas developed a leveling system for use with guided reading groups that is frequently used for leveling independent reading libraries. They provide lists of thousands of leveled books for grades K–8 in their book *Leveled Books, K–8: Matching Texts to Readers for Effective Teaching* (Heinemann, 2006) and on their website, fountasandpinnellleveledbooks.com.

- **The Lexile Framework**

  This leveling system uses a sophisticated formula to determine text difficulty, which it represents as a Lexile score, and then ranks the text on a graded scale. For example, a text with a score of 400 is "ranked" at approximately grade 2. Developers of the framework (MetaMetrics, Inc.) have created a database of more than 30,000 Lexiled titles plus software that allows teachers to search, sort, and view details on the titles. For more information, visit the Lexile Framework for Reading website at lexile.com.

SUPPORT FOR ENGLISH LANGUAGE LEARNERS (ELLs)

The *Making Meaning* program helps you implement effective teaching strategies to meet the needs of all children, including English Language Learners (ELLs). English Language Development strategies are an inherent part of the program's design. In addition, through ELL Notes, we provide you with suggestions for modifying the instruction to enhance support for ELLs.

While the *Making Meaning* program is an effective tool in teaching comprehension to ELLs, it is not intended to stand alone as a comprehensive linguistic development program. It is assumed that additional support in second language acquisition is occurring for ELLs outside of this program.

About Teaching Reading Comprehension to ELLs

One myth about teaching ELLs is that good teaching alone will meet their linguistic and academic needs, and that they will simply "pick up" the language in the typical classroom context. While certainly "good teaching" (developmental, research-based instructional strategies) enormously benefits learners of English, it is important to target their specific academic and linguistic strengths and needs. The first step is to develop an accurate picture of each child's English language proficiency level and previous academic experience.

Stages of Second Language Acquisition

As you know, learning a new language is a developmental process. The following chart outlines the generally accepted stages of acquiring a second language, and characteristics of students at each stage. Progress from one stage to the next depends on a wide variety of factors, including cognitive and social development and maturity, previous academic experience, family education and home literacy practices, personality, cultural background, and individual learning styles.

Stages of Second Language Acquisition	
Developmental Stages of Language Proficiency (under immersion)	**Student Characteristics**
Stage 1: Receptive or Preproduction (can last up to 6 months)	• Often "silent" during this period • Acquires receptive vocabulary (words and ideas that children "take in" or learn before they begin to produce words verbally) • Conveys understanding through drawing, writing, and gesturing • Gradually becomes more comfortable in the classroom
Stage 2: Early Production (can last up to 6 months)	• Uses one- to two-word answers • Verbally labels and categorizes • Listens more attentively • Writes words and some simple sentences
Stage 3: Speech Emergence (can last 6 months to 1 year)	• Speaks in phrases, short sentences • Sequences stories using words and pictures • Writes simple sentences
Stage 4: Intermediate Proficiency (can last 1 to 3 years)	• Uses increased vocabulary • Speaks, reads, and writes more complex sentences • Demonstrates higher order skills, such as analyzing, predicting, debating, etc.
Stage 5: Advanced Proficiency (can last 1 to 3 years)	• Demonstrates a high level of comprehension • Continues to develop academic vocabulary • Continues to speak, read, and write increasingly complex sentences

Considerations for Pairing ELLs

A key practice in the *Making Meaning* program is to have students work in unit-long partnerships. Random pairing is suggested as a way to ensure equity by reinforcing the value of each child in the classroom (see "Random Pairing" on page xviii). However, when considering the needs of English Language Learners, it may be advantageous to partner your ELLs in a more strategic way. For example, you might pair a beginning English speaker with a fluent English or bilingual speaker. It can be effective if the bilingual partner shares the ELL's native language, but we recommend prudence in asking the more fluent bilingual speaker to serve as translator. Another option is to place ELLs in trios with fluent English speakers to allow them more opportunity to hear the language spoken in conversation. In this case, it is important to make sure that all three students are participating and including one another in the work.

How the *Making Meaning* Program Supports ELLs

There are a number of effective English Language Development (ELD) instructional strategies integrated throughout the *Making Meaning* program. These strategies help make the content comprehensible, support students at their individual level of language proficiency, and help students see themselves as valuable members of the classroom community. They include the strategies shown in the chart below.

ELD Strategies in the *Making Meaning* Program	
Emphasis on making content comprehensible	• Opportunities for meaningful listening, speaking, and reading • Rereading text • Questions appropriate to proficiency level • Explicit teacher modeling • Drawing on prior knowledge and experience
Visual aids and engaging materials	• Rich, meaningful literature • Engaging book art
Explicit vocabulary instruction	• Opportunities to preview and discuss read-alouds before lessons • Building academic vocabulary • Brainstorming words
Creating a respectful, safe, learning community	• Active, responsible learning • High expectations for classroom interactions • Explicit classroom procedures and routines • Explicit social skills instruction • Regular discussions to reflect on classroom values and community
Cooperative learning	• Cooperative structures such as "Turn to Your Partner" and "Think, Pair, Share" • Ongoing peer partnerships • Opportunities to express thinking orally and listen to others' thinking • Sharing work and reflecting

Additional Strategies for Supporting ELLs

In addition to the practices embedded in the *Making Meaning* lessons, ELL Notes provide specific suggestions for adapting instruction to meet the needs of English Language Learners. In addition, you can implement a number of general strategies to help ELLs participate more fully in the program. These include:

- **Speaking slowly.** Beginning English speakers can miss a great deal when the language goes by too quickly. Modifying your rate of speech can make a big difference in helping your beginning English speakers understand you.

- **Using visual aids and technology.** Photographs, real objects, diagrams, and even quick sketches on the board can help to increase a student's comprehension. When giving directions, physically modeling the steps and writing the steps on the board while saying them aloud are effective ways to boost comprehension. Technology, such as books on tape or CD, can also be helpful.

- **Inviting expression through movement and art.** Having students express their thinking through movement and art can be enormously powerful. Drawing, painting, dancing, mimicking, role-playing, acting, singing, and chanting rhymes are effective ways for children to increase comprehension, build vocabulary, and convey understanding. The Total Physical Response (TPR) method, developed by James Asher, helps children build concepts and vocabulary by giving them increasingly complex verbal prompts (stand, sit, jump, etc.) that they act out physically and nonverbally (see the bibliography).

- **Building vocabulary.** ELL vocabulary is highlighted for most read-alouds in the program, and we recommend that you introduce this vocabulary and define it during the reading. In addition, prior to the read-aloud you might brainstorm words related to the text. The students can then illustrate each word and post the illustration next to the printed word, creating a visual chart to refer to as they listen to the read-aloud.

- **Preteaching.** It is always a good idea to preteach concepts with ELLs whenever possible. This could mean previewing vocabulary, doing a picture walk of a story, or looking at real objects or photographs before a lesson. Preteaching in a child's native language can be particularly effective— teachers, instructional aides, parents, or other community members can be enlisted to help.

- **Simplifying questions.** Open-ended questions are used throughout the *Making Meaning* program to elicit language and higher-order thinking from students. These questions are often more complex in structure than closed or one-word-answer questions. While all learners, including English Language Learners, benefit from the opportunity to consider such questions, you might periodically modify a complicated question into a simpler one to increase comprehension and participation by your ELLs. The chart below lists some suggestions for simplifying questions.

Suggestions for Simplifying Questions

Suggestion	Original Question	Simplified Question
Use the simple present tense.	What was happening at the beginning of the story?	What happens at the beginning of the story?
Use active rather than passive voice.	How was the window broken in the story?	Who broke the window in the story?
Ask *who/what/where/when* questions rather than *how/why* questions.	How are you and your partner working together?	What do you and your partner do to work well together?
Avoid the subjunctive.	After hearing this part of the book, what do you think raptors might have looked like?	The part of the book we read today describes raptors. What do you think raptors looked like?
Provide definitions in the question.	Why is the old woman so reluctant to name the dog?	The old woman does not want to name the dog. She is reluctant. Why?
Provide context clues as part of the question.	Why is Sally Jane's visit to the reservoir important?	At the end of the story, Sally Jane visits the reservoir and thinks about what her mother said. What is important about that?
Elicit nonverbal responses.	What do you see in this picture that tells about the words?	This picture shows the sentence "I like to paint." Point to the paints. Point to the paintbrushes.
Elicit 1- and 2-word answer responses.	What do you think will happen when Peter puts the snowball in his pocket?	Peter puts the snowball in his pocket. Is that a good idea?

- **Assessing comprehension.** When students are in the preproduction and early production stages of language acquisition, it can be hard to assess exactly what they understand. It is important not to confuse lack of verbal response with lack of understanding. Rather than force ELLs to produce language before they are ready (which can raise anxiety and inhibit their progress), you can assess nonverbal responses while the students are actively engaged by asking yourself questions such as:

  Q *Do the student's drawings and written symbols communicate thinking or show evidence of my teaching (such as drawing the problem and the solution in a story)?*

  Q *Does the student nod, laugh, or demonstrate engagement through other facial expressions?*

  Q *Does the student pick up academic and social cues from peers?*

  Q *Does the student follow classroom signals and routines?*

  Q *Does the student follow simple directions (such as "Please get out your pencils")?*

  Q *Does the student utter, chant, or sing some familiar words or phrases?*

Additional Modifications for English Language Learners

The English Language Development strategies outlined below can help you better meet the specific linguistic needs of your ELLs. These strategies can be implemented in small groups with your English Language Learners.

Read-aloud Lessons

- **Preview vocabulary.** Ask ELLs to draw or act out vocabulary and encourage them to give examples.

- **Take a picture walk.** Give ELLs an opportunity to become familiar with the illustrations in a story and make predictions to increase comprehension.

- **Modify cooperative structures.** Provide question prompts for verbal ELLs to use in partner conversations (for example, "Ask your partner, 'What will happen next?'") and allow nonverbal ELL students to gesture, draw, dramatize or write their ideas for their partners.

Strategy Lessons

- **Use multiple modalities.** Allow ELLs to use drama, drawing, realia, and writing in practicing comprehension strategies.

- **Create visual aids.** Use chart paper or the board to record the important parts of whole-class discussions.

- **Review vocabulary.** Emphasize vocabulary and story language to help ELLs make sense of the story and use vocabulary meaningfully.

Strategy Practice Lessons

- **Role-play or reenact parts of the text.** Encourage ELLs to demonstrate comprehension through active means.

- **Use journals.** Ask ELLs to draw or draw and label in a journal to express their ideas. Have them share their drawing or writing with a partner as a "rehearsal" before sharing with the whole group.

- **Use visualizing.** Provide opportunities for the students to create and describe mental pictures from the text as a way to enhance comprehension.

- **Review the strategy.** While students are working independently, have ELLs work in small groups to reinforce the strategy. Check in with groups to assess the students' comprehension.

- **Have pairs or small groups share.** Have ELLs work in pairs or small groups to present their ideas to the whole class.

- **Prepare for whole-class discussions.** Support participation in whole-class discussions by giving ELLs time to "rehearse" what they want to share. Encourage them to share examples from the text or bring in their own pictures or written materials.

Individualized Daily Reading (IDR)

IDR is an excellent opportunity to provide ELLs with targeted comprehension support. Here are several ways to differentiate instruction during IDR:

- **Provide books on tape or compact disc.** Provide a variety of stories on cassette or CD so ELLs can listen to a story, hear standard pronunciation, develop story language, and increase their understanding.

- **Use partner reading.** Have ELLs read a story with a partner.

- **Respond to literature.** Ask ELLs to draw or write a response to the book they are reading independently (for example, draw the main character or write a sentence describing the problem in the story).

- **Offer one-on-one support.** Enlist instructional assistants, student tutors, student teachers, native language speakers, and parents to read individually with ELL students during IDR.

By carefully observing your English Language Learners and employing some of the strategies suggested above (as well as those in the ELL Notes in the lessons), you will be able to support their development as readers and as caring, responsible participants in your writing community.

OTHER PROGRAM FEATURES

Assessment

The assessment component in the *Making Meaning* program is designed to help you (1) make informed instructional decisions as you teach the lessons and (2) track students' reading comprehension and social development over time. The expectation is that *all* of your students are developing at their own pace into readers with high levels of comprehension and that they can all develop positive, effective interpersonal skills and values.

The assessments in grade 1 are Class Progress Assessments (CPA), done once a week to help you assess the performance and needs of the whole class. As you follow the lessons in the *Teacher's Manual*, an assessment box and icon will alert you whenever a CPA is suggested. The assessment box will also direct you to the corresponding page in the *Assessment Resource Book*. During a CPA, you randomly observe students working in pairs or individually (selecting strong, average, and struggling readers) as you ask yourself key questions. Assessments target both reading comprehension and social development objectives. Each week's CPA record sheet in the assessment book gives you space to record your observations.

- **IDR Conference Notes**

  Your notes from the IDR conferences you have with students beginning in Unit 5 are an important source of information about each student's development over time. While you do not need to document every IDR conference you have, it is important to document at least one conference per unit per student, using the "IDR Conference Notes" record sheet (BLM14). We suggest that you create individual student folders to collect each student's conference notes for use in discussing the student's progress with the student or others.

The *Assessment Resource Book* and other reproducible materials are available on CD-ROM. Visit Developmental Studies Center's website at devstu.org for more information.

Facilitating Discussions

In the *Making Meaning* program, the students' learning relies on their ability to listen and respond to one another's ideas. As most teachers know, these skills are not innate for many students—students need to learn how to listen and how to take one another's thinking seriously.

In the *Making Meaning* program, these skills are taught directly through careful teacher facilitation of discussions. Facilitation tips included throughout the year suggest techniques you can use to facilitate class discussions among your students (for example, asking open-ended questions, using wait-time, and not paraphrasing or repeating students' responses).

The Teacher's Facilitation Bookmark (BLM12), which is introduced in Unit 3, is your resource for questions and suggestions you can use to facilitate these class discussions.

Parent Letters

Each unit in the *Making Meaning* program includes a letter informing parents about the most recent comprehension strategy and social skill their child has learned. Each letter also offers suggestions for supporting students' independent reading at home. Parent letters help strengthen the home-school connection and give parents a way to be actively involved in their children's reading lives. You will find a note referring to the blackline master of the parent letter at the end of each unit.

Making Meaning® Vocabulary

The *Making Meaning Vocabulary* program is a supplemental vocabulary component tied to *Making Meaning*. *Making Meaning Vocabulary* supports students' comprehension by giving them a deeper understanding of words taken directly from *Making Meaning* read-alouds. *Making Meaning Vocabulary* Notes at the end of each week of instruction direct you to the corresponding *Making Meaning Vocabulary* lessons. For more information about *Making Meaning Vocabulary*, see page xxxvii.

USING *MAKING MEANING* AS PART OF A COMPLETE LANGUAGE ARTS PROGRAM

While the *Making Meaning* program is designed to serve as the comprehension component of any reading program you may be using, Developmental Studies Center has developed a set of language arts curricula that can be used in conjunction with *Making Meaning* as components in a more complete language arts program. Following are suggestions for integrating the *Making Meaning* program with Developmental Studies Center's other programs. For information on any of Developmental Studies Center's programs, visit our website at devstu.org.

Being a Writer™

The *Being a Writer* program is a yearlong curriculum for grades K–6 designed to help each student develop the creativity and skills of a writer. *Being a Writer* provides inspiration and motivation and a clear scope and sequence to develop students' intrinsic desire to write regularly and to help students build a full understanding of and appreciation for the craft and conventions of writing.

The *Being a Writer* program can be used alongside *Making Meaning* to teach the craft, skills, and conventions of writing. Some read-aloud books are used in both the *Making Meaning* and *Being a Writer* programs. This allows the students to explore a book from the points of view of both writers and readers.

If you are teaching both programs, we recommend that you start teaching them simultaneously at the beginning of the year. This will ensure that the books used in both programs are encountered first in *Making Meaning*, where the students can gain both a surface-level and a deeper understanding of the text, before working with the books from the point of view of writers. The *Being a Write*r program includes specific suggestions for implementing it in conjunction with *Making Meaning* at your grade level.

Making Meaning Vocabulary

The *Making Meaning Vocabulary* program is intended as a supplement to *Making Meaning* lessons. In the program, students learn from four to six words each week (four words at grades K–2; six words at grades 3–6). The words in the *Making Meaning Vocabulary* program are taken from the *Making Meaning* read-aloud texts. Students at grades 2 and above also learn independent word-learning strategies, such as recognizing words with multiple meanings and using context and affixes (prefixes and suffixes) to figure out word meanings.

In *Making Meaning Vocabulary* lessons, the students are introduced to each word as it is used in the read-aloud, and then practice using the word through teacher-directed instruction and discussion. Review activities are provided each week to reinforce students' understanding of previously taught words. The program also includes class and individual student assessments.

Guided Spelling™

In Developmental Studies Center's *Guided Spelling* program, daily dictation is infused with instruction in spelling, phoneme awareness, phonics, and memorization strategies to promote understanding and improve accuracy and transfer to writing. The *Guided Spelling* program helps students be successful by providing them with guidance before and during writing so that they spell dictated words correctly. Because it assures success, *Guided Spelling* instruction leads to student self-confidence and interest in spelling. The *Guided Spelling* program is designed to be the spelling component in any language arts curriculum.

SIPPS®

In the *SIPPS* (Systematic Instruction in Phoneme Awareness, Phonics, and Sight Words) decoding program, instruction is explicit and teacher-directed, with group responses and extensive student involvement. *SIPPS* can be used in conjunction with *Making Meaning* lessons as part of a balanced language arts program in which you use *SIPPS* to teach decoding and the *Making Meaning* program to teach comprehension strategies.

INTEGRATING *MAKING MEANING* WITH OTHER READING/LANGUAGE ARTS PROGRAMS

The *Making Meaning* program is designed to replace or enhance any comprehension program you may be using. How you integrate it with other components of your language arts program depends on the type of program you have. Following are suggestions for integrating *Making Meaning* with basal programs and programs that use literature circles and guided reading.

Basal Programs

In many basal programs, comprehension instruction and language arts skills instruction are closely interconnected through each week's selection of literature. A single book or reading might be used to teach the week's comprehension, grammar, spelling, word study, and writing. The *Making Meaning* program can enhance the intellectual and social impact of these programs significantly. Here are some suggestions for integrating *Making Meaning* lessons with basal programs:

- *Making Meaning* grade 1 is designed in two- or three-day weeks. This allows you to read the week's basal anthology selection on Monday, so the week's spelling, writing, grammar, and other language arts skills instruction can be linked to that reading. *Making Meaning* lessons can then be used to replace the basal's comprehension lessons during the rest of the week.

- In addition to other reading materials, basal anthologies can be used as independent reading material during Individualized Daily Reading (IDR).

- The basal anthology selection can be used as the read-aloud text if you decide to repeat a week of instruction in the *Making Meaning* program.

Literature Circles

The *Making Meaning* program can support and enhance the work the students do in literature circles. The students can practice and strengthen the social development skills they have learned in *Making Meaning*, such as listening to others and explaining their thinking, as they interact in their circles. They can also apply the comprehension strategies they are learning to their literature circle selections, thereby building their understanding of the strategies and gaining experience in applying them to their personal, day-to-day reading. When the students are reading expository texts or narrative texts in the *Making Meaning* program, they can select the same type of text for their literature circle, and they can use IDR time in the program to read their circle selections.

Guided Reading

The *Making Meaning* program integrates well with a reading program that includes guided reading, which is also strategy-based. *Making Meaning* lessons can serve as the primary source of comprehension instruction, with guided reading providing extra support to students who need additional instruction and practice in using the strategies. The alternative books recommended in the weekly Overviews of *Making Meaning* can serve as texts for guided reading instruction.

Unit 1

The Reading Life

FICTION AND NARRATIVE NONFICTION

During this unit, the students make text-to-self connections and answer questions to understand stories. Socially, they learn the procedures for read-alouds and "Turn to Your Partner." As they build a reading community and take responsibility for their learning and behavior, they develop the group skill of listening to one another.

Week 1 *Quick as a Cricket* by Audrey Wood

Week 2 *When I Was Little* by Jamie Lee Curtis

Week 3 *Where Do I Live?* by Neil Chesanow

Week 4 *It's Mine!* by Leo Lionni

Week 1 Overview

UNIT 1: THE READING LIFE
Fiction and Narrative Nonfiction

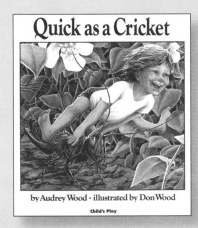

Quick as a Cricket
by Audrey Wood, illustrated by Don Wood
(Child's Play, 1982)

A young boy describes himself using characteristics of various animals.

ALTERNATIVE BOOKS

Animals Should Definitely <u>Not</u> Wear Clothing by Judi Barrett

Elephants Swim by Linda Capus Riley

Comprehension Focus

- Students *make text-to-self connections*.

- Students *answer questions* to understand a story.

Social Development Focus

- Teacher and students build a reading community.

- Students learn the procedure for a read-aloud.

- Students take responsibility for their learning and behavior.

- Students develop the group skill of listening to one another.

DO AHEAD

- Prepare a piece of chart paper with the title "Reading Together" for Day 2.

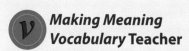

Making Meaning Vocabulary Teacher

Next week you will begin the *Making Meaning Vocabulary* program. (See page xxxvi for more information about the program.)

Read-aloud

In this lesson, the students:

- Hear and discuss a story
- Learn and practice the procedure for a read-aloud
- Listen to one another
- Take responsibility for themselves

1 Introduce the Reading Community

Introduce the *Making Meaning* program by telling the students that this year they will hear, think about, and talk about books together. They will share their ideas with the class. They will become a community of readers—a community in which everyone feels welcome and safe.

2 Learn and Practice the Read-aloud Procedure

Explain that today the students will learn some ways to act that will help them when they hear and talk about stories. Explain and model where you will sit and where and how the students will sit for read-alouds. (For example, you might ask two students to come to the rug and sit facing you, or sit in their seats facing you and the book.) Before asking the students to move, state your expectations clearly. (You might say, "I expect you to walk quietly without bumping into others. I want you to wait quietly and sit so that others have room on the rug.")

Have two students model getting ready for a read-aloud while the other students observe. Invite other pairs to join the group. As the students practice, comment on what you observe. (For example, you might say, "I notice people are sitting toward the front of the rug so that others can sit behind them.")

If necessary, have the students practice again until they are able to move to their places in an orderly way. Explain that you would like

Materials

- *Quick as a Cricket*

Teacher Note

Before the lesson, establish a place to come together for read-alouds (for example, you might have the students come to a rug area or sit at their tables or desks so that they can easily see the book and the illustrations). In the lessons, the gathering place is referred to as the rug; but you can use any place that is comfortable and convenient for your classroom situation.

them to do the same thing every time they gather for a read-aloud and that they will have other chances to practice.

After the students have moved to their places, ask:

Q *When we come together to listen to a story, what should we do?*

Before reading, state your expectations about the way the students will listen to and talk about the story. (You might say, "I would like you to sit facing forward, not touching anyone else. I would like you to look at the illustrations as I read. When we talk about the story, I want you to sit quietly and listen. When we talk as a class, one person will talk at a time and everyone else will look at the person who's talking.")

 Introduce *Quick as a Cricket*

Show the cover of *Quick as a Cricket* and read the title and names of the author and illustrator aloud. Explain that the author is the person who writes the story and the illustrator is the person who draws the pictures. Point to the words and have the students reread the title and names with you.

Point out the cricket and the boy. Explain that the boy in the story thinks he is like some animals and bugs. He thinks he is like a cricket because he is fast and crickets move fast. To help focus the students on the story, ask questions such as:

Q *One of the other animals in this story is a lion. What do you know about lions?*

Q *What sound do lions make?*

Q *What do you know about snails?*

Q *If you move like a snail, how do you move?*

Q *What do you know about sharks?*

Ask the students to listen for the animals that the boy thinks he is like. Explain that after they hear the story they will talk about it.

Teacher Note

The pages of *Quick as a Cricket* are unnumbered. For easy reference, you may wish to pencil in page numbers, beginning with the number 1 on the title page. Page 2 begins "I'm as quick as a cricket." Use this system for all read-aloud books with unnumbered pages.

 Note

Show the illustrations of the lion, snail, and shark as you ask these questions.

 Note

Before you read, you might want to show the illustrations of the animals in the story. You might also use the illustrations to clarify vocabulary.

4 ▶ Read Aloud

Read the story aloud slowly and clearly, showing the illustrations as you read.

Deal with each suggested vocabulary word as you come to it in the story by reading the word, defining it concisely, rereading it, and continuing (for example, "I'm as happy as a lark—a *lark* is a *small bird that likes to sing*—I'm as happy as a lark").

Suggested Vocabulary

lark: small bird that likes to sing (p. 9)
shy: timid, quiet (p. 24)
tame: not wild (p. 25)

ELL Vocabulary

English Language Learners may benefit from discussing additional vocabulary, including:

weak: not strong (p. 15)
lazy: not wanting to work or move around (p. 28; refer to the illustration)

5 ▶ Discuss the Story

At the end of the book, briefly discuss the story. Ask:

Q *What animals in the story do you like? Why do you like them?*

Have several students volunteer their ideas. As the students share their thinking, refer to the story and either reread the text or show the illustrations that correspond with the students' comments.

Students might say:

"I like the snail because I see them in my yard all the time."

"I like the shark because they are fast swimmers and have big teeth."

Help the students think about how they listened during the read-aloud and discussion. Offer some of your observations of their interactions.

Explain that they will have lots of chances to practice listening to stories and to one another. Tell the students that you will read *Quick as a Cricket* again in the next lesson and that the book will be in the class library for them to look at.

End the lesson by explaining how you expect the students to return to their seats or transition to the next activity. If necessary, practice the procedure until the students are able to move to the next activity in an orderly way.

◀ **Teacher Note**

Talking about books is an integral part of the *Making Meaning* program. Having the read-aloud book available for students to read on their own increases familiarity with the story and stimulates participation in class discussions.

Day 2

Materials

- *Quick as a Cricket*
- "Reading Together" chart and a marker (see "Do Ahead," page 3)

Listening Practice

In this lesson, the students:

- Hear and discuss a story
- Learn and practice the procedure for a read-aloud
- *Make text-to-self connections* to enjoy and understand a story
- Listen to one another
- Take responsibility for themselves

▶ 1 Introduce the "Reading Together" Chart

Review the procedure for getting ready for a read-aloud and your expectations about the way the students will listen to the story and one another. Ask the students how they should move to the rug and then have them move to their places. If necessary, review the procedure and have them practice again.

Refer to the chart paper entitled "Reading Together." Read the title aloud and explain that today the students will think of ideas that will help them during a read-aloud. Ask:

Q *When we get together to listen to a story, what is helpful?*

Q *What does it mean to be responsible during a read-aloud?*

Write the students' ideas on the chart paper. Explain that they will add ideas to the chart throughout the year. Tell the students that they will revisit the chart at the end of the lesson.

Teacher Note

Students might not know what it means to be responsible. If necessary, give some examples such as:

- *It's responsible to walk, not run, inside the classroom.*
- *It's responsible to push your chair in.*
- *It's responsible to sit and listen quietly.*

▶

Teacher Note ▶

The purpose of the "Reading Together" chart is to involve the students in thinking about getting ready for a read-aloud. If the students are not used to offering suggestions for how they might act, you may need to offer some.

Reread *Quick as a Cricket*

Show the cover of *Quick as a Cricket* and explain that today you will reread the story. Ask the students to listen carefully to hear anything that they might have missed during the first reading. Reading a story more than once helps the students think more about the story and remember it better, so that they can talk about it with the class. Explain that you will stop in the middle of the story to have them talk about it.

Reread the story aloud slowly and clearly, showing the illustrations. Stop after:

> **p. 16**   "I'm as strong as an ox."

Ask:

Q   *What animals has the boy compared himself to so far?*

Have a few volunteers share their ideas with the class.

Reread page 16 and continue reading to the end of the story.

◀ Teacher Note

Use self-stick notes to mark stopping places in the book. Self-stick notes can also be used to remind you of questions, instructions, or other information you want to convey to the students during the read-aloud.

 Note

English Language Learners especially benefit from hearing a story more than once. They may also benefit from more frequent stops and discussions during the reading (for example, you might stop after pages 9, 16, and 22 to discuss the story).

3 ▶ **Discuss the Story and Make Personal Connections**

At the end of the book, facilitate a brief discussion about the story. Remind the students that looking at the person who is talking helps them listen and shows respect for the other person. Ask one or more of the following questions, and have several students share their ideas with the class:

Q   *Name one animal the boy thinks he is like. Why does he think he is like that animal?*

Q   *What does the boy tell us about himself at the end of the story?*

Q   *What animals in the story are you like? Why?*

FACILITATION TIP

During this unit, help the students understand that they are talking to one another—not just you—during class discussions by asking them to **turn and look** at the person who will speak. Explain that looking at the speaker helps them listen, and it shows the speaker that everyone is interested in what she is saying. At the start of this discussion, model the procedure for the students; then during the discussion remind the students of the procedure as needed.

Teacher Note ▶

Save the chart to use in Week 2 and for periodic use throughout the rest of the year.

 Note

These Extension activities are particularly helpful for English Language Learners.

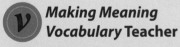 **Making Meaning Vocabulary Teacher**

Next week you will revisit *Quick as a Cricket* to teach Vocabulary Week 1.

4 ▶ Reflect on the "Reading Together" Chart

Help the students reflect on how they acted today during the read-aloud and discussion by reading and reviewing the "Reading Together" chart. Ask:

Q *What idea on our "Reading Together" chart did you practice today? Why is it important to do that?*

Tell the students that they will listen to stories and share ideas many times during this year.

EXTENSIONS

Act Out *Quick as a Cricket*

Have the students act out the story as you read it aloud.

Use the Story Language Pattern

In the book, pairs of antonyms are used to describe the animal characteristics. (For example, "I'm as weak as a kitten" is followed by "I'm as strong as an ox.") Reread the book and have the students focus on the words that describe opposing characteristics. Ask the students to think of animals that remind them of themselves. Have each student draw a picture of one of these animals and complete a frame sentence such as, "I am as [playful] as a [puppy]. " Have the students share their drawings and sentences with the class.

Week 2

Overview

UNIT 1: THE READING LIFE
Fiction and Narrative Nonfiction

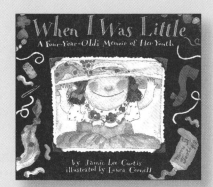

When I Was Little
by Jamie Lee Curtis, illustrated by Laura Cornell
(HarperTrophy, 1993)

A four-year-old girl describes how she has changed since she was a baby.

ALTERNATIVE BOOKS

Froggy Goes to School by Jonathan London

Much Bigger Than Martin by Steven Kellogg

Comprehension Focus

• Students *make text-to-self connections*.

• Students *answer questions* to understand a story.

Social Development Focus

• Teacher and students build a reading community.

• Students practice the procedure for a read-aloud.

• Students learn the procedure for "Turn to Your Partner."

• Students take responsibility for their learning and behavior.

• Students develop the group skill of listening to one another.

DO AHEAD

• Each student will begin working with a partner this week. Prior to Day 2, decide how you will randomly assign partners to work together. For suggestions about assigning partners randomly, see page xviii. For considerations for pairing English Language Learners, see page xxx.

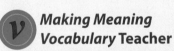

Making Meaning
Vocabulary Teacher

If you are teaching Developmental Studies Center's *Making Meaning Vocabulary* program, teach Vocabulary Week 1 this week. For more information, see the *Making Meaning Vocabulary Teacher's Manual*.

Day 1

Materials

- *When I Was Little*
- "Reading Together" chart and a marker

Teacher Note

The pages of *When I Was Little* are unnumbered. For easy reference, you may wish to pencil in page numbers, beginning with the number 1 on the title page. Page 5 says, "When I was little, I was a baby."

Teacher Note ▶

The "Students might say" notes help you anticipate possible student responses as you plan your lessons.

 Note

English Language Learners will benefit from previewing the story and illustrations prior to the read-aloud.

Read-aloud

In this lesson, the students:

- Hear and discuss a story
- Practice the procedure for a read-aloud
- *Make text-to-self connections* to enjoy and understand the story
- Listen to one another
- Take responsibility for themselves

▶ 1 Get Ready to Listen

Briefly review the procedure for a read-aloud and have the students move to their places. Make sure the students are facing you so they can hear the story and see the illustrations. After the students have moved, describe some ways you saw them taking responsibility. (For example, you might say, "I noticed that you pushed your chairs in, then walked quietly to the rug. Doing these things helps us be safe and not trip or bump into people.") Ask:

Q *What other things did you do to move in a safe and responsible way?*

> **Students might say:**
>
> "I waited for Jamie to sit down first."
>
> "I sat flat on the rug so people behind me can see."

Review the "Reading Together" chart and add new ideas.

▶ 2 Introduce *When I Was Little*

Show the cover of *When I Was Little* and read the title and names of the author and illustrator aloud. Point to the words and have the students reread the title and names with you.

Point out the girl and explain that in this story the girl compares what she was like when she was a baby to what she is like now. Ask the students to listen for what the girl says about when she was little, and explain that they will talk about how they listened at the end of the story.

 3 **Read Aloud**

Read the story aloud slowly and clearly, showing the illustrations as you read.

Deal with each suggested vocabulary word as you come to it in the story by reading the word, defining it concisely, rereading it, and continuing (for example, "Now I go to nursery school and I have teachers and cubbies—*cubbies* are *small closets or boxes where children keep their things*—Now I go to nursery school and I have teachers and cubbies and naptime and secrets").

◀ **Teacher Note**

Since listeners can easily miss details at the beginning of a story, consider reading the first one or two pages twice before going on with the rest of the story.

Suggested Vocabulary

braids, pigtails, ponytail, pom-pom: different hairstyles (p. 9)

handful: difficult to handle (p. 11)

Mommy and Me: place where mothers and babies do activities together (p. 14)

nursery school: preschool, a school for young children (p. 15)

cubbies: small closets or boxes where children keep their things (p. 15)

time-outs: times when you are sent to be by yourself for a while (p. 17)

floaties: (p. 20; refer to the illustration)

tickle torture: a tickling game (p. 28)

ELL Vocabulary

English Language Learners may benefit from discussing additional vocabulary, including:

granny: another name for grandmother, abuela, nona, bà, babushka (p. 23)

dreams: thoughts you have when you are sleeping (p. 31)

◀ **Teacher Note**

Use self-stick notes to mark the places the suggested vocabulary words appear. You might write the meanings of the words on the notes to help you define them smoothly without interrupting the reading.

ELL Note

You might support students with limited English proficiency by providing a prompt for responding to the question, such as, "The girl says…" or "She says…." (For more information about supporting English Language Learners at various levels of proficiency, see pages xxviii–xxxv.)

Teacher Note

Make the read-aloud books available for the students to read on their own after you read them aloud. This increases the students' familiarity with the stories and stimulates participation in class discussions.

4 ▸ Discuss the Story and Make Personal Connections

At the end of the book, facilitate a brief discussion of the story. Ask:

Q *What are some things the girl in the story says about when she was little?*

Q *Do you have some of the same ideas about being little as the girl in the story? What are they?*

Have a few volunteers share their ideas with the class. Be ready to reread and show the illustrations again to help the students recall what they heard.

5 ▸ Reflect on Listening

Have the students talk about how they listened to the story. Ask:

Q *What did you do to make sure that you listened to the story?*

Q *How did you listen to people when they were talking?*

Without mentioning students' names, offer some of your observations about what is working well and what they still need to practice. (For example, you might say, "I noticed that people were quiet when I was reading the story. This is important because it helps everyone hear the story. I noticed that sometimes people forgot to look at the person who is talking. This is something we will continue to practice.")

Explain that the students will have lots of chances to practice listening to stories and to one another. Tell them that you will read *When I Was Little* again in the next lesson and that it will be in the class library for them to look at on their own if they wish.

Day 2

Listening Practice

In this lesson, the students:

- Hear and discuss a story
- Learn and practice "Turn to Your Partner"
- *Make text-to-self connections* to enjoy and understand the story
- Listen to one another
- Take responsibility for themselves

1 ▶ Pair Students and Introduce "Turn to Your Partner"

Randomly assign partners and make sure they know each other's names. Ask partners to come to the rug and sit together for a read-aloud.

Tell the students that while you are reading today you will ask some questions and have each student turn to his partner to talk about the questions. Explain that talking to a partner gives everyone a chance to talk about what they're learning from the story before sharing ideas with the class. (For more information about the role of cooperative structures in social development, see "Focus on Social Development" on page xvii.)

Explain the "Turn to Your Partner" procedure. (You might say, "When I say 'turn to your partner,' you will turn to face your partner and start talking about the question that I ask. When I raise my hand, you will finish what you're saying and turn back to face me.") Explain that you expect the students to take turns talking and listening, and remind them to wait for their partners to finish before starting to talk.

Materials

- *When I Was Little*

◀ Teacher Note

You might give the partners several minutes to talk informally and get to know each other before continuing with the lesson. You might have them chat about questions such as:

Q *What do you like to play at recess?*

Q *What do you like to play at home?*

Q *How do you get to school?*

Model "Turn to Your Partner"

Have a student act as your partner and model turning to face each other. Ask the students to turn and face their own partners, and then have them turn back and face you when you give the signal. Have the students practice the procedure again if necessary.

With your student partner, model "Turn to Your Partner" again, but this time, add sharing. Turn to your partner and introduce yourself using your whole name. Have your partner introduce herself. Then on the prearranged signal, turn back to the class.

Have the class practice "Turn to Your Partner" with a sample question. Ask:

Q *What do you think is the most fun about school this year?*

 Say "turn to your partner," which is the signal to begin, and have the students turn and tell each other what they think is the most fun. Signal to bring the students' attention back to you. Have a few volunteers briefly share their partners' ideas with the class.

Remind the students that in the last lesson they heard a story about a young girl's ideas about what she was like when she was little. Practice "Turn to Your Partner" again, using the question:

Q *What do you think you were like when you were little? Tell your partner one idea you have about that.*

 Say "turn to your partner" and follow the same procedure. After partners share, have a few volunteers briefly share their partners' responses with the class.

If the students need more practice, review your expectations and have them practice again.

 Review *When I Was Little*

Show the cover of *When I Was Little* and say that today the students will hear the book again and partners will talk about the story. Remind them that reading a story more than once helps them remember and understand the story.

Teacher Note ▶

Having the students share their partners' ideas rather than their own helps them be accountable for listening carefully.

Ask:

Q   *What do you remember about this story?*

Say "turn to your partner" and have the students take turns answering the question. After 20–30 seconds, signal for them to end their conversations and turn their attention back to you. Ask one or two students to share with the class what their partners said.

4 ▶ Reread the Story

Reread the story aloud slowly and clearly, showing the illustrations. Stop after:

> **p. 12**   "When I was little, I rode in a baby car seat. Now I ride like a grown-up and wave at policemen."

Ask:

Q   *What do you remember about the story so far?*

Say "turn to your partner" and have partners turn to face each other and take turns answering the question. After 20–30 seconds, signal for their attention. Have a couple of volunteers share with the class what their partners said. Reread page 12 and continue reading to page 20. Stop after:

> **p. 20**   "I still do, but now we wear bathing suits but we don't wear floaties."

Ask:

Q   *What do you remember about the story so far?*

Say "turn to your partner" and have partners discuss the question. Have a few volunteers share their partners' ideas with the class.

Reread the last sentence on page 20 and continue reading to the end of the story.

FACILITATION TIP

During this discussion, continue to prompt the students to **turn and look** at the person who will speak. (You might say, "Tyler is going to speak. Let's all turn and look at him.") Throughout the discussion, scan the class to ensure that the students are looking at the speaker and, if necessary, interrupt the discussion to remind them of your expectations.

5 ▶ Discuss the Story and Make Personal Connections

At the end of the book, facilitate a brief discussion about the story. Ask questions such as:

Q *What are some differences between the girl now and when she was a baby?*

Q *What parts of this story remind you of when you were little?*

6 ▶ Reflect on "Turn to Your Partner"

Remind the students that today they learned to use "Turn to Your Partner." Help them reflect on how they did working with their partners. Ask:

Q *What was helpful when you talked to your partner about your thinking?*

If the students have difficulty answering this question, share your observations with the class. (For example, you might say, "I noticed that you looked at your partner when I said, 'turn to your partner.' I saw partners looking at each other, but I am not sure everyone was listening to each other because one partner would start talking before the other partner was finished. It is very important to listen to what your partner is saying.")

Tell the students they will have many more opportunities to use "Turn to Your Partner" during read-alouds.

Teacher Note

You will assign new partners for next week's lesson and at the beginning of Week 4.

EXTENSION

Make a Class Book

Ask the students to think about how they did something when they were little and how they do it now. Divide sheets of drawing paper in half. Have each student draw a picture of what they did when they were little on one half and what they do now on the other half. Under each drawing, have them complete a frame sentence: "When I was little, I _____." or "Now I _____."

Collect the papers and compile them into a class book entitled *When We Were Little.* Read the book aloud and place it in the classroom library.

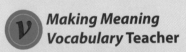

ELL Note

Drawing activities are especially helpful for English Language Learners. Consider helping your students with limited English proficiency complete the frame sentence.

***v* Making Meaning Vocabulary Teacher**

Next week you will revisit *When I Was Little* to teach Vocabulary Week 2.

Week 3

Overview

UNIT 1: THE READING LIFE
Fiction and Narrative Nonfiction

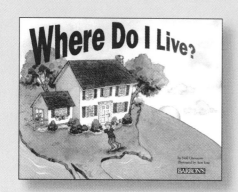

Where Do I Live?
by Neil Chesanow, illustrated by Ann Iosa
(Barron's, 1995)

This book explains where people live, beginning with a single room and expanding in scale to a street, a town, and beyond.

ALTERNATIVE BOOKS

Who's in a Family? by Robert Skutch

What Lives in a Shell? by Kathleen Widner Zoehfeld

Comprehension Focus

- Students *make text-to-self connections*.

- Students *answer questions* to understand a story.

- Students read independently.

Social Development Focus

- Teacher and students build a reading community.

- Students practice the procedure for "Turn to Your Partner."

- Students take responsibility for their learning and behavior.

- Students develop the group skill of listening to one another.

DO AHEAD

- Prior to Day 1, decide how you will randomly assign partners to work together. For suggestions about assigning partners randomly, see page xviii. For considerations for pairing English Language Learners, see page xxx.

- Collect a variety of fiction and nonfiction picture books for independent reading.

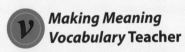

Making Meaning Vocabulary Teacher

If you are teaching Developmental Studies Center's *Making Meaning Vocabulary* program, teach Vocabulary Week 2 this week. For more information, see the *Making Meaning Vocabulary Teacher's Manual*.

Day 1

Materials

- *Where Do I Live?* (pages 1–21)
- Selection of nonfiction and fiction picture books for independent reading

Read-aloud

In this lesson, the students:

- Hear and discuss a story
- Practice "Turn to Your Partner"
- Read independently for up to 10 minutes
- Listen to one another
- Take responsibility for themselves

▶1 Pair Students and Get Ready to Work Together

Randomly assign new partners. Ask the students to come to the rug for read-aloud. Have partners sit together.

Ask:

Q *What is important to remember when you use "Turn to Your Partner"?*

 Say "turn to your partner" and have the students take turns answering the question. Signal for their attention, and ask a few volunteers to share their thinking with the class.

> *Students might say:*
>
> "It is important to look at your partner when you talk."
>
> "It is important to stop talking and turn and face the teacher at the signal."
>
> "It is important to give your partner a turn to talk."

Remind the students that "Turn to Your Partner" gives everyone a chance to think more about the story by talking with another person.

▶2 Introduce *Where Do I Live?*

Show the cover of *Where Do I Live?* and read the title and names of the author and illustrator aloud. Point to the title and have the

Teacher Note

The students will only hear the first part of this book read aloud. After page 21, the text calls for progressively more sophisticated and abstract thinking. If the students seem interested, you might read the rest of the book aloud at another time or make it available in the class library for them to read on their own.

students reread the title with you. Explain that this book is about all the different places people live. Ask:

Q *Some people live in houses; some live in apartments or other places. Where do you live?*

Have a few volunteers share with the class.

Ask the students to listen for what they find out about where people live. Explain that you will stop during the reading and ask the students to turn to their partner to talk about the story.

 ## Read Aloud

Read the story aloud through page 21, slowly and clearly, showing the illustrations as you read and stopping as described below. Deal with each suggested vocabulary word as you come to it in the story by reading the word, defining it concisely, rereading it, and continuing (for example, "It runs right past—*runs right past* means *is next to*—It runs right past the home where you live").

Suggested Vocabulary

dozens or even hundreds: very many (p. 18)

ELL Vocabulary

English Language Learners may benefit from discussing additional vocabulary, including:

runs right past: is next to (p. 10)
form: make (p. 14)
dotting: on (p. 18)

Read pages 4–10 and stop after:

p. 10 "Everyone who lives next to a street can say, 'This is my street.'"

Ask:

Q *Where are some of the places people live?*

 ELL Note

English Language Learners will benefit from hearing the story and seeing the illustrations prior to the read-aloud. They also may benefit from more frequent stops during the reading to discuss what they are hearing (for example, after pages 6 and 15).

 ELL Note

To increase comprehension, consider asking a volunteer to act out "runs right past."

 Say "turn to your partner" and have the students take turns answering the question. Signal for the students to return their attention to you. Have a few pairs briefly share their ideas with the class.

Reread page 10 and continue through page 21.

4 Discuss the Story and Make Connections

 After the reading, facilitate a brief discussion of the story. Use "Turn to Your Partner" during this discussion to increase students' thinking and participation. Ask:

Q *Where are some of the places people live?*

Q *Where are some of the places you live?*

> **Students might say:**
>
> "I live in a house in the state of Massachusetts."
>
> "I live in an apartment in the North End of Boston."

5 Reflect on Working Together

Help the students reflect on their discussions. Ask questions such as:

Q *What did you do to make sure you both had a chance to talk?*

Q *What did the class do well during our read-aloud?*

Q *What do we still need to practice?*

Tell the students that in the next lesson they will hear *Where Do I Live?* again.

6 Read Independently

Provide a wide selection of nonfiction and fiction picture books at various reading levels. Have the students choose books and read independently for 5–10 minutes. Have students who are unable to read independently look at the pictures in their books. Then have partners take turns sharing their books with each other.

FACILITATION TIP

During this and other discussions today, continue to remind the students to **turn and look** at the person who is speaking. Remind them that looking at the speaker helps them listen and shows the speaker they are interested in what he says.

Teacher Note

Individualized Daily Reading (IDR) will be formally introduced in Unit 5. During IDR the students read books at appropriate reading levels independently for up to 15 minutes each day. Many informal experiences with independent reading will prepare the students for more formalized IDR. For information about providing and leveling books, setting up a classroom library, and your role in IDR, see "Individualized Daily Reading" on page xxv. For information about Developmental Studies Center's Individualized Daily Reading Libraries, see page xxvii and visit Developmental Studies Center's website at devstu.org.

Day 2

Listening Practice

In this lesson, the students:

- Hear and discuss a story
- Practice "Turn to Your Partner"
- *Make text-to-self connections* to enjoy and understand the story
- Read independently for up to 10 minutes
- Listen to one another
- Take responsibility for themselves

1 ▶ Review *Where Do I Live?*

Have the students come to the rug with their partners from the previous lesson. Show the cover of *Where Do I Live?* and read the title aloud. Remind the students that they listened to the story and looked at the pictures to help them understand the book.

Ask:

Q *What do you remember about where people live?*

Have two or three volunteers share what they remember with the class.

Explain that today the students will hear parts of the story again. Ask them to listen carefully and notice what they learn about the place that is described in each part of the book. Tell them that you will ask them to use "Turn to Your Partner" to talk about what they heard.

Materials

- *Where Do I Live?* (pages 1–21)
- *Assessment Resource Book*
- Selection of nonfiction and fiction picture books for independent reading

◀ **Teacher Note**

If the students have difficulty recalling the story, you might show them some of the illustrations and ask them to say what place is being described.

Read Selections from the Story and Make Personal Connections

Read pages 8 and 9 aloud twice, showing the illustrations. Ask:

Q *What did you learn about "land" in the part you just heard?*

Say "turn to your partner," and have partners discuss the question. After 20–30 seconds, signal to bring the students' attention back to you. Have a few students share what they learned. As they share, refer to the text to help them remember what they heard.

> **Students might say:**
>
> "Land is the ground."
>
> "Some people play in the yard and some people play in the park."

Use "Turn to Your Partner" again to have the students discuss:

Q *When have you been in a park? What do you remember about it?*

Have two or three volunteers share their experiences with the class.

Read pages 14–17 aloud twice, showing the illustrations.

Use "Turn to Your Partner" to have the students discuss:

Q *What did you learn about towns and cities in the part you just heard?*

Q *Where are some of the places you go in your [town/city]?*

Point out that readers often think about things in their own lives to help them understand a story.

CLASS PROGRESS ASSESSMENT

As the students share their thinking, ask yourself:

Q *Are the students making connections to the story?*

Q *Are the students listening to each other?*

Q *What problems, if any, do I want to bring up at the end of the lesson?*

Record your observations on page 2 of the *Assessment Resource Book*.

 3 **Discuss Working Together**

Facilitate a brief discussion about how the students worked together. Ask:

Q *What did you and your partner do to help each other today?*

Q *How did that help you talk together?*

If necessary, without using names, point out any problems you noticed during "Turn to Your Partner." (For example, you might say, "I noticed that in some pairs one person did all of the talking. It is good if both people have a chance to talk when you turn to your partner. What is one way you can make sure you both talk?")

Tell the students that they will have new partners next time they work together.

 ELL Note

Ask your English Language Learners to pay attention to what they like and don't like in their books as they read. At the end of the independent reading, you may want to provide a prompt for their response, such as, "I liked my book because…."

4 **Read Independently**

Provide a wide selection of nonfiction and fiction picture books at various reading levels. Have the students choose books and read independently for 5–10 minutes. Have students who are unable to read independently look at the pictures in their books. At the end of independent reading time, ask each student to find the part of the book he liked the best. Then in pairs, have each student share his favorite part and tell why he likes it.

Teacher Note

Being a Writer, a writing curriculum from Developmental Studies Center, provides lessons that will help your students write in many different genres.

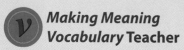

Making Meaning
Vocabulary Teacher

Next week you will revisit *Where Do I Live?* to teach Vocabulary Week 3.

EXTENSION

Make a Class Book

Remind the students that in *Where Do I Live?* they learned that their room at home is a special place. Reread page 4 of the book. Then ask the students to think about one thing that is special about their room at home. Explain that it might be because that's where they keep a special toy or stuffed animal, or because their bed is comfortable, or it's a place where they like to do fun things. Have a few volunteers share their thinking about their rooms with the class. Then distribute writing paper and have the students write and illustrate a story about their room. (You might provide a frame sentence to support the students' writing such as "My room is special because _____." or "In my room I like to _____.") Have the students share their completed stories with the class or their partners.

Week 4

Overview

UNIT 1: THE READING LIFE
Fiction and Narrative Nonfiction

It's Mine!
by Leo Lionni
(Knopf, 1985)

In this fable, a group of frogs learn that it is better to share.

ALTERNATIVE BOOKS

Chubbo's Pool by Betsy Lewin

Wemberly Worried by Kevin Henkes

Comprehension Focus

- Students *make text-to-self connections*.

- Students *answer questions* to understand a story.

- Students informally *identify important ideas* in the story.

- Students read independently.

Social Development Focus

- Teacher and students build a reading community.

- Students practice "Turn to Your Partner."

- Students take responsibility for their learning and behavior.

- Students develop the group skill of listening to one another.

DO AHEAD

- Prior to Day 1, decide how you will randomly assign partners to work together. For suggestions about assigning partners randomly, see page xviii. For considerations for pairing English Language Learners, see page xxx.

- Make copies of the Unit 1 Parent Letter (BLM1) to send home with the students on the last day of the unit. (For more information about the Parent Letters, see page xxxvi.)

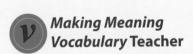

Making Meaning
Vocabulary Teacher

If you are teaching Developmental Studies Center's *Making Meaning Vocabulary* program, teach Vocabulary Week 3 this week. For more information, see the *Making Meaning Vocabulary Teacher's Manual*.

Day 1

Materials

- *It's Mine!*
- "Reading Together" chart and a marker
- Selection of picture books for independent reading

Teacher Note

The pages of *It's Mine!* are unnumbered. For easy reference, pencil in page numbers, beginning with the number 1 on the title page. Page 2 begins "In the middle of Rainbow Pond there was a small island."

Teacher Note

At this time of the year the students may have difficulty articulating their thinking about their social interactions. Model talking about social interactions by selecting one idea from the "Reading Together" chart that the students are doing particularly well and talking about how you see it working in the classroom. In addition, if the students are having difficulty interacting, you might want to have them focus on improving their interactions in one area at a time.

Save the "Reading Together" chart for Unit 3.

Read-aloud

In this lesson, the students:

- Hear and discuss a story
- Practice "Turn to Your Partner"
- Read independently for up to 10 minutes
- Take turns talking and listening
- Take responsibility for themselves

1 ▶ Pair Students and Get Ready to Work Together

Randomly assign partners and make sure they know each other's names. Ask the pairs to come to the rug for a read-aloud. Explain that the students who came to the rug together will be partners today. Explain that you will read a book aloud and they will use "Turn to Your Partner" so everyone will have a chance to talk about the story.

Remind the students that they are a community of readers. Read the "Reading Together" chart aloud and explain that these ideas will help them create a feeling of community. Ask:

Q *What is one thing on the chart you want to remember when you listen to your partner and others in the class? Why will that be helpful?*

Students might say:

"It is important to look at your partner."

"If your partner is not facing you, it makes you feel sad and like you don't have a partner."

"It is important to let your partner talk."

Add any new ideas to the chart.

Introduce *It's Mine!*

Show the cover of *It's Mine!* and read the title and author's name aloud. Explain that Leo Lionni also is the illustrator of this book. Point to the words and have the students reread the title and name with you. Explain that this is a story about three frogs—Milton, Rupert, and Lydia—and a toad. Explain that frogs live in or near the water and toads live on land. The story takes place on an island in the middle of Rainbow Pond. Be sure that the students understand *island* and *pond*.

 Note

English Language Learners will benefit from previewing the story and illustrations before you read it to the class.

 Read Aloud

Explain that you will stop during the reading and ask the students to turn to their partners to talk about the story. Read the story aloud slowly and clearly, showing the illustrations, and stopping as described on the next page.

Deal with each suggested vocabulary word as you come to it in the story by reading the word, defining it concisely, rereading it, and continuing (for example, "On the island lived three quarrelsome frogs—*quarrelsome frogs* are *frogs who argue or disagree a lot*—On the island lived three quarrelsome frogs named Milton, Rupert, and Lydia").

Note

You may wish to add a stop to give the students another opportunity to discuss the story (for example, after page 23).

Suggested Vocabulary

quarrelsome: arguing or disagreeing a lot (p. 5)

quibbled: argued or disagreed about something unimportant (p. 5)

bickering: quarreling; arguing (p. 13)

thunder: a loud rumbling noise that comes after lightning during a storm (p. 16)

The island…was swallowed up by the rising flood: The island disappeared under the rising water (p. 16)

trembling: shaking (p. 20)

subsided: went down (p. 20)

minnows: tiny fish (p. 25)

peaceful: quiet and calm with no arguing (p. 29)

ELL Vocabulary

English Language Learners may benefit from discussing additional vocabulary, including:

appeared: came into sight (p. 13; refer to the illustration)

disappear: go out of sight (p. 18)

recognized the toad: saw the toad and remembered him from before (p. 23)

Read pages 2–10 and stop after:

> **p. 10** "'The air is mine!' screamed Lydia as she leaped to catch a butterfly. And so it went."

Ask:

Q *What do you know about Rupert, Milton, and Lydia so far?*

 Say "turn to your partner" and have the students take turns answering the question. Signal for the students to return their attention to you. Have a few pairs briefly share their ideas with the class. It is important not to interfere with the flow of the story and to keep the students engaged.

Reread page 10 and continue to page 18. Stop after:

> **p. 18** "But soon these too began to disappear."

 Use "Turn to Your Partner" again to have the students discuss:

Q *What do you think will happen next?*

Have a few students briefly share their thinking with the class. Reread the last sentence on page 18 and continue reading to the end of the story.

4 ▶ Discuss as a Whole Class

At the end of the book, briefly discuss the story as a class. Ask:

Q *What happens in this story?*

Students might say:

"The frogs keep saying, 'That's mine.'"

"When they found out the rock was the toad, they said, 'You saved us.'"

Facilitate a brief discussion about how the students talked and listened to one another today. Have them share any problems they had. Facilitate a discussion about how they might solve these problems.

Tell the students they will have another chance to talk about *It's Mine!* in the next lesson.

Teacher Note ▶

The purpose of this discussion is to provide a surface-level understanding of the story. On Day 2 the students will think and talk in more detail about the story.

Read Independently

Provide a wide selection of picture books at various reading levels. Have the students choose books and read independently for 5–10 minutes. Have students who are unable to read independently look at the pictures in their books. Then have a few volunteers share their books with the class.

Day 2

Materials

- *It's Mine!*
- *Assessment Resource Book*
- Selection of picture books for independent reading
- Unit 1 Parent Letter (BLM1)

Note

Not showing the illustrations encourages the students to listen carefully and make meaning from the words; however, your English Language Learners will benefit from reviewing the illustrations prior to the read-aloud.

Listening Practice

In this lesson, the students:

- Hear and discuss a story
- Practice "Turn to Your Partner"
- Read independently for up to 10 minutes.
- Listen to one another
- Take responsibility for themselves

1 Get Ready to Listen for Leo Lionni's Message

Have partners from Day 1 sit together. Explain that they will hear *It's Mine!* and talk about the story again today.

Tell the students that *It's Mine!* is a special kind of story called a fable. Fables often have animals talking and acting like people. Fables usually have ideas or messages to help us live happier lives. Ask the students to think about what Leo Lionni, the author, is trying to tell us in this fable.

2 Reread the Story

Reread the story slowly and clearly, without showing the illustrations, and stopping as described below.

Read pages 2–13 aloud and stop after:

> **p. 13** "With that the toad slowly turned around and hopped away through the weeds."

Ask:

Q *Why does the toad visit Rupert, Milton, and Lydia?*

Have several students share their thinking with the class. Refer to the text to model the connection between the students' thinking and the story. (For example, a student might say that the toad was unhappy with the frogs because they were always arguing. Read the text on page 13 that supports this thinking: "There is no peace because of your endless bickering.")

Reread the last sentence on page 13 and continue reading to page 20. Stop after:

> **p. 20**   "The rain fell gently and then stopped altogether."

 Have the students use "Turn to Your Partner" to discuss:

Q   *I just read the middle part of the story. What happens to the frogs in the middle part of the story?*

Have a few students briefly share their thinking with the class. Reread the last sentence on page 20 and continue reading to the end of the story.

▶3 Discuss the Story

 Remind the students that a fable has a message for the reader. First in pairs, and then as a class, briefly discuss:

Q   *What do you think Leo Lionni is trying to tell us in this fable?*

Q   *What part of the story made you think that?*

> **Students might say:**
>
> "It will be sad if you don't share."
>
> "If you don't share, you can have bad luck."
>
> "They learned how to share because they were scared."

As the students offer their ideas, refer to the text that supports their thinking.

FACILITATION TIP

Continue to have the students **turn and look** at the person who is speaking during discussions. Notice the effect that using this facilitation technique has on the students' engagement in class discussions over time.

CLASS PROGRESS ASSESSMENT

During the discussion, note the students' understanding of the story and their interactions with partners and as a class. Ask yourself:

Q *Do the students understand the surface level of the story? Are they able to follow the plot?*

Q *Are they able to connect their thinking to the text?*

Q *Are the students practicing the procedures for a read-aloud? What procedures do they have difficulty with?*

Q *How are they interacting and listening during "Turn to Your Partner"?*

Record your observations on page 3 of the *Assessment Resource Book*.

 4 ▶ **Reflect on Partner and Class Discussions**

Ask the students to think about one way they shared ideas with their partners or with the class. Have volunteers share with the class. If the students do not offer any examples, share some of your own observations. (You might say, "I noticed that both partners were talking about the story. I also heard a lot of people giving ideas when we all talked together.")

If there were problems, discuss the problems and possible solutions. (You might say, "I noticed that some of you are eager to share your own ideas, but find it harder to listen well to others' ideas.")

 ELL Note

You may want to help your English Language Learners select books at the appropriate level.

5 ▶ **Read Independently**

Provide a wide selection of picture books at various reading levels. Have the students choose books and read independently for 5–10 minutes. Have students who are unable to read independently look at the pictures in their books. Then have partners take turns sharing their books with each other.

EXTENSION

Draw and Write About Sharing

Remind the students that the frogs in *It's Mine!* learn that it is important to work together and share. Have the students briefly discuss ways they share in the classroom and why that is important. Ask them to draw a picture showing a time they shared something in the classroom. Help each student dictate or write a sentence about her picture. Then have the students share their work with the class or compile the pictures into a class book entitled "How We Share."

Parent Letter

Send home with each student the Parent Letter for this unit (see "Do Ahead," page 33). Periodically, have a few students share with the class what they are reading at home.

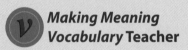

***Making Meaning Vocabulary* Teacher**

Next week you will revisit *It's Mine!* to teach Vocabulary Week 4.

Unit 2

Making Connections

FICTION

During this unit, the students informally identify important ideas in stories. They also make text-to-self connections and answer questions to understand the stories. Socially, they continue to take responsibility for their learning and behavior as they develop the group skill of talking and listening to one another.

Week 1 *Matthew and Tilly* by Rebecca C. Jones

Week 2 *McDuff and the Baby* by Rosemary Wells

Week 3 *Chrysanthemum* by Kevin Henkes

UNIT 2: MAKING CONNECTIONS
Fiction

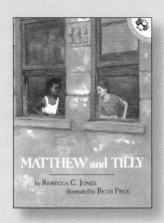

Matthew and Tilly
by Rebecca C. Jones, illustrated by Beth Peck
(Puffin, 1995)

Matthew and Tilly are two friends who enjoy each other's company until one day they have a disagreement.

ALTERNATIVE BOOKS

Best Friends by Steven Kellogg

Luka's Quilt by Georgia Guback

Comprehension Focus

- Students *make text-to-self connections*.

- Students informally *identify important ideas* in a story.

- Students answer questions to understand the story.

- Students read independently.

Social Development Focus

- Students take responsibility for their learning and behavior.

- Students develop the group skill of talking and listening to one another.

DO AHEAD

- Prior to Day 1, decide how you will randomly assign partners to work together during this unit. For suggestions about pairing students randomly, see page xviii. For considerations for pairing English Language Learners, see page xxx.

Making Meaning
Vocabulary Teacher

If you are teaching Developmental Studies Center's *Making Meaning Vocabulary* program, teach Vocabulary Week 4 this week. For more information, see the *Making Meaning Vocabulary Teacher's Manual*.

Day 1

Materials

- *Matthew and Tilly*

Being a Writer™ **Teacher**

You can either have the students work with their *Being a Writer* partner or assign them a different partner for the *Making Meaning* lessons.

 Note

English Language Learners will benefit from hearing the story and seeing the illustrations prior to the read-aloud. Continue this procedure throughout the *Making Meaning* program.

Read-aloud

In this lesson, the students:

- Hear and discuss a story
- Refer to the text to support their thinking
- Read independently for up to 10 minutes
- Begin working with new partners
- Talk and listen to one another

1 ▶ Pair Students and Get Ready to Work Together

Randomly assign partners. Have pairs sit together and make sure they know each other's names. Check to see that all the students can see the book and illustrations clearly. Explain that for the next few weeks each student will work with the same partner. During today's lesson, you will read a book aloud and the students will talk about the story in pairs and then with the class. Remind the students that it is important to listen carefully as you read so that they can remember and talk about the story.

2 ▶ Introduce *Matthew and Tilly*

Show the book's cover and read the title and the names of the author and illustrator aloud. Explain that this is a story about two friends, Matthew and Tilly. Matthew and Tilly live in the same city apartment building. Explain that you will stop during the reading to have partners talk about what is happening in the story.

3 ▶ Read Aloud

Read pages 5–15 aloud slowly and clearly, showing the illustrations and stopping as described on the following page.

Deal with each suggested vocabulary word as you come to it in the story by reading the word, defining it concisely, rereading it, and continuing. (See page 35 for an example of how to deal with vocabulary during a reading.)

Suggested Vocabulary

sidewalk games: games that you play on the sidewalk, such as hopscotch (p. 9)

rescued: saved (p. 12)

crabbiest: most complaining (p. 19)

picky: fussy or choosy (p. 19)

ELL Vocabulary

English Language Learners may benefit from discussing additional vocabulary, including:

hide-and-seek: game in which one player looks for other players who are hiding (p. 7)

when business was slow: when no one was buying lemonade (p. 8)

bubble-gum machines: containers that hold candy (p. 14)

got sick of each other: got tired of playing together (p. 16)

stomped: thumped as he walked (p. 20)

cash register: machine that holds money and adds numbers (p. 24; refer to the illustration)

Stop after:

> **p. 15** "So later they chewed gum together and remembered how brave they had been."

Ask:

Q *What have you learned about Matthew and Tilly so far?*

 Use "Turn to Your Partner" to have the students discuss the question. Then have one or two volunteers briefly share their ideas with the class.

Reread the last sentence on page 15, and continue reading.
Stop after:

> **p. 19** "'Well, you're so stupid,' Tilly said. 'You're so stupid and stinky and mean.'"

 Note

Consider asking the students to act out vocabulary words, such as "hide and seek" and "stomped." For "crabbiest," ask the students to make their crabbiest face. This type of nonverbal participation will support the students' understanding and engage their interest. Be sure to wrap up this activity quickly to maintain the flow of the story.

Ask:

Q *What has happened to Matthew and Tilly?*

 Use "Turn to Your Partner" to have the students discuss the question. Then have one or two volunteers briefly share their ideas with the class. Reread the last sentences on page 19, and continue reading.

Stop after:

p. 27 "And a sidewalk game wasn't much fun without another player."

Ask:

Q *What do you think might happen next? Why?*

 Use "Turn to Your Partner" to have the students discuss the question. Then have one or two volunteers briefly share their ideas with the class. Reread the last sentence on page 27 and continue reading to the end of the story.

4 ▶ Discuss the Story

 First in pairs, and then as a class, discuss:

Q *What happens in this story?*

Q *What happens so that Matthew and Tilly stop enjoying each other's company?*

Q *What happens at the end of the story?*

Explain that in the next lesson the students will talk again about *Matthew and Tilly* and how the story might remind them of things that happen in their own lives.

Read Independently

Have the students independently read books they choose for 5–10 minutes. Have students who are unable to read independently look at the pictures in their books. If time permits, have a few students share their books with the class. Ask each volunteer to tell one thing she liked about her book.

Note

Before your English Language Learners read independently, preview the question you will ask at the end. For example, you might say, "After you read, I will ask you about a part you liked."

Materials

- *Matthew and Tilly* (pages 16–23)
- *Assessment Resource Book*

ELL Note

Provide the students with the verbal prompt "I remember...."

Teacher Note ▶

If the students have difficulty recalling the story, you might reread all or parts of the story.

Strategy Lesson

In this lesson, the students:

- *Make text-to-self connections* to enjoy and understand a story
- Refer to the text to support their thinking
- Read independently for up to 10 minutes
- Talk and listen to one another

About Making Connections

One of the ways that young students naturally make sense of text is by making personal, or text-to-self, connections to the plot or characters in the story. Later, as they continue to hear stories, students begin to see similarities and make connections between stories or themes. In reading and talking, they accumulate experiences and background knowledge that help them make sense of text. Making connections increases both enjoyment and understanding of stories and language. (For more discussion about *making connections,* please see "Using Schema" on page xv.)

1 ▶ Review *Matthew and Tilly*

Have partners sit together. Show the cover of *Matthew and Tilly* and tell the students that today they will talk more about the book. Ask:

Q *What do you remember about the story?*

Use "Turn to Your Partner" to have the students discuss what they remember. Then have a few volunteers share their thinking with the class.

As the students share, turn to the story text that supports their thinking and read it aloud. (For example, if the students say that Matthew accidentally broke Tilly's crayons and Tilly got mad, turn to page 19 and read aloud, "'You broke my crayon,'Tilly said in her crabbiest voice.")

▶2 Introduce Making Connections

Explain that one thing good readers do is think about how the story they are reading reminds them of their own lives—of experiences they have had or people they know. Making a connection between the story and their lives helps readers make sense of the story. Explain that today you will reread part of *Matthew and Tilly*. Tell the students that as they listen you would like them to think about how the story reminds them of their own lives.

▶3 Reread Pages 16–23

Reread pages 16–23, slowly and clearly, stopping to show the illustrations.

▶4 Discuss the Students' Connections

Ask the students to think about the part of the story they just heard, then ask:

Q *How does what happened remind you of your own life?*

 Give the students time to think individually; then have them share with their partners. Have two or three volunteers share their experiences with the class. As the students share their connections, probe their thinking with questions such as:

Q *How did you feel when that happened to you? How do you think Matthew and Tilly feel?*

Q *How did you solve your disagreement?*

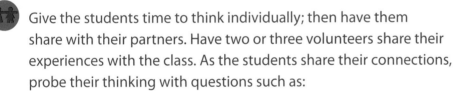 **ELL Note**

To support your English Language Learners, consider restating the question to provide clarification. You might say, "Matthew and Tilly had a disagreement. Have you ever had a disagreement with a friend?"

◀ **Teacher Note**

Allow plenty of time for the students to initiate the discussion. If they have difficulty making connections, you might stimulate their thinking by thinking aloud about a situation in your own life or asking questions such as:

Q *Have you ever had a disagreement with anyone? What did you disagree about?*

Q *How did you feel?*

Q *How was your disagreement like Matthew and Tilly's? How was it different?*

FACILITATION TIP

During this unit, we encourage you to focus on two questioning techniques that deepen the students' thinking and broaden participation in discussions: **asking open-ended questions** and **using wait-time**. Notice that most of the questions we suggest are open-ended, inviting many responses. They cannot be answered with a single word and often begin with words like *what*, *how*, and *why*. We encourage you to ask the questions as they are written and notice how the students respond. Because the questions require thought, we suggest that you use at least 5–10 seconds of wait-time after asking a question before calling on anyone to respond. This gives everyone a chance to think before talking.

5 Reflect on the Story's Message

Tell the students that sometimes stories teach us lessons that can help us in our own lives. Explain that *Matthew and Tilly* is a story about friendship. Ask:

Q *What do you think Matthew and Tilly find out about friendship in this story?*

Q *How can what happens to Matthew and Tilly help you be a better friend?*

Review that today the students thought about a story and connected the story to their own lives. Tell them that in the coming weeks they will continue to hear stories and make connections.

6 Discuss Talking Together

Share some of your observations about the students' interactions. Mention things that went well and, if appropriate, any problems you noticed. Have the students suggest possible solutions.

Read Independently

Have the students independently read books they choose for 5–10 minutes. Have students who are unable to read independently look at the pictures in their books. If time permits, have a few volunteers share their books with the class. Help each student read the title of his book to the class. Then have each volunteer discuss the book. Ask questions such as:

Q *What is your book about?*

Q *What is your favorite part of the book?*

Note

Previewing the questions with your English Language Learners before they begin to read independently will help them focus on their reading.

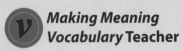

Making Meaning
Vocabulary **Teacher**

Next week you will revisit *Matthew and Tilly* to teach Vocabulary Week 5.

UNIT 2: MAKING CONNECTIONS
Fiction

McDuff and the Baby
by Rosemary Wells, illustrated by Susan Jeffers
(Hyperion, 1997)

McDuff's life changes after a baby arrives and Lucy and Fred are too busy to pay attention to him.

ALTERNATIVE BOOKS

Koala Lou by Mem Fox

The Cow That Went OINK by Bernard Most

Comprehension Focus

- Students *make text-to-self connections*.

- Students informally *identify important ideas* in a story.

- Students answer questions to understand the story.

- Students read independently.

Social Development Focus

- Students take responsibility for their learning and behavior.

- Students develop the group skill of talking and listening to one another.

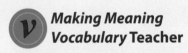

Making Meaning
Vocabulary Teacher

If you are teaching Developmental Studies Center's *Making Meaning Vocabulary* program, teach Vocabulary Week 5 this week. For more information, see the *Making Meaning Vocabulary Teacher's Manual.*

Day 1

Materials

- *McDuff and the Baby*
- *Assessment Resource Book*

Read-aloud

In this lesson, the students:

- Hear and discuss a story
- Refer to the story to support their thinking
- Read independently for up to 10 minutes
- Talk and listen to one another

1▶ Get Ready to Work Together

Have partners sit together. Explain that today you will read a story aloud, and then the students will talk in pairs and with the class about it. Remind the students that it is important to listen carefully as you read so they can talk about the story.

2▶ Introduce *McDuff and the Baby*

Show the cover of *McDuff and the Baby* and read the title and names of the author and illustrator aloud. Explain that McDuff is a dog that belongs to a couple named Fred and Lucy. Ask:

Q *What do you think this story might be about?*

 Use "Turn to Your Partner" to have pairs discuss the question. Then have one or two volunteers share their ideas with the class.

3▶ Read Aloud

Explain that you will show the pictures as you read and that you will stop to have partners talk about the story.

Read the book aloud slowly and clearly, showing the illustrations and stopping as described on the next page.

FACILITATION TIP

As you **ask open-ended questions** this week, remember to use 5–10 seconds of **wait-time** to give everyone a chance to think before talking. If you often hear from the same few students during class discussions, extend the wait-time to encourage more students to participate.

 Note

Consider previewing the story with your English Language Learners prior to the read-aloud.

Deal with each suggested vocabulary word as you come to it in the story.

Suggested Vocabulary

comics: stories told in cartoons; funny pages (p. 3)

stranger: person you don't know (p. 6)

arrived: came (p. 6)

carriage: stroller (p. 10; refer to the illustration)

admired: liked (p. 11)

radio concerts: live music performances heard on the radio (p. 12)

ELL Vocabulary

English Language Learners may benefit from discussing additional vocabulary, including:

skunk trails: tracks left by skunks (p. 4)

kept Lucy and Fred hopping: kept Lucy and Fred busy (p. 8)

woodland path: path in the woods (p. 10)

neighbors: people who live near you (p. 11; refer to the illustration)

interrupted: stopped for a short time (p. 12)

terrible: very bad or unpleasant (p. 15)

squinting: squeezing his eyes (p. 15)

footprints: marks made by a foot or shoe (p. 19)

 Note

Consider providing visual support for your English Language Learners by drawing a quick sketch of some of the vocabulary words, such as *skunk trails*, *woodland path*, and *footprints*.

Stop after:

p. 5 "Every day in every way McDuff was happy."

Ask:

Q *What have you learned about Lucy, Fred, and McDuff so far?*

Use "Turn to Your Partner" to have the students discuss the question. Then have one or two volunteers share their ideas with the class. Reread the last sentence on page 5, and continue reading. Stop again after:

p. 16 "'McDuff has stopped eating!' said Lucy."

Ask:

Q *What happens after the baby arrives?*

Teacher Note ▶

Hearing from only one or two
students at each stop helps
maintain the flow of the story and
keeps the students engaged.

ELL Note

If necessary, reread parts of the
story to clarify any confusion.

 Use "Turn to Your Partner" to have the students discuss the question
and then have one or two volunteers share their thinking with the
class. Reread the last sentence on page 16, and then read to the end
of the story.

4 ▶ Discuss the Story

 First in pairs, and then as a class, discuss questions such as:

Q *What happens at the end of the story?*

Q *What surprises you about McDuff and the Baby?*

As the students share, turn to the story text that supports their
thinking and read it aloud.

> ### CLASS PROGRESS ASSESSMENT
>
> As partners talk, observe them and ask yourself:
>
> **Q** *Are both partners sharing their thinking?*
>
> **Q** *Are they making connections to the part of the story
> they heard?*
>
> **Q** *Are they connecting to the big ideas and feelings in that
> part of the story?*
>
> Record your observations on page 5 of the *Assessment
> Resource Book*.

Tell the students that they will talk more about *McDuff and the Baby*
in the next lesson and think about how the story reminds them of
things that happen in their own lives.

5 ▶ Read Independently

Have the students independently read books they choose for 5–10
minutes. Have students who are unable to read independently look
at the pictures in their books. If time permits, have a few students
share their books with the class. Ask volunteers to tell one thing
they liked about their books.

Day 2

Strategy Lesson

In this lesson, the students:

- *Make text-to-self connections* to enjoy and understand a story
- Refer to the story to support their thinking
- Read independently for up to 10 minutes
- Talk and listen to one another

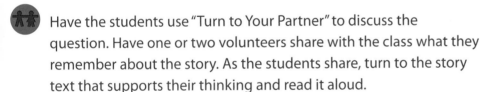 **Review *McDuff and the Baby***

Have partners sit together. Show the cover of *McDuff and the Baby* and remind the students that in the previous lesson they heard the story and talked about it. Ask:

Q *What is this story about?*

 Have the students use "Turn to Your Partner" to discuss the question. Have one or two volunteers share with the class what they remember about the story. As the students share, turn to the story text that supports their thinking and read it aloud.

Probe the students' thinking with questions such as:

Q *What problem does McDuff have?*

Q *How does McDuff feel about the baby at the beginning of the story? Why does he feel this way?*

Q *How does McDuff feel about the baby at the end of the story? Why do his feelings change?*

Materials

- *McDuff and the Baby* (pages 6–17)
- A sheet of writing/drawing paper for each student
- Crayons or markers

ELL Note

You might support students with limited English proficiency by providing prompts for responding to the questions such as "McDuff's problem is…" and "McDuff feels…."

Think About Making Connections

Remind the students that previously they heard the story *Matthew and Tilly* and thought about how the story reminded them of their own lives. Explain that today you will reread the part of *McDuff and the Baby* in which McDuff feels left out because of the new baby. Tell them that as they listen you would like them to think about a time in their own lives when they felt left out like McDuff. Explain that later they will draw a picture about this time in their lives.

 Reread Pages 6–17

Reread pages 6–17, slowly and clearly, stopping to show the illustrations.

 Briefly Discuss Personal Connections

Have the students think quietly about a time when they felt left out. Have one or two students respond to the following question. (Later in the lesson more students will have opportunities to share their connections.)

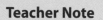
Teacher Note

If the students have difficulty making connections, you may want to share a connection from your own life.

Q *When have you felt left out like McDuff?*

Students might say:

"I remember when my baby sister came home from the hospital. Everyone came to see her. I felt left out and sad."

"When I started school this year, I didn't have any friends and felt lonely. Now I have friends, and I'm happy."

"Sometimes my brother won't play with me. That makes me feel left out and mad like McDuff felt in the story."

 Note

Having the opportunity to express their thinking through drawing is especially helpful for your English Language Learners.

 Draw Personal Connections

Distribute a sheet of writing/drawing paper to each student. Explain that they will each use the paper to draw a picture of a time when they felt left out. Have each student dictate or write a sentence about his picture.

 When the students complete their drawings, ask them to share and talk about the drawings with their partners. Then, have a few volunteers share and describe their drawings for the class.

Remind the students that when they think about how a story reminds them of their own lives they are doing something that good readers do—making connections. Explain that the students will continue to make connections as they hear stories in the coming weeks.

6 Read Independently

Have the students read books they choose independently for 5–10 minutes. Have students who are unable to read independently look at the pictures in their books. Then have partners take turns sharing their books with each other. Ask the pairs to talk about why they liked or did not like their books.

EXTENSION

Think About the Classroom Community

Review that the students heard you read *McDuff and the Baby* and thought about times in their lives when they felt left out like McDuff. Remind the students that they are building a classroom community this year in which everyone feels safe and welcome and no one feels left out. Ask:

Q *What can we do in our classroom to make sure that everyone feels welcome and no one feels left out?*

Ask the students to think about the question individually; then have them share in pairs. After a few moments, ask volunteers to share their thinking with the class. You might list the students' ideas on a sheet of chart paper entitled "Making Everyone Feel Welcome." Alternatively, you might have the students make drawings about ways to make everyone feel welcome and then collect the drawings in a class book.

ELL Note

Before your English Language Learners read independently, preview the question you will ask at the end. You might say, "After you read, I will ask you about what parts of your book you liked and didn't like."

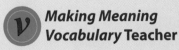

*Making Meaning
Vocabulary* **Teacher**

Next week you will revisit *McDuff and the Baby* to teach Vocabulary Week 6.

Week 3

Overview

UNIT 2: MAKING CONNECTIONS
Fiction

Chrysanthemum
by Kevin Henkes
(Mulberry, 1991)

Chrysanthemum loves her name, until she starts school and the other children make fun of it.

ALTERNATIVE BOOKS

Oliver Button Is a Sissy by Tomie dePaola

Arthur's Eyes by Marc Brown

Comprehension Focus

• Students *make text-to-self connections.*

• Students informally *identify important ideas* in a story.

• Students *answer questions* to understand the story.

• Students read independently.

Social Development Focus

• Students take responsibility for their learning and behavior.

• Students develop the group skill of talking and listening to one another.

DO AHEAD

• Prepare a sheet of chart paper labeled "What Good Readers Do" (see Day 2, Step 5 on page 69).

• Make copies of the Unit 2 Parent Letter (BLM2) to send home with the students on the last day of the unit. (For more information about the Parent Letters, see page xxxvi.)

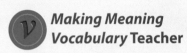

Making Meaning
Vocabulary Teacher

If you are teaching Developmental Studies Center's *Making Meaning Vocabulary* program, teach Vocabulary Week 6 this week. For more information, see the *Making Meaning Vocabulary Teacher's Manual.*

Day 1

Materials

- *Chrysanthemum*

 Note

You might prepare English Language Learners to hear the story by having a brief conversation about teasing. They may also benefit from previewing the story. Continue to preview the read-alouds with your English Language Learners throughout the *Making Meaning* program.

Read-aloud

In this lesson, the students:

- Hear and discuss a story
- Refer to the story to support their thinking
- Read independently for up to 10 minutes
- Talk and listen to one another

1 ▶ Get Ready to Work Together

Have partners sit together. Explain that today you will read a book aloud and the students will talk about the story in pairs and then with the class. Remind them that it is important to listen carefully so that they can remember what happens in the story.

2 ▶ Introduce *Chrysanthemum*

Show the book's cover and read the title and name of the author aloud. Explain that the story is about a girl mouse named Chrysanthemum and that a chrysanthemum is also a type of flower.

3 ▶ Read Aloud

Explain that you will stop during the reading to have partners talk about the story.

Read the book aloud slowly and clearly, showing the illustrations and stopping as described on the next page.

Deal with each suggested vocabulary word as you come to it in the story.

Suggested Vocabulary

wilted: went from feeling happy to feeling sad (p. 10)

dreadful: very bad (p. 10)

winsome: cheerful (p. 13)

speechless: so surprised you cannot talk (p. 24)

indescribable wonder: a very special person or event (p. 24)

musicale: a play that includes singing and dancing (p. 25)

humorous: funny or amusing (p. 27)

blushed, beamed, bloomed: was very happy (p. 29)

marigold, carnation, lily of the valley: names of flowers (p. 30)

ELL Vocabulary

English Language Learners may benefit from discussing additional vocabulary, including:

perfect: wonderful and beautiful; the very best ever (p. 3)

giggled: laughed (p. 9)

nightmare: scary dream (p. 22)

They went out of their way to make a nice impression: They tried very hard to be good so that Mrs. Twinkle would like them (p. 24)

Read pages 3–8 and stop after:

p. 8   "Chrysanthemum thought her name was absolutely perfect."

Ask:

Q   *What have you learned about Chrysanthemum so far?*

 Use "Turn to Your Partner" to have the students discuss the question. Then have one or two volunteers share their ideas with the class.

Reread the last sentence and continue reading. Follow this procedure at the next two stops:

p. 15   "It was an extremely pleasant dream."

p. 22   "It was the worst nightmare of Chrysanthemum's life."

Reread the last sentence, and continue reading to the bottom of page 31. Do not read the "Epilogue" on page 32 now. You may wish to read it as an extension activity (see page 70).

4 ▶ Discuss the Story

Facilitate a brief whole-class discussion of the story. Ask:

Q *After her first day at school, Chrysanthemum says, "School is no place for me." Why does she say that?*

Q *What happens that makes Chrysanthemum feel happy about her name again?*

Have one or two volunteers share their ideas with the class. Be ready to reread passages and show illustrations to help the students recall what they heard.

5 ▶ Reflect on the Partner Discussions

Have the students reflect on their partner discussions. Ask:

Q *What went well when you talked with your partner today?*

Q *What might you and your partner do differently the next time you work together?*

Explain that in the next lesson the students will talk more about the story and think about how it reminds them of experiences in their own lives.

6 ▶ Read Independently

Have the students read books they choose independently for 5–10 minutes. Then have partners take turns sharing their books with each other. Ask partners to talk about why they liked or did not like their books.

 ELL Note

Preview the question you will ask at the end of independent reading by asking the students to pay attention to what they like or don't like in their book as they read. At the end of independent reading, provide a response prompt for your students with limited English proficiency, such as "I liked my book because…."

Day 2

Strategy Lesson

In this lesson, the students:

- *Make text-to-self connection*s to enjoy and understand a story
- Refer to the story to support their thinking
- Read independently for up to 10 minutes
- Talk and listen to one another

Materials

- *Chrysanthemum* (pages 17–19)
- "What Good Readers Do" chart, prepared ahead, and a marker
- *Assessment Resource Book*
- Unit 2 Parent Letter (BLM2)

1 Review Making Connections

Have partners sit together. Review that in previous lessons the students heard *Matthew and Tilly* and *McDuff and the Baby* and thought about how the stories reminded them of their own lives. Explain that today they will hear part of *Chrysanthemum* again and think about how that part reminds them of something that has happened to them.

2 Review *Chrysanthemum*

Show the book and read the title and author's name. Ask:

Q *What is this story about?*

Probe the students' thinking with questions such as:

Q *What happens to Chrysanthemum on her first day at school?*

Q *How does Mrs. Twinkle help Chrysanthemum like her name again?*

◀ **Teacher Note**

If the students have difficulty recalling the story, you might reread all or parts of it. Alternatively, you might show the students some of the illustrations and ask them to say what is happening (for example, you might show the pictures on pages 7, 12–13, 18–19, 22–23, 28–29, and 31).

FACILITATION TIP

Reflect on your experience over the past three weeks with **asking open-ended questions** and **using wait-time**. Do these techniques feel comfortable and natural? Do you find yourself using them throughout the school day? What effect has repeated use of them had on your students' thinking and participation in discussions? We encourage you to continue to use and reflect on these techniques throughout the year.

 Note

To provide more support to your English Language Learners, consider showing them the illustrations prior to rereading with the whole class.

Have a few volunteers share their thinking with the class. To extend the discussion and involve other students, ask follow-up questions such as:

Q *What did you hear [Rosa] say about the story?*

Q *What would you like to add to what [Rosa] said?*

▶ **3** **Reread Pages 17–19 and Make Connections**

Explain that you will reread part of *Chrysanthemum* today without showing the illustrations so that the students can listen more carefully to the words. Tell them that as they listen you would like them to think about how the story reminds them of their own lives.

Reread pages 17–19, slowly and clearly, without showing the illustrations.

▶ **4** **Discuss the Students' Connections**

Ask the students to think quietly about this question:

Q *When has someone said something to you that hurt your feelings?*

 Use "Turn to Your Partner" to have the students discuss the question. Ask a few volunteers to share their experiences with the class.

> **CLASS PROGRESS ASSESSMENT**
>
> As partners talk, circulate among them and listen to the connections they make between their lives and the story. Ask yourself:
>
> **Q** *Are the students making connections to the part of the story they heard?*
>
> **Q** *Are they connecting to the big ideas and feelings in that part of the story?*
>
> Record your observations on page 6 of the *Assessment Resource Book*.

As the students share their connections, probe their thinking with questions such as:

Q *How did you feel when that happened to you?*

Q *How do you think Chrysanthemum feels? Why do you think she feels [sad]?*

5 Begin the "What Good Readers Do" Chart

Remind the students that as they thought about *Chrysanthemum,* they did something that good readers do—they made connections between what happens in stories and their own lives. Explain that making connections can help them enjoy and understand a story.

Direct the students' attention to the chart paper labeled "What Good Readers Do." Read the title of the chart aloud and explain that you are going to use the chart to keep a record of the things good readers do to help them make sense of what they read. Write *make connections to our lives* on the chart. Explain that the students will continue to make connections as they hear stories throughout the year and that they will also practice making connections in their independent reading.

6 Reflect on Working Together

Help the students think about their interactions. Ask:

Q *What did you do to take responsibility for listening to your partner today?*

Have a few volunteers share their ideas with the class.

7 Read Independently

Have the students independently read books they choose for 5–10 minutes. Ask the students if they made any connections between what happened in their books and their own lives. Have one or two students share their thinking with the class.

ELL Note

You might support your English Language Learners by providing prompts for their responses to the questions, such as "I felt…" and "I think Chrysanthemum feels…."

◀ **Teacher Note**

Display the "What Good Readers Do" chart where the students can refer to it throughout the year. You will add strategies to the chart as they are introduced. Refer to the chart often to remind the students to use the strategies as they listen to stories and read independently throughout the day.

Teacher Note

This is the last week of Unit 2. You may want to repeat this unit's lessons with alternative books, which are listed on the Week Overview page.

You will reassign partners for Unit 3.

Teacher Note

The second question is an opportunity for the students to explore the effect of one's actions on the feelings of others. You might probe their thinking about what Chrysanthemum did with questions such as "How did Chrysanthemum feel when the students giggled at her name? How do you think Victoria would feel if she knew Chrysanthemum was giggling at her? Would you have giggled at Victoria? Why or why not?"

▶

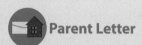

Parent Letter

Send home with each student the Parent Letter for this unit (see "Do Ahead," page 63). Periodically have a few students share with the class what they are reading at home.

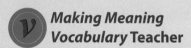

Making Meaning Vocabulary Teacher

Next week you will revisit *Chrysanthemum* to teach Vocabulary Week 7.

E X T E N S I O N

Read and Discuss the Epilogue

Show the "Epilogue" page to the students and explain that an *epilogue* is a short piece of writing added to the end of a story. Remind the students that in *Chrysanthemum* Mrs. Twinkle, the music teacher, assigned Chrysanthemum and the other students roles in the class musicale. Explain that as you read the epilogue you would like the students to listen for what happened at the musicale. Read the epilogue aloud slowly and clearly.

After the reading, facilitate a whole-class discussion. Ask:

Q *What happened at the musicale?*

Q *Chrysanthemum giggled when Victoria forgot her lines. What do you think about that?*

Unit 3

Retelling

FICTION

During this unit, the students use the sequence of events to retell stories with a simple narrative structure. They discuss important characters in the stories and answer questions to understand the stories. Socially, they relate the values of respect and responsibility to their behavior and continue to develop the group skills of speaking clearly and taking turns talking and listening.

UNIT 3: RETELLING
Fiction

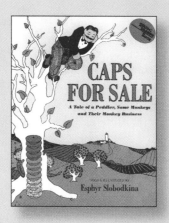

Caps for Sale
by Esphyr Slobodkina
(HarperTrophy, 1987)

A hat peddler has an encounter with some monkeys.

ALTERNATIVE BOOKS

Little Mouse's Painting by Diane Wolkerson

Annie and the Wild Animals by Jan Brett

Comprehension Focus

• Students use the sequence of events to *retell* a story with a simple narrative structure.

• Students answer questions to understand the story.

• Students read independently.

Social Development Focus

• Students relate the values of respect and responsibility to their behavior.

• Students develop the group skills of speaking clearly and taking turns talking and listening.

DO AHEAD

• Prior to Day 1, decide how you will randomly assign partners to work together during the unit. For suggestions about assigning partners randomly, see page xviii. For considerations for pairing English Language Learners, see page xxx.

• Prepare the "Teacher's Facilitation Bookmark," following the directions on BLM12. Refer to the questions and suggestions throughout the year to help you facilitate whole-class discussions.

• Collect a variety of narrative texts for the students to read independently throughout the unit. For information about Developmental Studies Center's Individualized Daily Reading Libraries, see page xxvii and visit Developmental Studies Center's website at devstu.org.

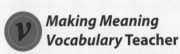

Making Meaning Vocabulary **Teacher**

If you are teaching Developmental Studies Center's *Making Meaning Vocabulary* program, teach Vocabulary Week 7 this week. For more information, see the *Making Meaning Vocabulary Teacher's Manual.*

Day 1

Materials

- *Caps for Sale*
- A sheet of writing/drawing paper for each student
- Markers or crayons
- "Teacher's Facilitation Bookmark" (BLM12), to be used throughout the program

***Being a* Writer™ Teacher**

You can either have the students work with their *Being a Writer* partner or assign them a different partner for the *Making Meaning* lessons.

Teacher Note ▶

Model speaking in a very soft, a very loud, and an appropriate voice.

Read-aloud

In this lesson, the students:

- Begin working with new partners
- Hear and discuss a story
- Refer to the story to support their thinking
- Read independently for up to 10 minutes
- Speak so that others can hear

▶1 Get Ready to Work with New Partners

Randomly assign partners and ask the students to come to the rug for a read-aloud. Make sure all the students can see the book and illustrations clearly. Explain that the students will work in these pairs for the next three weeks.

During today's lesson you will read a book aloud and the students will use "Turn to Your Partner" so everyone will have a chance to talk about the story. Remind the students that by talking and listening in pairs, the students get a chance to think more about the story.

Tell the students that during the next few weeks they will listen to stories and then retell them in their own words. Explain that it is important for speakers to talk clearly so that their partners and the class can hear and understand. Let them know that they will talk about how they did speaking clearly later in the lesson.

▶2 Introduce *Caps for Sale*

Show the cover of *Caps for Sale* and read the title and author's name aloud. Explain that Esphyr Slobodkina is also the illustrator. Point to the words on the cover and have the students reread the title and author's name with you.

Explain that this is a story about a peddler. A peddler is a person who travels around selling things—in this case, caps. Point out the peddler and the caps in the illustration on the cover.

Explain that *Caps for Sale* is a story that children have enjoyed for many years, so some of them might have heard it before. Listening to a story again can help them notice things they might have missed or forgotten.

 ## 3 ▶ Read Aloud

Explain that you will stop during the reading to have partners talk.

Read the story aloud slowly and clearly, showing the illustrations and stopping as described below.

Suggested Vocabulary

peddler: person who travels around selling things (p. 5)

wares: things for sale (p. 5)

upset: tip, turn, or knock something over (p. 7)

disturb: bother or upset (p. 11)

refreshed: feeling stronger and wide awake (p. 15)

ELL Vocabulary

English Language Learners may benefit from discussing additional vocabulary, including:

stamped his foot: lifted his foot and put it down hard (p. 30; act out stamping your foot)

Read pages 5–13, and stop after:

p. 13 "He slept for a long time."

Ask:

Q *What do you know about the peddler so far?*

 Use "Turn to Your Partner" to have the students discuss the question. Then have one or two volunteers briefly share their ideas with the class.

ELL Note

English Language Learners may benefit from more frequent stops and discussions during the story. For example, you might stop after page 7 (to discuss what the students know about the peddler so far), and after page 30 (to discuss what they think might happen next in the story).

Reread page 13 and continue reading pages 15–21. Stop after:

p. 21 "And what do you think he saw?"

 Have the students discuss, first in pairs, and then as a class:

Q *What do you think might happen next in the story?*

Reread page 21 and continue reading to the end of the story.

Teacher Note ▶
Remind students familiar with the story that it is important not to tell their partners what happens in the story.

4 ▶ Discuss the Story

Teacher Note ▶
The purpose of this discussion is to make sure the students have a surface-level understanding of the story. If necessary, reread parts of the story to clarify any confusion.

At the end of the book, facilitate a brief whole-class discussion of the story. Ask:

Q *What is the peddler's problem in the story?*

Q *How is his problem solved?*

Explain that in the next lesson, the students will talk again about *Caps for Sale*.

5 ▶ Reflect on Speaking Clearly

Teacher Note

Use your "Teacher's Facilitation Bookmark" to help you facilitate discussions in a way that creates opportunities for the students to respond to one another and that increases student accountability. For example:

- Use "Turn to Your Partner" when only a few students are responding or if many students want to talk.

- Teach listening directly by saying, "[Mary] is going to speak. Let's all look at her and think about what [she] says."

Remind the students that one goal for the class today was to talk in voices others could hear and understand. Ask questions such as:

Q *What did you do to make sure others could hear you?*

Q *Why is it important for you and your partner to hear one another?*

6 ▶ Read Independently

Have the students read books they choose independently for 5–10 minutes. Ask several students to share their books with the class. Have each student read his title to the class and tell one or two things he liked about the story.

EXTENSIONS

Draw Mental Pictures of a Cap

Ask the students to think about the color and kind of cap they would buy if they could buy any kind they wanted. After a few minutes of thinking time, have a few students share their ideas with the class. Then distribute a sheet of writing/drawing paper to each student and have the students draw and write about the cap they have in mind.

Form pairs into groups of four students. Have the students take turns sharing their work in the small groups.

Act Out the Story

Combine retelling and physical movement to enhance understanding of the story. Form small groups and assign character roles from the story. Reread sections of the story and have the students act them out, using their own words or performing in pantomime as you read the story.

ELL Note

This extension is especially helpful for your English Language Learners. Acting out the story will help them understand the story more fully.

Day 2

Materials

- *Caps for Sale*
- *Assessment Resource Book*

Strategy Lesson

In this lesson, the students:

- Use the sequence of events to *retell* a story with a simple narrative structure
- Refer to the story to support their thinking
- Read independently for up to 10 minutes
- Speak so that others can hear

About Retelling

Narrative text is the primary type of text that young students listen to and read. Through teacher questioning and class discussions, the students begin to recognize that narrative stories follow certain patterns and evolve through a sequence of events.

As the students practice *retelling* stories, they become increasingly familiar with the way plots develop and with other story elements, such as character, setting, and problems and solutions. Retelling a sequence of events helps the students make logical sense of the story and forms a foundation for talking about books.

1 ▶ Review the Importance of Speaking Clearly

Have partners sit together. Briefly review the importance of talking so that others can hear. Ask for volunteers to model speaking at very soft, very loud, and appropriate levels.

2 ▶ Introduce Retelling

Explain that today the students will talk more about the story *Caps for Sale* by retelling it in their own words. Point out that retelling a story helps them think about what happens in the story and talk about the story with other people. Retelling also helps them understand and enjoy the story.

ELL Note

You may wish to explain to the students that when they *retell* a story, they *use their own words to say what happened* in the story.

3 ## Model Retelling with *Caps for Sale*

Show the cover of *Caps for Sale* and read the title and author's name aloud. Explain that you will begin retelling the story. Then you will show the students the pictures to help them think about the story, and ask them to continue the retelling.

Point out the illustrations on pages 4, 6, and 8, stopping at each illustration to model retelling the story in your own words. (For example, you might say, "Once there was a peddler who carried the caps that he sold on his head. He had his own checked cap on the bottom, then he had gray caps, brown caps, and blue caps. On the very top he had red caps. He walked up and down calling out, 'Caps! Caps for sale! Fifty cents a cap!' One day he couldn't sell any caps so he decided to take a walk in the country.")

ELL Note

It may benefit English Language Learners to retell the story in smaller sections. You might read a section, stop to show the illustrations, and then ask the students to retell just that section.

4 ## Have the Class Retell the Story

Show the illustration on page 10. Ask:

Q *What is happening in the story?*

Have a volunteer retell that part of the story to the class (for example, "The peddler sits down to rest under a tree"). Continue to show the illustrations, stopping as indicated and having individual students retell that part of the story to the class. Group the illustrations as follows: pages 12–14, 16–20, 22–33, 35–39, and 41–43.

◀ **Teacher Note**

Retelling as a whole class allows you to check for understanding. Help the students focus on retelling the sequence of events, using questions such as:

Q *What part of the story have we missed?*

Q *Where does that part fit?*

> ### CLASS PROGRESS ASSESSMENT ·············
>
> Listen to and observe the students as they share.
> Ask yourself:
>
> **Q** *Are the students referring to the text to retell the story?*
>
> **Q** *Are they speaking so they can hear one another?*
>
> Record your observations on page 7 of the *Assessment Resource Book*.

FACILITATION TIP

During this unit, we invite you to practice **asking a question once** and then waiting for the students to respond before repeating or rephrasing it. If the students are confused by a question or need to hear it again, have them ask you to repeat it or ask it again in a different way. This helps the students learn to take responsibility for listening carefully during a discussion.

 Discuss Retelling

Remind the students that today they practiced retelling *Caps for Sale*. Ask:

Q *What does it mean to retell a story?*

Have a few students share their thinking with the class.

Tell the students that they will retell more stories with the class and their partners during the coming weeks.

 Read Independently

Have the students read independently for 5–10 minutes. Continue to have individual students share their books with the class.

EXTENSION

Sequence the Events in *Caps for Sale*

Write the main events in the story on sentence strips. Include a picture clue for each event. For example:

- *The peddler walks through the town yelling "Caps! Caps for sale!"*

- *The peddler sits down under a tree and falls asleep.*

- *The peddler wakes up and his caps are gone.*

- *The monkeys in the tree have the caps.*

- *The peddler shakes his finger and stamps his feet.*

- *The peddler throws his cap on the ground.*

- *The monkeys throw the caps on the ground.*

- *The peddler puts the caps on his head.*

Place the strips randomly in a pocket chart. Read each sentence with the students and have them put the events in order. Be ready to reread from the story as necessary. Later, put the strips in an envelope and have them available for pairs to work with on their own.

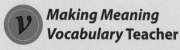

Making Meaning
Vocabulary **Teacher**

Next week you will revisit *Caps for Sale* to teach Vocabulary Week 8.

Week 2

Overview

UNIT 3: RETELLING
Fiction

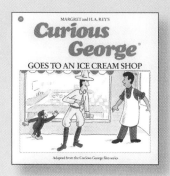

Curious George Goes to an Ice Cream Shop
edited by Margret Rey and Alan J. Shalleck
(Houghton Mifflin, 1989)

A funny monkey creates some chaos as he tries to decide on an ice cream flavor, but he redeems himself in the end.

ALTERNATIVE BOOKS

The Hat by Jan Brett

Curious George Takes a Job by H. A. Rey

Comprehension Focus

- Students use the sequence of events to *retell* a story with a simple narrative structure.

- Students discuss important characters in a story.

- Students read independently.

Social Development Focus

- Students relate the values of respect and responsibility to their behavior.

- Students develop the group skills of speaking clearly and taking turns talking and listening.

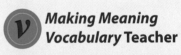 **Making Meaning Vocabulary Teacher**

If you are teaching Developmental Studies Center's *Making Meaning Vocabulary* program, teach Vocabulary Week 8 this week. For more information, see the *Making Meaning Vocabulary Teacher's Manual.*

Day 1

Materials

- *Curious George Goes to an Ice Cream Shop*

- "Reading Together" chart (from Unit 1) and a marker

Read-aloud

In this lesson, the students:

- Hear and discuss a story
- Discuss important characters in the story
- Refer to the story to support their thinking
- Read independently for up to 10 minutes
- Speak clearly, listen responsibly, and take turns

1 ▶ **Discuss Speaking Clearly and Listening Responsibly**

Have partners sit together. Explain that this week the students will listen to a story and retell it to their partners and the class. Remind them that last week they talked about the importance of speaking loudly and clearly.

Explain that listeners have a responsibility to ask speakers to speak more clearly when they are unable to hear them. Ask:

Q *How can you ask someone in a respectful way to speak a little louder or to repeat what she said? Why is this important?*

Record ideas on the "Reading Together" chart.

> **Students might say:**
>
> "Please talk a little louder because I can't hear you."
>
> "Can you say that again, please?"
>
> "Please look at me when you talk. That will help me hear you."

Ask the students to think about being responsible listeners as they work with their partners today.

Reading Together

- *listen to and talk about the story*

- *listen to what your partner says*

Introduce *Curious George Goes to an Ice Cream Shop*

Show the cover of *Curious George Goes to an Ice Cream Shop* and read the title aloud. Explain that this is a story about a monkey named Curious George, and that there are many stories about Curious George and his adventures. Point out that *curious* means *wanting to find out about things.* Ask:

Q *What do you think might happen to George in this story?*

Have one or two volunteers share their ideas with the class.

Read Aloud

Explain that you will stop during the reading and ask partners to talk about the story. Ask the students to listen for times when George is curious.

Read the story aloud slowly and clearly, showing the illustrations and stopping as described on the next page.

Suggested Vocabulary

curious: wanting to find out about things (title)

errands: short trips to pick up, buy, or deliver something (p. 8)

sprinkles: small, colorful pieces of candy (p. 24)

masterpiece: very special or outstanding piece of work (p. 26)

scold: tell someone that you are unhappy with what he did (p. 27)

customers: people who buy something (p. 30)

ELL Vocabulary

English Language Learners may benefit from discussing additional vocabulary, including:

Let's treat ourselves to some ice cream: Let's do something special and get some ice cream (p. 3)

owner: person the ice cream shop belongs to (p. 5)

a mountain of ice cream: lots and lots of ice cream (p. 22; refer to the illustration)

The orders kept pouring in: Lots of people were asking to buy ice cream (p. 29; refer to the illustration on p. 28)

Note

Support your students with limited English proficiency by providing prompts for their responses, such as "I think George is thinking…" and "I think George feels…." (For more information about supporting English Language Learners at various levels of proficiency, see page xxviii.)

FACILITATION TIP

Continue to support the students in taking responsibility for listening carefully during discussions by **asking a question once** without repeating or rewording it. Remember to use wait-time before calling on anyone so the students have a chance to think before talking. Encourage the students to have you repeat a question if they didn't hear it, or say it in a different way if they are confused.

Read pages 3–10 aloud, and stop after:

> **p. 10** "There were so many flavors to choose from."

Ask:

Q *What do you think George might be thinking?*

 Have pairs use "Turn to Your Partner" to discuss the question and have one or two volunteers share with the class.

Reread page 10 and continue reading. Follow the same procedure for the next two stops and questions.

> **p. 17** "'Get away from here!' Mr. Herb was angry."

Ask:

Q *How do you think George feels?*

Stop after:

> **p. 23** "Outside, there was a crowd watching."

Q *What do you think might happen next?*

Reread the last sentence and continue to the end of the story.

4 ▶ Discuss the Story

At the end of the story, have the class discuss:

Q *What is George's problem in this story?*

Q *How is his problem solved?*

Tell the students that they will talk more about *Curious George Goes to an Ice Cream Shop* in the next lesson.

5 ▶ Read Independently

Have the students read books they choose independently for 5–10 minutes. Ask one or two students who have finished their books to retell their stories to the class. Have each student read the title of her book and tell what happens in the story. If necessary, support the students by asking questions such as:

Q *What happens first in the story?*

Q *What happens next?*

Q *What happens at the end of the story?*

EXTENSION

Make Personal Connections to the Story

Facilitate a discussion about students' personal connections to *Curious George Goes to an Ice Cream Shop* using the following questions:

Q *George has a hard time deciding on an ice cream flavor. Does that ever happen to you? How do you make up your mind about the flavor of ice cream you want?*

Q *What are some other things you have to make up your mind about? How do you decide?*

 ELL Note

Support your English Language Learners by helping them rehearse retelling the stories they are reading.

 ELL Note

Consider giving examples of decisions the students might make at school, such as what game to play at recess or what activity to do during free time. Ask the students how they make decisions.

Day 2

Materials

- *Curious George Goes to an Ice Cream Shop*
- "What Good Readers Do" chart (from Unit 2)
- *Assessment Resource Book*

Strategy Lesson

In this lesson, the students:

- Use the sequence of events to *retell* a story with a simple narrative structure
- Refer to the story to support their thinking
- Discuss important characters in the story
- Read independently for up to 10 minutes
- Speak clearly, listen to one another, and take turns

1 Prepare to Do Partner Retelling of *Curious George Goes to an Ice Cream Shop*

Have partners sit together. Remind the students that after listening to *Caps for Sale* they retold the story as a class. Show the cover of *Curious George Goes to an Ice Cream Shop* and quickly review the names of the characters (George, the man in the yellow hat, and Mr. Herb) and where the story takes place. Explain that today partners will take turns retelling *Curious George Goes to an Ice Cream Shop* to each other.

Explain that you will show them some pictures and then ask partners to talk about what happens up to that point in the story. Then you will show them some more pictures and ask them to continue to retell the story in pairs.

 Have partners briefly discuss how they plan to take turns retelling the story. Ask a few volunteers to share their ideas with the class.

ELL Note

You might need to remind the students that when they *retell* a story, they *use their own words to say what happened* in the story.

2 Use Illustrations to Retell the Story

Explain that you will show the students the illustrations from a part of the story and they will talk in pairs about what is happening in that part. Remind them to talk about only the part of the story that you show, even though they may know what happens next.

Teacher Note ▶

If the students need additional support, reread as you show the illustrations.

Slowly show the illustrations on pages 3–7 and stop. Have pairs discuss:

Q *What happens in the part of the story I just showed you?*

When most pairs have finished, continue, using the same procedure for the following sections of the story: pages 8–13, 14–19, 20–25, and 26–32.

> **CLASS PROGRESS ASSESSMENT**
>
> As partners retell the story, ask yourself:
>
> **Q** *Are the students referring to the text to retell the story?*
>
> **Q** *Are partners speaking so they can hear each other?*
>
> **Q** *Do they help each other fill in gaps in the retelling?*
>
> Record your observations on page 8 of *the Assessment Resource Book.*

 ELL Note

Provide the students with prompts to help begin their partner conversation, such as "In the story, I remember…."

▶3 Add Retelling to the "What Good Readers Do" Chart

Review that the "What Good Readers Do" chart reminds the students of things they can do to enjoy and understand stories. Remind the students that they have been practicing retelling. Retelling can help them remember what happens in stories and talk to others about them. Write *retell* on the "What Good Readers Do" chart and let the students know they will have more chances to practice retelling in the coming weeks.

*What Good
Readers Do*

*- make connections to
our lives*

▶4 Reflect on Taking Turns

Have the students think about how they worked together retelling the story. Ask:

Q *What did you and your partner do to make sure you both had a chance to retell the story?*

Q *What would you do [the same way/differently] next time?*

Q *What can you do to help if your partner forgets part of the story?*

Offer some of your observations of ways the students worked well together. Tell the students they will have many chances to practice retelling stories.

5▶ Read Independently

Have the students read independently for 5–10 minutes. Continue to ask students who have finished their books to retell their stories to the class. Support the students by asking them what happens first, next, and at the end of the story.

EXTENSION

Think About Being Curious

Facilitate a discussion about the students' experiences with curiosity using the following questions:

Q *What does it mean to be curious?*

Q *What are you curious about?*

Teacher Note ▶

Keep a list of things the students are curious about. It will be an excellent resource for selecting classroom library books.

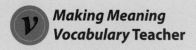 *Making Meaning Vocabulary* **Teacher**

Next week you will revisit *Curious George Goes to an Ice Cream Shop* to teach Vocabulary Week 9.

Week 3

Overview

UNIT 3: RETELLING
Fiction

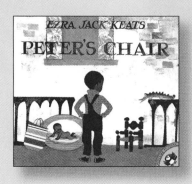

Peter's Chair
by Ezra Jack Keats
(Puffin, 1998)

A boy finds his blue furniture has been painted pink for his new baby sister. He decides to take his blue chair and run away.

ALTERNATIVE BOOKS

Jamaica and Brianna by Juanita Havill

The Tiny Seed by Eric Carle

Comprehension Focus

- Students use the sequence of events to *retell* a story with a simple narrative structure.

- Students discuss important characters in a story.

- Students read independently.

Social Development Focus

- Students relate the values of respect and responsibility to their behavior.

- Students develop the group skills of speaking clearly and taking turns talking and listening.

DO AHEAD

- Make copies of the Unit 3 Parent Letter (BLM3) to send home with the students on the last day of the unit. (For more information about the Parent Letters, see page xxxvi.)

 Making Meaning Vocabulary Teacher

If you are teaching Developmental Studies Center's *Making Meaning Vocabulary* program, teach Vocabulary Week 9 this week. For more information, see the *Making Meaning Vocabulary Teacher's Manual.*

Day 1

Materials

- *Peter's Chair*

Read-aloud

In this lesson, the students:

- Hear and discuss a story
- Use the sequence of events to *retell* a story with a simple narrative structure
- Refer to the story to support their thinking
- Read independently for up to 10 minutes
- Speak clearly, listen to one another, and take turns

 Introduce *Peter's Chair*

Have partners sit together. Show the cover of *Peter's Chair* and read the title and author's name aloud. Explain that Ezra Jack Keats is also the illustrator.

Tell the students that in *Peter's Chair,* Peter is the main character. Peter's father and mother, his sister Susie, and his dog Willie are also in the story. Remind the students that the main character in a story usually has a problem that is solved by the end of the story.

 Read Aloud

Explain that you will stop during the reading so that partners can talk. Read the story aloud slowly and clearly, showing the illustrations and stopping as described on the next page.

Suggested Vocabulary

fussing: paying a lot of attention to something (p. 8)

cradle: baby bed on rockers (p. 8)

muttered: spoke in a quiet, low voice (p. 13)

rascal: mischievous person (p. 25)

ELL Vocabulary

English Language Learners may benefit from discussing additional vocabulary, including:

stretched: reached out (p. 4; refer to the illustration)

high chair: special chair for a baby to sit in when being fed (p. 11)

dog biscuits: treats for dogs (p. 17)

arranged his things very nicely: put his things where he wanted them (p. 18)

his mother saw signs that Peter was home: his mother saw some of Peter's things (p. 25)

grown-up chair: chair for adults (p. 28)

Read pages 4–14 slowly and clearly, stopping to show the illustrations. Stop after:

p. 14   "He picked it up and ran to his room."

Ask:

Q *How does Peter feel in the part of the story you just heard?*

 Have the students use "Turn to Your Partner" to discuss the question; then have one or two volunteers share with the class. Reread page 14 and continue reading to page 22. Stop after:

p. 22   "But Peter got an idea."

Q *What do you think Peter's idea might be?*

 Have the students use "Turn to Your Partner" to discuss the question. Have one or two volunteers share with the class. Reread the last sentence on page 22 and continue reading to the end of the story.

3 ▶ **Discuss the Story**

Facilitate a discussion of the story using the following questions:

Q *What problem does Peter have in this story?*

Q *Why do you think Peter decides to paint the chair at the end?*

Q *What do you want to add to what [Carmen] said? Does anyone have a different idea?*

Tell the students they will have a chance to talk about *Peter's Chair* again in the next lesson.

4 ▶ **Read Independently**

 Have the students read books they choose independently for 5–10 minutes. Ask partners to take turns retelling the stories they have been reading. Circulate as partners share and provide support as needed.

EXTENSION

Make Personal Connections to the Story

Remind the students that they have talked before about how stories remind them of their own lives. Ask them to think about ways *Peter's Chair* reminds them of things that have happened to them. Prompt their thinking with questions such as:

Q *Why does Peter decide to run away in the story? How does he feel?*

Q *When have you felt [left out] the way Peter feels? Tell us about it.*

Q *What are some ways to make sure no one feels left out in our reading community?*

Day 2

Strategy Lesson

In this lesson, the students:

- Use the sequence of events to *retell* a story with a simple narrative structure
- Discuss important characters in the story
- Refer to the story to support their thinking
- Read independently for up to 10 minutes
- Listen to one another and take turns

1 Review Partner Retelling

Have partners sit together. Remind them that they have been listening to stories and retelling them to their partners and the class. Retelling a story helps them think more about what happens in the story and about the characters in it.

2 Reread and Retell the Story

Tell the students that you will read *Peter's Chair* again, and that you will stop at the beginning, middle, and end of the story to have partners retell it. Remind partners to take turns talking.

Reread pages 4–13 aloud, slowly and clearly, showing the illustrations. Stop after:

p. 13 "'My crib. It's painted pink too.'"

Ask partners to tell each other what has happened so far in the story.

Reread the last sentences before the stop and continue reading to page 20. Stop after:

p. 20 "He was too big!"

Ask partners to tell each other what happened in the part of the story they just heard.

Materials

- *Peter's Chair*
- Chart paper and a marker
- Sheet of drawing paper for each student
- Markers or crayons
- *Assessment Resource Book*
- Unit 3 Parent Letter (BLM3)

◀ **Teacher Note**

Not taking time to share as a class maintains the flow of the story and helps the students learn to rely on sharing their thinking with their partners, rather than always depending on the teacher or the whole class to confirm or support their thinking.

Reread page 20 and continue reading to the end of the story.

Ask partners to tell each other what happens in the last part of the story.

 Note

This activity will be especially helpful for your English Language Learners.

 Draw Pictures of the Story

Explain that each student will draw a picture of one thing that happens in the story. Ask:

Q *What are some of the things Peter does?*

> **Students might say:**
>
> "Peter hides behind the curtain."
>
> "Peter plays with his blocks."
>
> "Peter watches his mother with the baby."
>
> "Peter helps his father paint the chair."

Distribute a sheet of drawing paper to each student. Ask the students to draw a picture of something that happens in the story.

Give the students about 10 minutes to complete their drawings, alerting them when they have 2–3 minutes left.

CLASS PROGRESS ASSESSMENT

Reflect on the students' participation and ask yourself:

Q *Are the students able to sequence the events in the story?*

Q *Do they speak clearly when they share their thinking?*

Record your observations on page 9 of the *Assessment Resource Book.*

 Share Drawings

When the students finish their drawings, if time permits, have partners share them and decide which of their pictured events happens first in the story.

Teacher Note

This is the last week of Unit 3. You will need to reassign partners in Unit 4.

5 Read Independently

Have the students read independently for 5–10 minutes. Then have each student take turns retelling the story she has been reading to her partner. As before, circulate and provide support as needed.

EXTENSION

Make Text-to-text Connections Informally

Show the students the cover of *McDuff and the Baby*. Remind them that they heard and talked about this story earlier. Briefly review the story using questions such as:

Q *What happens in this story?*

Q *What do you remember about McDuff?*

If the students have difficulty, you might show some of the illustrations and ask the students to recall what happens at that point in the story. Ask:

Q *How is what happens to McDuff in* McDuff and the Baby *like what happens to Peter in* Peter's Chair?

Have the students use "Turn to Your Partner" to discuss the question. Then have volunteers share their thinking with the class.

> **Students might say:**
>
> "McDuff is like Peter because they both don't like the new baby."
>
> "No one is paying attention to them."
>
> "They're both nice to the baby at the end."

 Parent Letter

Send home with each student the Parent Letter for this unit (see "Do Ahead," page 93). Periodically, have a few students share with the class what they are reading at home.

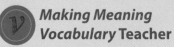 ***Making Meaning Vocabulary* Teacher**

Next week you will revisit *Peter's Chair* to teach Vocabulary Week 10.

Unit 4

Visualizing

POETRY AND FICTION

During this unit, the students visualize to make sense of text and make informal use of schema and inference. Socially, they learn the cooperative structure "Think, Pair, Share." They also relate the values of caring and respect to their behavior and develop the group skills of listening and respecting one another's time to think.

Week 1 *Did You See What I Saw? Poems about School* by Kay Winters
"The Balloon Man" by Dorothy Aldis

Week 2 *In the Tall, Tall Grass* by Denise Fleming

Week 3 *Sheep Out to Eat* by Nancy Shaw

Week 4 *The Snowy Day* by Ezra Jack Keats

Week 1

Overview

UNIT 4: VISUALIZING
Poetry and Fiction

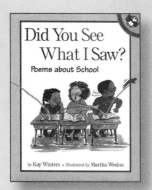

Did You See What I Saw? Poems about School
by Kay Winters, illustrated by Martha Weston
(Puffin, 2001)

Twenty-four poems bring school days to life.

"The Balloon Man"
by Dorothy Aldis

This poem is about a man who sells balloons to children.

ALTERNATIVE BOOKS

Have You Seen Birds? by Joanne Oppenheim
Grandparent Poems compiled by John Miklos Jr.

Comprehension Focus

- Students *visualize* to make sense of text.

- Students informally *use schema* and *inference* as they visualize.

- Students read independently.

Social Development Focus

- Students relate the values of respect, caring, and responsibility to their behavior.

- Students develop the group skills of speaking clearly and giving one another time to think.

- Students learn procedures for "Think, Pair, Share" and class meetings.

DO AHEAD

- Prior to Day 1, decide how you will randomly assign partners to work together during the unit. For suggestions about assigning partners randomly, see page xviii. For considerations for pairing English Language Learners, see page xxx.

- Prepare the "Class Meeting Ground Rules" chart (see the "Teacher Note" on page 105).

- Collect a variety of narrative and expository texts for the students to read independently throughout the unit. For information about Developmental Studies Center's Individualized Daily Reading Libraries, see page xxvii and visit Developmental Studies Center's website at devstu.org.

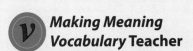

Making Meaning Vocabulary Teacher

If you are teaching Developmental Studies Center's *Making Meaning Vocabulary* program, teach Vocabulary Week 10 this week. For more information, see the *Making Meaning Vocabulary Teacher's Manual.*

Day 1

Materials

- Space for the class to sit in a circle
- "Class Meeting Ground Rules" chart, prepared ahead

Teacher Note ▶

There is a class meeting in each week of this unit. This gives the students an opportunity to become comfortable with the procedure. In later units, class meetings are less frequent.

Being a Writer™ **Teacher**

You can either have the students work with their *Being a Writer* partner or assign them a different partner for the *Making Meaning* lessons.

Class Meeting

In this lesson, the students:

- Learn the procedure and rules for a class meeting
- Listen to one another
- Begin working with new partners
- Read independently for up to 15 minutes

About Class Meetings

Class meetings are an important tool for fostering a nurturing classroom community and they will occur throughout the remainder of the year in the *Making Meaning* program. Unlike other classroom discussions, these meetings bring the students together around the common goal of creating a welcoming and accepting environment that enhances their academic achievement and encourages responsibility. Through class meeting discussions, the students learn to solve problems, develop empathy, and grow socially and ethically.

During the first part of the school year, the students have had many experiences working together and discussing their work together. Class meetings will give them the opportunity to discuss and further develop their reading community. If possible, arrange the students in a circle for class meetings. A circle puts everyone on equal footing, and the students are able to address one another directly. If there is not enough space to form a circle, have the students arrange their chairs so that most students can see one another.

▶ 1 ▶ Pair Students and Get Ready to Work Together

Randomly assign partners and have them sit together. Tell the students that they will work with these partners for the next few weeks. Have a few students briefly share what has been working well during their past partner work.

▶ 2 ▶ Introduce Class Meetings

Remind the students that they have been working together to create a comfortable classroom community. Explain that for the rest of the year, they will come together for class meetings to talk about how they are doing at creating a caring and safe reading community. Explain that today they will learn the procedure and rules for a class meeting.

3 Teach and Practice the Class Meeting Procedure

Explain how you would like the students to move into a circle and state your expectations. (For example, you might say, "When I call you and your partner, you will quietly get up and move carefully into a circle. You will form this side of the circle first, then the other side.") Before asking pairs to move, ask:

Q *What do you want to remember to make moving into a circle go smoothly?*

Have the students move to the circle with partners sitting together. If necessary, practice the procedure again until they can move in an orderly way. Explain that you would like them to use the same procedure every time they gather for a class meeting.

4 Discuss the Class Meeting Ground Rules

Refer to the "Class Meeting Ground Rules" chart and read each rule aloud. Explain that these are the rules that everyone follows during a class meeting. To help the students understand the rules, facilitate a brief discussion about each rule using the following questions. Have the students use "Turn to Your Partner" to discuss the questions; then have a few pairs share their thinking with the class. Ask:

Q *Why is it important that only one person talks at a time? Why is it important to listen during whole-class discussions?*

Q *What does it mean to disagree? How can we act in a caring way when we disagree with someone's idea?*

Q *We've worked a lot on speaking clearly so that others can hear. What are some other things we can do to be respectful when we're talking to each other?*

◀ **Teacher Note**

Before the lesson, prepare a chart with rules for the students to follow during class meetings. You might want to use or adapt the following rules:

- One person talks at a time.
- Listen to one another.
- Allow people to disagree.
- Talk respectfully to one another.

Students might say:

"I can listen better when I turn and look at the person talking."

"I can be nice to my partner even if I disagree."

Tell the students that they will have class meetings regularly from now on, and they will have opportunities to think about and practice these rules.

▶5 Reflect and Close the Class Meeting

Facilitate a brief discussion about how the class meeting went for the students. Ask:

Q *What did you think of our first class meeting?*

Tell the students how you would like them to return to their desks, and have them return. If necessary, have them practice this again until they are able to move from the circle to their desks in an orderly way.

▶6 Read Independently/Monitor the Students' Reading Levels and Understanding

Teacher Note ▶

During this unit take time to decide each student's appropriate independent reading level for Individualized Daily Reading (IDR), which will be formally introduced in Unit 5. (Please read "Individualized Daily Reading" on page xxv for additional information about placing the students with appropriate books, monitoring their progress, and conducting IDR in your classroom.)

Tell the students that as they read today you will circulate among them and talk to them about the books they are reading. Because you will ask them to read some of their book aloud to you, it will be important to have books they can read.

Explain that it will be particularly important that they read without disturbing others so that you can hear the individual students read aloud and talk about their books. Briefly discuss questions such as:

Q *What can you do to make sure you do not disturb others during reading?*

Students might say:

"I can read quietly and not talk."

"I can have more than one book. That way I won't have to get out of my seat."

"I can reread my book when I get done."

Have the students read independently for up to 15 minutes.

As the students read, circulate among them to make sure they have books they can read and understand. Stop and talk with individuals about their reading. Have each student read aloud from his book, and ask questions such as:

Q *What is your book about? What is happening in your book right now?*

Q *What do you think will happen next?*

At the end of independent reading, give the students a few minutes to share what they read with the class.

ELL Note

Consider providing reading materials in the students' primary languages.

Day 2

Materials

- *Did You See What I Saw? Poems about School* (pages 5 and 14)

Read-aloud/Strategy Lesson

In this lesson, the students:

- *Visualize* to understand and enjoy poems
- Connect their mental images to the poems
- Learn and practice the cooperative structure "Think, Pair, Share"
- Read independently for up to 15 minutes
- Give one another time to think

About Visualizing

Readers create mental images about texts based on their own background knowledge and experiences. They can visualize the topics of nonfiction texts, as well as the setting, character, and action in stories, by inferring from descriptive language. Visualizing enhances readers' understanding and enjoyment of texts. While some young readers may visualize naturally, others benefit from instruction about visualizing. All students benefit from reflecting on the fact that they are visualizing. In this unit, the students visualize as they listen to read-alouds and read independently. (For more information about *visualizing,* see page xv.)

FACILITATION TIP

During this unit, continue to practice **asking a question once** and **using wait-time** to give the students an opportunity to think before responding. Wait-time becomes especially important when the students begin to use the cooperative structure "Think, Pair, Share," a variation of "Turn to Your Partner" in which the students think quietly to themselves about a question before responding to it.

▶1 Introduce "Think, Pair, Share" and Visualizing

Have partners sit together. Explain that for the next few weeks, they will hear poems and stories and use the words they hear to make pictures in their minds. To help them think and talk about the pictures they make, you will teach them "Think, Pair, Share." Explain that "Think, Pair, Share" is similar to "Turn to Your Partner." The difference is that they get time to think quietly for a few moments before they talk in pairs.

▶2 Practice "Think, Pair, Share" and Visualizing

Explain that today the students will hear two poems about school. Ask them to close their eyes and create a picture in their minds of a school and things they would see at the school.

After a few moments, ask the students to open their eyes. Then on a given signal (such as "talk to your partner about the things you pictured in your mind"), have the students share their mental pictures in pairs. Then have one or two students share their mental pictures with the class.

3 ▶ Introduce *Did You See What I Saw? Poems about School*

Explain that the two poems you will read are from *Did You See What I Saw? Poems about School* by Kay Winters. Tell the students that you will read the poems without showing the pictures. The students will close their eyes and use the words in the poem to create a picture in their own minds. Explain that closing their eyes will help them get a picture in their mind without being distracted by things in the classroom.

Explain that you will read each poem twice before asking them to talk about their mental pictures.

4 ▶ Read "School Bus" Aloud and Visualize

Read "School Bus" (page 5) aloud twice, slowly and clearly, pausing between the readings.

> **ELL Vocabulary**
>
> English Language Learners may benefit from discussing the following vocabulary:
>
> **bumpy:** bouncing up and down
> **stuffed:** very full

Ask the students to think about the pictures that the words in the poem bring to mind. Then, give the signal and have partners describe their mental pictures to each other.

Have one or two volunteers share their mental images with the class. As the students describe their visualizations, reread the part of the text that connects their images to the poem. Follow up by asking:

Q *The poem says, "Stuffed with kids." How do you picture the kids in the bus? What do you think it feels like to be on a bus "stuffed with kids"?*

Teacher Note

Hearing from only a couple of students at a time in whole-class discussion helps to keep the lesson moving. All the students have the opportunity to discuss their thinking when they share with their partners.

Teacher Note

The purpose of rereading is to help the students recall what they heard and focus on the words that trigger their mental images. Talking about their mental images helps partners identify words or phrases that trigger those images. The students will realize that each person's visual image is unique.

ELL Note

Consider previewing all the read-alouds in this unit with your English Language Learners. Help them understand the language in each read-aloud and practice creating pictures in their minds.

Students might say:

"I saw a picture of getting squished on the bus."

"I imagined all the kids talking and shouting when the poem said that the bus was loud."

"I thought about how the bus stops a lot to pick up more kids."

5 ▶ Read "Sliding Board" Aloud and Visualize

Explain that the students will hear another poem and picture it in their minds. Read the title and explain that this is a poem about a playground slide.

Read the poem "Sliding Board" (page 14) aloud using the same procedure you used with "School Bus."

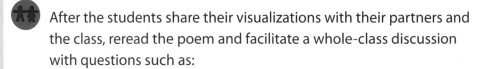 After the students share their visualizations with their partners and the class, reread the poem and facilitate a whole-class discussion with questions such as:

Q *Who did you picture on the slide? How is that person coming down the slide?*

Q *What sounds did you imagine? What do the words "swish, whish" bring to your mind?*

6 ▶ Review Visualizing

Explain that today the students had a chance to listen to some poems and think about their mental images. They also imagined sounds and feelings. Point out that picturing what they read helps readers enjoy and understand what they read. Tell the students to think about creating pictures in their minds the next time they read or listen to a poem or story.

7 ▶ Read Independently/Monitor the Students' Reading Levels and Understanding

Teacher Note

If necessary, review the procedures for selecting books and reading quietly.

Tell the students that you will continue to have individual students read aloud and talk about their books with you. Remind them that it is important to have a book that they can read.

Have the students read independently for up to 15 minutes.

Continue to monitor whether the students are reading books at appropriate reading levels and whether they are making sense of what they read. Probe their thinking with questions like those listed on page 107.

At the end of independent reading, give the students a few minutes to share with their partners what they read. Tell the students to start their sharing by telling their partners the title and author of their books. Circulate as the students share and note conversations and anything that you would like to bring up with the class or attend to later.

EXTENSIONS

Read Other Poems from *Did You See What I Saw?*

Read other poems from *Did You See What I Saw?* and have the students continue to practice visualizing. After the students share their mental images of each poem, show the illustrations and look for similarities and differences between their mental pictures and the book's illustrations.

Compare "Sliding Board" and "Swinging"

Reread "Sliding Board" to the students. Then read "Swinging" aloud (page 15 in *Did You See What I Saw?*). Facilitate a discussion comparing the two poems using questions such as:

Q *What are these two poems about?*

Q *How are they alike? How are they different?*

Day 3

Materials

- "The Balloon Man" (see page 115)
- A sheet of drawing paper for each student
- Crayons or markers
- *Assessment Resource Book*

Guided Strategy Practice

In this lesson, the students:

- *Visualize* to understand and enjoy a poem
- Draw mental images of the poem
- Read independently for up to 20 minutes
- Give one another time to think
- Act in a caring and respectful way

1 ▶ Review "Think, Pair, Share"

Have partners sit together. Explain that today the students will hear another poem and create a picture of it in their minds. Then they will use "Think, Pair, Share" to talk about their thinking. Ask:

Q *Why is it important to give each other time to think about your own pictures before talking?*

Have two or three students share their thinking with the class.

Teacher Note

You might want to give the students a few moments to visualize balloons before you read the poem.

 Note

Prior to today's read-aloud, consider asking one of your students to act out each line of the poem as you read, to increase comprehension.

2 ▶ Introduce "The Balloon Man"

Tell the students that you will read "The Balloon Man" by Dorothy Aldis. Explain that this is a poem about a man who sells balloons to children.

3 ▶ Read "The Balloon Man" Aloud and Visualize

Tell the students you will read the poem aloud twice. Ask them to close their eyes and make pictures in their minds as you read. Read the poem (on page 115) aloud twice, slowly and clearly, pausing between the readings.

Suggested Vocabulary

bob and tug: float up and down and pull gently (p. 115)

ELL Vocabulary

English Language Learners may benefit from discussing this additional vocabulary:

puddles: small pools of water on the ground (p. 115)

After the second reading, ask:

Q *How do you picture the balloon man in your mind?*

Have partners use "Think, Pair, Share" to discuss their images. Have one or two students share their mental pictures with the class.

4 ▶ Draw Mental Pictures of the Balloon Man

After partners have had a chance to talk, tell them that they will draw their mental pictures of the balloon man. Distribute drawing paper and crayons or markers to each student. Ask the students to think quietly about their mental pictures first and then draw them.

As the students draw, read the poem aloud a third time. Reread parts of the poem to individual students as needed.

Teacher Note

If the students have difficulty drawing, you might model by doing a brief sketch on a sheet of chart paper using the ideas of a few volunteers. Students can use your model to help them get started and continue adding their own details. Point out that their mental pictures are more important than their drawings. They should try to capture on paper what they saw in their minds.

CLASS PROGRESS ASSESSMENT

As you observe the students drawing, ask yourself:

Q *Are the students' visualizations connected to words and phrases in the poem?*

Record your observations on page 10 of the *Assessment Resource Book.*

Give the students a few minutes to complete their drawings, alerting them when they have about two minutes left.

Reread and Share Drawings

Reread "The Balloon Man." Explain that partners will show each other their drawings and talk about how their drawings remind them of the poem. Remind them to be caring and respectful as they view each other's drawings.

 Have pairs share and discuss their drawings.

Teacher Note ▶

As partners share their drawings, circulate and notice caring and respectful ways the students are interacting. Be ready to share your observations at the end of the lesson.

 ## Reflect on Sharing Drawings

Facilitate a brief discussion about respectful and caring ways the students talked about their partners' drawings. Share some of your own observations.

Tell the students that they will continue to practice making pictures in their minds and talking with their partners during the next lesson.

Read Independently/Monitor the Students' Reading Levels and Understanding

Have the students read independently for up to 20 minutes. Continue to monitor the students and probe their thinking with questions like those listed on page 107.

At the end of independent reading, give the students time to share with their partners.

Teacher Note ▶

Consider increasing the time students read independently to 20 minutes a day. Reading books at the appropriate level independently every day for at least 20 minutes will help the students build their reading stamina and become better readers.

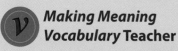

***Making Meaning Vocabulary* Teacher**

Next week you will revisit "Sliding Board" and "The Balloon Man" to teach Vocabulary Week 11.

The Balloon Man

by Dorothy Aldis

Our balloon man has balloons.
He holds them on a string.
He blows his horn and walks about
Through puddles, in the spring.

He stands on corners while they bob
And tug above his head—
Green balloons, and blue balloons
And yellow ones, and red.

He takes our pennies and unties
The two we choose; and then
He turns around, and waves his hand,
And blows his horn again.

Overview

UNIT 4: VISUALIZING
Poetry and Fiction

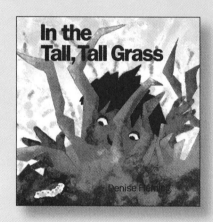

In the Tall, Tall Grass
by Denise Fleming
(Henry Holt, 1995)

This book describes the many insects and animals that make their homes in the tall grass.

ALTERNATIVE BOOKS

In the Small, Small Pond by Denise Fleming

Night in the Country by Cynthia Rylant

Comprehension Focus

• Students *visualize* to make sense of text.

• Students informally *use schema* and *inference* as they visualize.

• Students read independently.

Social Development Focus

• Students relate the values of respect, caring, and responsibility to their behavior.

• Students develop the group skills of listening and speaking clearly.

• Students participate in a class meeting.

DO AHEAD

• Neatly write each line of text from *In the Tall, Tall Grass* on its own sheet of blank drawing paper. You will have 15 sheets. The students will illustrate these on Day 2. (See page 122.)

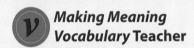

Making Meaning Vocabulary Teacher

If you are teaching Developmental Studies Center's *Making Meaning Vocabulary* program, teach Vocabulary Week 11 this week. For more information, see the *Making Meaning Vocabulary Teacher's Manual.*

Day 1

Materials

- *In the Tall, Tall Grass*

Read-aloud

In this lesson, the students:

- Hear and discuss a story
- Read independently for up to 20 minutes
- Listen to one another

▶1 Get Ready to Work Together

Have pairs sit together. Explain that today they will have a chance to talk about what happens in a story you read aloud. Explain that you will stop in the middle of the story and partners will talk about what has happened so far.

▶2 Introduce *In the Tall, Tall Grass*

Show the cover of *In the Tall, Tall Grass,* and read the title and author's name aloud. Ask:

Q *What do you think the child might find in the tall, tall grass?*

▶3 Read *In the Tall, Tall Grass* Aloud

Read *In the Tall, Tall Grass* aloud, showing the illustrations and stopping as described on the next page.

 Note

English Language Learners may benefit from additional stops to discuss the reading—for example, after pages 9 and 23.

> ### Suggested Vocabulary
>
> **dart:** move quickly (p. 6)
>
> **dip:** go down (p. 6)
>
> **strum:** brush your fingers over (p. 8)
>
> **lug:** carry something with great difficulty (p. 13)
>
> **ritch, ratch:** noise made when scratching (p. 16)
>
> **moles:** small, furry mammals that dig tunnels and live underground (p. 16)
>
> **fireflies:** small beetles that fly at night and give off flashes of light from their bodies (p. 25)

ELL Vocabulary

English Language Learners may benefit from discussing additional
vocabulary, including:

sip: drink a little bit at a time (p. 7)

hum: make a soft singing sound (p. 9; make a humming sound)

glide: move very smoothly (p. 15; model a gliding movement)

glow: shine or give off light (p. 25)

Read pages 3–5 aloud twice, and then continue reading to page 15.
Stop after:

pp. 14–15 "slip, slide, snakes glide"

Ask:

Q *What has the child seen in the tall, tall grass so far?*

Have the students use "Turn to Your Partner" to discuss the question.
Have a few pairs share with the class.

Reread page 15 and continue reading to the end of the story.

▶4 Discuss the Story

Facilitate a whole-class discussion about the book. Have the
students use "Turn to Your Partner" to discuss the questions before
sharing as a whole class. Ask:

Q *What does the child find in the tall, tall grass?*

Q *How high do you picture the tall, tall grass? What in the story
makes you think the grass is that tall?*

Explain that in the next lesson the students will hear *In the Tall, Tall
Grass* again and create mental pictures.

Read Independently/Monitor the Students' Reading Levels and Understanding

Have the students read books at appropriate reading levels independently for up to 20 minutes.

Continue to monitor whether the students are reading books at appropriate levels and whether they are making sense of what they read.

Day 2

Strategy Lesson

In this lesson, the students:

- *Visualize* to understand and enjoy a story
- Draw their mental images of the story
- Read independently for up to 20 minutes
- Speak clearly
- Act in a caring and respectful way

Materials

- *In the Tall, Tall Grass*
- Drawing sheets with lines from *In the Tall, Tall Grass*, prepared ahead (see page 117)
- Crayons or markers
- *Assessment Resource Book*

1 ▶ Get Ready to Work Together

Have partners sit together. Explain that today the students will hear parts of *In the Tall, Tall Grass* again and picture parts of the story in their minds. They will use "Think, Pair, Share" to talk about their mental pictures with their partners. Remind the students that it is important to speak clearly so their partners can hear them. Ask:

Q *If you can't hear your partner, what are some caring and respectful ways to let your partner know?*

2 ▶ Review *In the Tall, Tall Grass*

Show the book's cover and ask:

Q *What do you remember about the story* In the Tall, Tall Grass?

 Have pairs share, and then briefly share as a class.

3 ▶ Model Visualizing with the Read-aloud

Explain that you will reread parts of *In the Tall, Tall Grass*. Ask the students to notice what pictures come to mind and what words in the story help them make the pictures. Model by reading page 13 aloud ("pull, tug, ants lug") and thinking aloud about how the words bring an image to your mind. (For example, you might say, "When I

ELL Note

Consider rereading the entire text to your English Language Learners if you think they might benefit from additional support.

hear the words 'pull, tug, ants lug,' I see a long line of ants carrying large seeds through the grass.")

4 ▶ Practice Visualizing with the Read-aloud

Explain that you will read parts of *In the Tall, Tall Grass* as the students close their eyes and picture the words. Then, they will describe their mental images in pairs and with the class. Remind the students that even though they have seen the illustrations, they can still create their own mental pictures. Be sure to conceal the illustrations during this part of the lesson.

Have the students close their eyes, and read:

> **p. 10**   "crack, snap, wings flap"

Ask:

Q   *What do you picture in the tall, tall grass?*

Have the students think first, and then talk in pairs. Call on two or three volunteers to share their ideas with the class. Repeat this procedure with the following line:

> **pp. 22–23**   "hip, hop, ears flop"

5 ▶ Reread the Story as a Whole Class

Reread *In the Tall, Tall Grass,* showing the illustrations and having the students join in the reading.

6 ▶ Draw Mental Pictures and Make a Class Book

Tell the students that now that they have practiced making pictures in their minds and heard *In the Tall, Tall Grass* again, they will have a chance to illustrate parts of the story. Hand out one of the prepared drawing sheets to each student. Have each student think quietly about the words on the page, make a picture in her mind, and then illustrate her page. Circulate among the students and be ready to reread passages from the story to individual students, if necessary.

Teacher Note ▶

If the students respond with only the animals pictured in the illustrations, you might ask, "What other animal could you picture in your mind using the words 'crack, snap, wings flap'?"

Teacher Note

There should be 15 drawing sheets with lines of text. If there are more than 15 students in your class, have some students work in pairs. If pairs are not experienced in drawing together, offer them assistance in planning their drawing.

CLASS PROGRESS ASSESSMENT

Circulate as the students draw and ask yourself:

Q *Is there evidence in the students' drawings that they are thinking about the words in the text?*

Record your observations on page 11 of the *Assessment Resource Book.*

Compile the students' drawings and add a cover to create a class book. Make the book available for students to read in the classroom.

7 ## Read Independently

Have the students read books at appropriate reading levels independently for 10 minutes. Stop the students and ask them to reread those same pages and notice if they are making pictures in their minds as they read. Then have the students read for another 10–15 minutes.

At the end of independent reading, ask students who made pictures in their minds as they read to share with the class the part of the story they pictured.

EXTENSION

Compare *In the Tall, Tall Grass* and *In the Small, Small Pond*

Read the book *In the Small, Small Pond* to the students and facilitate a discussion comparing the two stories using questions such as:

Q *What are these two stories about?*

Q *How are they alike? How are they different?*

ELL Note

Students with limited English proficiency will benefit from reading the class book during independent reading.

Day 3

Materials

- "Reading Together" chart
- "Class Meeting Ground Rules" chart (from Week 1, Day 1)

Class Meeting

In this lesson, the students:

- Review the class meeting procedure and rules
- Think about and discuss how they work together
- Read independently for up to 20 minutes
- Listen and speak clearly
- Act in a caring and respectful way

▶1 Review Procedure and Gather for a Class Meeting

Explain that today the students will have a class meeting. Remind them how you would like them to get into a circle, including your expectations about how they will move. Before you signal them to move, ask:

Q *What do you want to remember to make getting into our circle go smoothly?*

Have the students move into the circle. Take time to have them practice this again if necessary, until they are able to move to the circle in an orderly way.

▶2 Review the Class Meeting Ground Rules

Refer to the "Class Meeting Ground Rules" chart and quickly review the rules. Ask:

Q *What are some ways we can let the person talking know that we're listening?*

Have two or three students share their thinking with the class.

Class Meeting Ground Rules

- one person talks at a time

3 Discuss the Reading Community

Remind the students that a class meeting is a time to talk about their reading community and how they are working together. Point out that this is a time to share and express their opinions and that it is okay to disagree respectfully.

Refer to the "Reading Together" chart and facilitate a brief discussion. Ask the students to think about how they have been treated by other students and how they have treated others. Ask:

Q *What do you like about how you treat each other? What do you think we can do better?*

 Have the students use "Think, Pair, Share" to discuss the question. Then have two or three students share their thinking with the class.

> **Students might say:**
>
> "I like how we take turns talking."
>
> "I show my partner that I am listening by looking at her."
>
> "I think we can do better with sitting so that everyone can see the book."

4 Reflect and Close the Class Meeting

Refer to the "Class Meeting Ground Rules" chart and facilitate a brief discussion about how the class meeting went. Ask:

Q *What class meeting rules did you follow well today?*

Q *Which ones do we need to work on?*

Let the students know they will have many chances to share and discuss their opinions.

Tell the students how you would like them to return to their desks, and have them return. If necessary, have them practice this again until they are able to move from the circle to their desks in an orderly way.

Reading Together

- listen to and talk about the story

ELL | Note

On occasion during independent reading, consider pairing your English Language Learners who need support in reading with a more fluent reader and have them read together.

Making Meaning Vocabulary Teacher

Next week you will revisit *In the Tall, Tall Grass* to teach Vocabulary Week 12.

5 ▶ Read Independently/Monitor the Students' Reading Levels and Understanding

Have the students read books at appropriate reading levels independently for up to 20 minutes. Remind the students to notice if they are picturing their stories in their minds as they read.

Week 3

Overview

UNIT 4: VISUALIZING
Poetry and Fiction

Sheep Out to Eat
by Nancy Shaw, illustrated by Margot Apple
(Houghton Mifflin, 1992)

Five sheep stop to eat and get themselves in a mess.

ALTERNATIVE BOOKS

Sheep in a Shop by Nancy Shaw

Buzz by Janet S. Wong

Comprehension Focus

- Students *visualize* to make sense of text.

- Students informally *use schema* and *inference* as they visualize.

- Students read independently.

Social Development Focus

- Students relate the values of respect, caring, and responsibility to their behavior.

- Students develop the group skills of speaking clearly and giving one another time to think.

- Students participate in a class meeting.

DO AHEAD

- Prior to Day 3, prepare a sheet of chart paper with space for drawing at the top and this sentence starter at the bottom: "I like this book because _____." (See Step 6, pages 138–139.)

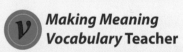 **Making Meaning Vocabulary Teacher**

If you are teaching Developmental Studies Center's *Making Meaning Vocabulary* program, teach Vocabulary Week 12 this week. For more information, see the *Making Meaning Vocabulary Teacher's Manual.*

Day 1

Materials

- *Sheep Out to Eat*

Read-aloud

In this lesson, the students:

- Hear and discuss a story
- Read independently for up to 20 minutes
- Listen to one another
- Act in a responsible way

 Introduce *Sheep Out to Eat*

Have partners sit together. Show the cover of *Sheep Out to Eat* and read the title and names of the author and illustrator aloud. Show the five sheep on the page opposite the title page and explain that these sheep are going to a restaurant to eat. Show the cat on the title page and tell them that the cat works in the restaurant. Ask:

Q *What do you think might happen in* Sheep Out to Eat?

Have one or two students share their thinking with the class.

Ask the students to listen carefully and think about what's happening in the story and how the sheep act in the restaurant. Explain that you will read the story, stopping in the middle for partners to talk about what has happened so far.

 Note

English Language Learners may benefit from additional stops to discuss the reading—for example, after pages 11, 19, and 25.

 Read *Sheep Out to Eat* Aloud

Read the book aloud, showing the illustrations and stopping as described on the next page.

Suggested Vocabulary

menus: lists of food served in a restaurant (p. 10)

feed: food for animals (p. 10)

spinach custard: a food like pudding with spinach mixed in (p. 14)

appetites: desires for food (p. 15)

slop: splashed or spilled liquid (p. 24)

lawn: grass (p. 29)

tips: extra money given to waiters as thanks for their good service (p. 31)

Point out the two different uses of the word "tips," on pages 20 and 31. Let the students know that when they read a word that has more than one meaning, they can often tell which meaning is right by thinking about the other words in the sentence.

ELL Vocabulary

English Language Learners may benefit from discussing additional vocabulary, including:

teashop: small restaurant that serves tea and snacks (p. 7)

bite to eat: (idiom) small meal or snack (p. 8)

tips: leans or falls over (p. 20)

You might want to act out the meaning of words like *scoop, slurp, chomp, pout,* and *smack lips* when you come to them in the reading.

Read pages 7–8 twice; then continue reading to page 15. Stop after:

> **p. 15**   "Sheep lose their appetites."

 Ask, and have the students use "Turn to Your Partner" to discuss:

Q   *What has happened so far?*

Reread the last sentence on page 15 and continue reading to the end of the story.

 ### Discuss the Story and Make Personal Connections

At the end of the story, facilitate a whole-class discussion about the book. Ask:

Q   *What problem do the sheep have in the story? How does their problem get solved?*

FACILITATION TIP

This week and next, continue to practice **asking a question once** and using wait-time (at least 5–10 seconds) to give the students an opportunity to think before responding.

Teacher Note ▶

During this discussion, encourage the students to listen to one another's comments by asking questions such as:

Q *What do you think about what [Damon] just said?*

Q *What do you want to add to what [Damon] said?*

Q *How do the sheep act in the restaurant? Why do they make such a mess?*

Q *How could the sheep be more responsible the next time they visit the teashop? Why will that be important?*

Tell the students that partners will have a chance to talk about the story in the next lesson.

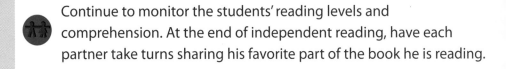

▶ **Monitor the Students' Reading Levels and Understanding**

Have the students read independently for up to 20 minutes.

Continue to monitor the students' reading levels and comprehension. At the end of independent reading, have each partner take turns sharing his favorite part of the book he is reading.

Day 2

Strategy Lesson

In this lesson, the students:

- *Visualize* to understand and enjoy a story
- Connect their mental images to the story
- Read independently for up to 20 minutes
- Act in a caring and respectful way
- Give one another time to think

1▶ Review *Sheep Out to Eat*

Have partners sit together. Explain that today the students will revisit *Sheep Out to Eat.* They will have a chance to picture the story in their minds and talk about their pictures with their partners. Show the cover of the book and read the title and names of the author and illustrator aloud. Ask:

Q *What do you remember about the story* Sheep Out to Eat*?*

Have two or three students share what they remember.

Explain that while you reread *Sheep Out to Eat,* you want the students to close their eyes, listen carefully, and make a picture in their minds of what's happening. Point out that making a picture in your mind is like creating a movie of the story. Explain that you will stop during the reading to have partners talk about what they see happening.

2▶ Reread *Sheep Out to Eat* with Visualizing

Read the story aloud without showing the illustrations and stopping as described below.

Stop after:

p. 11 "They point to words that they can't read."

Materials

- *Sheep Out to Eat*
- *Assessment Resource Book*

 Note

You may want to page through the book and show the pictures to help the students recall the story.

◄ **Teacher Note**

You may want to remind the students that the reason for closing their eyes is to help them get a clearer picture in their mind.

Have the students use "Think, Pair, Share" to talk about what they see happening in the part you just read. Remind them to give their partners time to think and to speak clearly so their partners can hear.

Without sharing as a class, reread the last sentence and continue reading to the next stop. Follow this procedure at the next three stops:

> **p. 17** "Sheep add pepper by mistake."
>
> **p. 23** "Tea and cake are everywhere."
>
> **p. 29** "The lawn is what they want for lunch."

Continue reading to the end of the story.

CLASS PROGRESS ASSESSMENT

Listen to partners as they discuss their mental pictures and ask yourself:

Q *Do the students refer to the text as they describe their mental images?*

Record your observations on page 12 of the *Assessment Resource Book*.

 3 ▶ **Discuss Visualizing the Story**

 Facilitate a discussion about how the students pictured the story. First in pairs, and then as a class, discuss questions such as:

Q *What did you picture happening when the tea and cake are everywhere?*

Q *What do the sheep look like in your mind when they are asked to leave the shop?*

Encourage the students to notice when they make pictures in their minds when they read or listen to other stories.

Reflect on Visualizing and Partner Work

Have the students think about how visualizing helped them understand and enjoy the story. Ask:

Q *What do you like about discussing your mental pictures with your partner?*

Q *What did you do to be respectful while your partner was talking?*

Tell the students they will have another chance to talk about their mental pictures with their partners in the next lesson.

Monitor the Students' Reading Levels and Understanding

Have the students read independently for up to 20 minutes.

Continue to monitor the students' reading levels and comprehension. At the end of independent reading, ask the students to think about parts of their books where they could picture the story in their minds. Have a few students share what they visualized with the class.

EXTENSIONS

Read and Illustrate Another Story from the *Sheep* Series

As you did for Week 2, Day 2, write out the words of another story from the *Sheep* series (*Sheep in a Jeep, Sheep in a Shop,* or *Sheep on a Ship*) on individual sheets of drawing paper. Pair students and hand out a sheet to each pair and have them read and illustrate their part of the story. Have each pair read their part of the story to another pair and compare their illustrations. Also, have the students compare the illustrations in the book with their own illustrations and discuss similarities and differences.

◀ **Teacher Note**

This activity is another opportunity to reinforce the idea that mental images are unique to the reader (including the illustrator).

Think About Lists, Menus, and Signs

Have the students identify some of the things the sheep read in *Sheep Out to Eat*. Show pages 10 and 11 and ask:

Q *What does the waiter give the sheep to read?*

Point out that a menu is a list of foods served in a restaurant, and that a list is any series of things that go together. Ask:

Q *What kinds of lists have you seen in our classroom?*

Show page 7 or page 32 and ask:

Q *What might the sheep read on these pages? What would those things tell the sheep?*

Q *What kinds of signs have you seen, in or out of our classroom?*

Encourage the students to notice the signs and lists they read in their own lives.

Day 3

Class Meeting

In this lesson, the students:

- Review class meeting procedure and rules
- Discuss their reading lives
- Draw pictures of their favorite books
- Read independently for up to 20 minutes

1 Review Procedure and Gather for a Class Meeting

Explain that today the students will be having a class meeting. Remind them how you would like them to get into a circle, including your expectations about how they will move. Before you signal them to move, ask:

Q *Why is it important to move into the class meeting circle slowly and quietly?*

Have the students move into the circle.

2 Review the Class Meeting Ground Rules

Refer to the "Class Meeting Ground Rules" chart and quickly review the rules. Ask:

Q *Why is it important to speak clearly so others can hear you during the meeting?*

Have two or three students share their thinking with the class.

3 Introduce and Share Reading Lives

Explain that the purpose of this class meeting is for the students to think about and share their reading lives. Tell the students that a person's reading life includes what kind of books she likes to read and where and when she likes to read.

Materials

- "Class Meeting Ground Rules" chart
- Sheet of chart paper with starter sentence and space for drawing (see "Do Ahead," page 129)
- Sheet of writing/drawing paper for each student
- Crayons or markers

> Class Meeting
> Ground Rules
>
> - one person talks
>   at a time

Teacher Note ▶
You may want to use a book
you are currently reading
when you model sharing
about your reading life.

Model by sharing a little bit about your own reading life. (You might say, "I love to read stories, and I try to read every day. Usually, I read in the evening after dinner. I sit in a rocking chair in the corner of my living room. I enjoy reading many kinds of books. Right now I'm reading a book about a family that lived a long time ago.")

4 **Have the Students Think About Their Reading Lives**

Ask the students to think quietly as you pose the following questions. Give the students time to think after each question. Ask:

Q *What are some books you've read or heard that you really love?*

Q *Where is your favorite place to read or listen to a book?*

ELL Note

Support your students with
limited English proficiency
by providing them with the
following prompts: "I love…"
and "My favorite place
to read is…."

Have the students use "Turn to Your Partner" to talk about what they thought. Have two or three students share what they talked about with the whole class. Let the students know that they will have a chance to talk more about their reading lives at the next class meeting.

5 **Reflect and Close the Class Meeting**

Refer to the "Class Meeting Ground Rules" chart and facilitate a brief discussion about how the class meeting went. Ask:

Q *Which meeting rules did you notice others following today?*

Q *What do you like about having class meeting rules?*

Remind the students of how you expect them to move back to their desks, and have them return to their desks.

ELL Note

This activity will be especialy
helpful for your English
Language Learners.

6 **Draw and Write About Favorite Books**

Remind the students that during the class meeting they thought about books they love. Ask them to close their eyes and visualize something they remember from their favorite books. Let them know it can be a book they read in class or outside of class.

After the students have had a chance to think, direct their attention to the sheet of chart paper you prepared with space for a drawing and the sentence starter "I like this book because _____." Explain that you will give each student a sheet of paper. Read the sentence starter aloud and explain that the students will copy the sentence on their sheets of paper and then finish the sentence by telling why they like their books. The students will then draw their mental pictures of their books.

Distribute a sheet of writing/drawing paper to each student. Have the students draw their mental pictures and copy and complete the sentence starter. Circulate as the students draw and write, and talk to them about their books and why they like them. Let them know when they have approximately two minutes of drawing and writing time left.

Collect the students' drawings. Explain that at the next class meeting, they will have a chance to share their drawings.

7 Monitor the Students' Reading/Get to Know the Students' Reading Lives

Have the students read independently for 20 minutes.

Continue to monitor whether the students are reading books at appropriate levels and whether they are making sense of what they are reading.

As you confer with individual students about their reading and monitor their reading levels, use this time to get more acquainted with their reading attitudes, preferences, and experiences. To guide your discussion, ask questions such as:

Q *What do you like to read or listen to? What do you like about these books?*

Q *What kinds of books would you like to add to our classroom library?*

Q *How do you feel about reading? Why do you like to read? Why do you dislike reading?*

◀ **Teacher Note**

If the students are struggling to draw their mental pictures or complete the sentence, call for the class's attention and model drawing and completing the sentence, using the chart paper you prepared and a visualization from a favorite book of your own.

 Note

Give your students with limited English proficiency the option of drawing their responses or showing you books they like to read.

Q   *What would you like me to do to help you this year?*

Q   *What books do you like to read at home? What is your favorite place to read at home or outside of school?*

Record notes on individual students and use this information to help you make decisions about instruction and your classroom library.

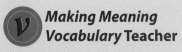

**Making Meaning
Vocabulary Teacher**

Next week you will revisit
Sheep Out to Eat to teach
Vocabulary Week 13.

Week 4

Overview

UNIT 4: VISUALIZING
Poetry and Fiction

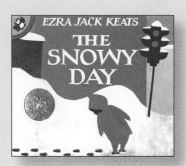

The Snowy Day
by Ezra Jack Keats
(Puffin, 1976)

Peter enjoys a day in the snow.

ALTERNATIVE BOOKS

Time to Sleep by Denise Fleming

Sunflower House by Eve Bunting

Comprehension Focus

- Students *visualize* to make sense of text.

- Students informally *use schema* and *inference* as they visualize.

- Students read independently.

Social Development Focus

- Students relate the values of respect, caring, and responsibility to their behavior.

- Students develop the group skills of speaking clearly and giving one another time to think.

- Students participate in a class meeting.

DO AHEAD

- Make copies of the Unit 4 Parent Letter (BLM4) to send home with the students on the last day of the unit. (For more information about the Parent Letters, see page xxxvi.)

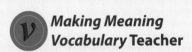

**Making Meaning
Vocabulary Teacher**

If you are teaching Developmental Studies Center's *Making Meaning Vocabulary* program, teach Vocabulary Week 13 this week. For more information, see the *Making Meaning Vocabulary Teacher's Manual.*

Class Meeting

In this lesson, the students:

- Practice class meeting procedure and rules
- Analyze the ways they have been interacting
- Share drawings of their favorite books
- Appreciate and respect one another's drawings
- Read independently for up to 20 minutes

Materials

- "Class Meeting Ground Rules" chart
- Students' drawings from Week 3

▶ 1 Get Ready for a Class Meeting

Explain that today the students will have a class meeting. Remind them that class meetings are times to get to know one another and to check in on how they are working together. Review the procedure for coming to a class meeting. Then have partners move to the circle and sit together.

After the students have gathered, ask:

Q *What are our class meeting rules?*

If necessary, use the "Class Meeting Ground Rules" chart to prompt the students' thinking.

Class Meeting Ground Rules

- one person talks at a time

▶ 2 Discuss How to Share Drawings

Explain that during today's class meeting, partners will share with the class the drawings about a favorite story that they made during the last lesson.

Ask:

Q *What can we do to be caring and respectful when people are sharing their drawings?*

Have a few students share their ideas with the class. Then distribute the students' drawings.

Share and Discuss Drawings

 Have the students use "Turn to Your Partner" to discuss their drawings and writing. Ask them to listen very carefully because later they will share with the class what their partners said.

After a few moments, have several volunteers share their partners' favorite books and drawings with the class, and explain why their partners like these books. Encourage class participation in the discussion using questions such as:

Q *What would you like to tell [Jamal] about [his] picture?*

Q *What do you like about [Maureen's] picture?*

Q *Do you think this is a book you would like to read or hear? Why?*

Continue until all the pairs have shared. You may want to have a few pairs share today and others share at another time.

 ## Reflect and Close the Class Meeting

Facilitate a brief discussion about the class meeting. Ask questions such as:

Q *How do you think you did following our class meeting rules today?*

Review the procedures for returning to their desks or tables and adjourn the meeting.

 ## Monitor the Students' Reading/Get to Know the Students' Reading Lives

Have the students read independently for up to 20 minutes.

Continue to monitor the students' reading levels and comprehension using the questions on page 107. Also continue to talk to individual students about their reading lives using the ideas and questions on pages 139–140.

Day 2

Materials

- *The Snowy Day*
- "What Good Readers Do" chart and a marker

What Good
Readers Do

- make connections to
  our lives

Read-aloud

In this lesson, the students:

- *Visualize* to understand and enjoy a story
- Read independently for up to 20 minutes
- Act in a caring and respectful way
- Give one another time to think

▶1 Add *Visualizing* to the "What Good Readers Do" Chart

Have partners sit together. Refer to the "What Good Readers Do" chart and remind them that they have been learning about what helps them understand stories they hear and read. Review the strategies *retelling* and *making connections to our lives*. Explain that in the past few weeks they have been using *visualizing*. Ask:

Q *What does it mean to* visualize *a story?*

Add *visualize* to the chart, and explain that today you will read a story aloud and they will have a chance to visualize the story and talk about it in pairs.

▶2 Introduce *The Snowy Day* and Build Background Knowledge

Show the cover of *The Snowy Day* and read the title and author's name aloud. Explain that the boy in this story is also the one in *Peter's Chair*. In this story, Peter goes walking in the snow.

To help them think about the story's setting, ask the students to close their eyes and visualize being out in the snow. Stimulate their thinking with questions such as:

Q *Picture your neighborhood covered with snow. What would that look like?*

Teacher Note

Allow the students a few moments to create an image in their minds before asking the questions. Pause between the questions to give them time to create their images.

Q *What would it feel like to walk in the snow?*

Have the students talk in pairs about what they visualized. Have one or two students share their thinking with the class.

Explain that you will read the story without showing the pictures, and that they will use their own imaginations to see the story in their minds.

3 Read *The Snowy Day* Aloud and Visualize

Read the book as described below without showing the illustrations.

◀ **Teacher Note**

The purpose of reading without showing the illustrations is to encourage the students to create their own mental pictures. If they have difficulty visualizing or retelling, you may want to act out some of the things Peter does or show some of the illustrations.

Suggested Vocabulary

snowsuit: heavy jacket and pants worn in the snow to keep warm (p. 7)

tracks: marks left on the ground by a moving person, animal, or vehicle (p. 10)

smacking: hitting (p. 13)

snowball fight: game in which players make balls of snow and throw them at one another (p. 17)

made angels: lay down on the snow, spreading arms and legs back and forth to make the shape of an angel in the snow (p. 19)

packed: pressed together (p. 22)

adventures: exciting and sometimes dangerous experiences (p. 23)

ELL Vocabulary

English Language Learners may benefit from discussing additional vocabulary, including:

heaping: piled high (p. 20)

slid: moved smoothly (p. 21)

firm: solid (p. 22)

Read pages 5–7 aloud twice, and then continue to page 10. Stop after:

p. 10 "Then he dragged his feet s-l-o-w-l-y to make tracks."

Have the students use "Think, Pair, Share" to talk about what they see happening so far in the story.

Have one or two volunteers share their mental pictures with the class. As each student shares, ask what he heard that helped him create the picture in his mind. Reread the last sentence and continue to the end of page 14. Follow the same procedure at the next three stops.

p. 14 "Down fell the snow—plop!—on top of Peter's head."

p. 22 "Then he went into his warm house."

p. 26 "He felt very sad."

Reread the last sentence on page 26 and continue reading to the end of the story.

4 Discuss the Story

At the end of the story, facilitate a whole-class discussion about the book. Ask:

Q *What are some of the things Peter does in the snow?*

Q *Why do you think Peter put the snowball in his pocket?*

Q *What are some of the pictures you have in your mind of Peter in the snow?*

Explain that in the next lesson, the students will talk more about *The Snowy Day* and how they pictured the story.

5 Monitor the Students' Reading/Get to Know the Students' Reading Lives

Have the students read independently for up to 20 minutes. Remind the students to notice if they are visualizing as they read.

Continue to monitor the students' reading levels and comprehension using the questions on page 107. Also continue to talk to individual students about their reading lives using the ideas and questions on page 139–140.

Teacher Note ▶

The purpose of this discussion is to establish the students' surface-level understanding of the story before they draw their images in the next lesson. If necessary, reread parts of the text to clarify confusion or to help the students recall what they heard.

EXTENSION

Use Context to Understand Different Uses of a Word

Have the books *Sheep Out to Eat*, *The Snowy Day*, and *In the Tall, Tall Grass* on hand. Remind the students that many words in the English language have more than one meaning. One example is *tip,* which is in *Sheep Out to Eat.* Ask the students to listen as you read sentences aloud from the books, and have them listen for the word that is in all three books.

Show and read aloud page 8 in *The Snowy Day*, page 28 in *Sheep Out to Eat*, and pages 4–5 in *In the Tall, Tall Grass.* Ask:

Q *What word is on all three of these pages?*

Q *What does* crunch *mean?*

Q *How is the meaning the same in these stories? How is it different?*

Remind the students that when they read a word that has more than one meaning, they can often use the other words and illustrations around it to help them figure out what the author means.

ELL Note

This is a very helpful strategy for your English Language Learners.

Day 3

Materials

- *The Snowy Day*
- A sheet of drawing paper for each student
- Crayons or markers
- *Assessment Resource Book*
- Unit 4 Parent Letter (BLM4)

Guided Strategy Practice

In this lesson, the students:

- *Visualize* to understand and enjoy a story
- Draw their mental images of the story
- Read independently for up to 20 minutes
- Act in a caring way

▶1 Review *The Snowy Day* and Prepare to Draw Mental Pictures

Have partners sit together. Explain that today you will reread *The Snowy Day* without stopping or showing the illustrations. After talking in pairs about what they visualized, the students will each draw a picture of part of the story. Show the cover of the book and ask:

Q *What happens in* The Snowy Day*?*

 Have partners talk about what they remember.

▶2 Discuss Acting in Caring Ways

Facilitate a brief discussion about caring and kind ways to talk about other people's drawing and writing. Ask questions such as:

Q *What do we want to keep in mind when we're talking about our drawings today to make sure we're acting in a caring way toward one another?*

Q *Why is this important?*

Let the students know you will check in with them later in the lesson to see how they did.

Reread *The Snowy Day* Aloud

Reread the story, without showing the illustrations. At the end of the story, ask:

Q   *What are some pictures you have in your mind of* The Snowy Day?

 Have partners discuss their mental pictures.

 Draw Mental Images of *The Snowy Day*

Explain that the students will draw a picture of a part of the story that they can visualize very clearly, and they will write about what is happening in their drawings. Distribute a sheet of drawing paper and crayons or markers to each student. Ask the students to first think, and then quietly draw their pictures. Tell them they will share their pictures in the next part of the lesson.

Circulate among the students as they draw their pictures. Help students who have difficulty getting started or who need to add story details to their drawings.

 Note

If many students need help writing about their pictures, consider sketching a picture for the class and modeling writing a sentence about it.

CLASS PROGRESS ASSESSMENT

As you observe the students drawing and writing, ask yourself:

Q   *Are the students connecting their drawings to the story?*

Q   *Are they using background knowledge to visualize the story?*

Record your observations on page 13 of the *Assessment Resource Book.*

 Share and Discuss Drawings

Explain that partners will discuss their drawings and writing. Remind them to think about caring and respectful ways to talk about each other's work.

 Have partners tell each other how their drawings reminds them of *The Snowy Day* and talk about how their drawings are similar.

As the students share their drawings and writing, circulate among them. Observe the students' interactions and responsiveness to each other's ideas. Note whether they are expressing their interest in and appreciation of their partners' work.

6 ▶ Talk About Acting in Caring Ways

Have the students reflect on how they acted in caring ways during the lesson. Point out examples you noticed of students working in caring ways. If you noticed problems, point these out without mentioning the students' names, and discuss:

Q *How might it feel to have someone [say something mean about your drawing]?*

Q *Why is it important that we try to avoid hurting one another's feelings?*

Q *What can we do to make things better if we realize we have hurt someone's feelings?*

Tell the students they will have more opportunities to practice acting in caring ways.

7 ▶ Monitor the Students' Reading Levels and Understanding

Have the students read independently for up to 20 minutes.

 Continue to monitor the students' reading levels and comprehension. If time permits, have partners take turns reading favorite parts of their books to each other.

Teacher Note

This is the last week in Unit 4. You will reassign partners for Unit 5.

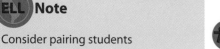 **Note**

Consider pairing students who speak the same primary language for this activity.

EXTENSION

Stroll with *The Snowy Day*

Have the students display their drawings of *The Snowy Day* on their desks. Then have them stroll around to view one another's work. As a class, discuss what the students noticed about others' pictures and writing.

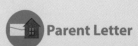

Parent Letter

Send home with each student the Parent Letter for this unit (see "Do Ahead," page 143). Periodically, have a few students share with the class what they are reading at home.

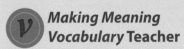

***Making Meaning Vocabulary* Teacher**

Next week you will revisit *The Snowy Day* to teach Vocabulary Week 14.

Unit 5

Wondering

FICTION AND NARRATIVE NONFICTION

During this unit, the students continue to use a sequence of events to retell a story. They also use wondering and visualization to help them understand and enjoy a story. They learn the procedure for Individualized Daily Reading (IDR). Socially, the students relate the value of responsibility to their behavior. They develop the group skill of sharing their ideas with one another and have a check-in class meeting.

Week 1 *An Extraordinary Egg* by Leo Lionni

Week 2 *George Washington and the General's Dog* by Frank Murphy

Week 3 *Down the Road* by Alice Schertle

Week 1

Overview

UNIT 5: WONDERING
Fiction and Narrative Nonfiction

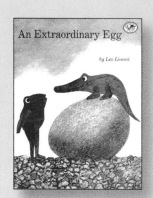

An Extraordinary Egg
by Leo Lionni
(Knopf, 1998)

Three frogs make friends with an animal that hatches from an egg they find.

ALTERNATIVE BOOKS

Little Polar Bear and the Husky Pup by Hans de Beer

Pet Show! by Ezra Jack Keats

Comprehension Focus

• Students use the sequence of events to *retell* a story.

• Students use *wondering* to help them understand a story.

• Students learn the procedure for Individualized Daily Reading (IDR) and read independently.

Social Development Focus

• Students relate the value of responsibility to their behavior.

• Students develop the group skill of sharing ideas with one another.

DO AHEAD

• Prior to Day 2, decide how you will randomly assign partners to work together during the unit.

• Copy the "Resource Sheet for IDR Conferences" on BLM13 and refer to it throughout the year for questions to ask and suggestions to make during IDR conferences. You may want to laminate it to protect it for long-term use. (For more about IDR conferences, see page xxvi.)

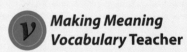
Making Meaning
Vocabulary Teacher

If you are teaching Developmental Studies Center's *Making Meaning Vocabulary* program, teach Vocabulary Week 14 this week. For more information, see the *Making Meaning Vocabulary Teacher's Manual.*

Day 1

Materials

- Books of various genres and levels that the students can read independently
- Chart paper and a marker

Individualized Daily Reading

In this lesson, the students:

- Learn the procedure for Individualized Daily Reading
- Read independently

About Individualized Daily Reading

Today the students will begin Individualized Daily Reading (IDR), which will continue through the rest of the year. In IDR, the students read books at their own reading levels independently each day, then reflect on and discuss what they read. The students read for up to 20 minutes a day.

During IDR, it is critical that the students read books at appropriate reading levels. If you have a library organized by reading level and have identified students' reading levels, they should be taught how to find their own books. If you do not have such a library, you will need to provide reading material. This might include library books, basal readers, or children's newspapers and magazines. It is important to have a system to help the students identify appropriately leveled material. (Please read "Individualized Daily Reading" on page xxv for additional information about organizing a leveled library and conducting IDR in your classroom. For information about Developmental Studies Center's Individualized Daily Reading Libraries, see page xxvii and visit Developmental Studies Center's website at devstu.org.)

1 ▶ Introduce Individualized Daily Reading

Remind the students that they already have been selecting books and reading silently. Explain that they will continue to have time each day to read silently and that during Individualized Daily Reading, or IDR, time they are going to focus on reading books that are at just the right reading level for each of them. Explain that you will help them select the books, because reading books that are at the right reading level will help them become better readers. Reading books that are too hard or too easy will not help them improve as readers.

Ask and briefly discuss:

Q *How might you know a book is just right for you?*

Explain that a "just right" book is a book that has words they can read and understand, and a story they enjoy. Write the following list on a sheet of chart paper and post it where everyone can see it:

A "just right" book is a book that:

- I enjoy
- I can read
- I can understand

2 Select the Books

Explain the way you have organized the books for IDR, model the procedure you would like the students to follow for selecting books, and have a brief discussion about how the students will follow the procedure.

Have the students, a few at a time, select their books for IDR while the other class members observe. As the students select books, comment on what is working well.

After the students have selected their books, tell them that as they are reading you will be coming around to listen to individual students read and to talk about the books.

3 Read Independently

Remind the students that it is important to read quietly so that they don't disturb others. They will have a chance to talk about their books at the end of reading time. Have the students read independently for up to 20 minutes.

◀ **Teacher Note**

There are several ways to ensure that the students select books that are right for them. If you have students seated at tables, an option is to place books in a variety of genres and levels in a basket on each table. Color code each book and tell the students which colors they can select. Rotate the baskets every few days. If you organize the classroom library according to reading levels, the students can either choose a book from the library each day or select several books and keep them in an individual "bookcase," such as a cubby, box, book bag on the back of their chair, or magazine holder.

As the students read, circulate among them and check to see whether they are reading books at appropriate reading levels. Have individual students each read a passage aloud and tell you what her book is about. If the book is not at an appropriate reading level, help the student find another book.

4 Discuss the Independent Reading

Signal the end of the independent reading time. Have several students share their reading with the class. Ask:

Q *What did you read today?*

Briefly share some of the observations you made during IDR. (For example, you might say, "I noticed that you settled down very quickly to read your books," "I noticed that some people read their books more than one time," and "I noticed that you were respectful of others' reading time, because you did not interrupt or talk. ")

Explain that they will have many opportunities during the rest of the year to share and discuss what they read during IDR.

ELL Note

You may wish to give English Language Learners the opportunity to act out a part of their reading—perhaps their favorite part.

Teacher Note ▶

From this point, each lesson ends with an Individualized Daily Reading section. You may choose to have IDR at another time during the school day. We strongly recommend that the students spend up to 20 minutes reading books at appropriate reading levels independently each day.

Day 2

Read-aloud/Strategy Lesson

In this lesson, the students:

- *Wonder* about a story read aloud
- Begin working with new partners
- Read independently for up to 20 minutes
- Share ideas with one another

About Wondering

Wondering is a strategy that good readers use to construct understanding. In this unit, the students build this understanding through teacher modeling, wondering on their own during a read-aloud, and independent reading. (For more information about *wondering,* please see page xv.)

▶1 Pair Students and Get Ready to Work Together

Randomly assign partners and have them sit together. Tell them that you will read a story aloud, and then partners will talk about it. Explain that they will be responsible for both thinking on their own and sharing in pairs and that you will ask them to talk about their partner work at the end of the lesson.

▶2 Introduce *An Extraordinary Egg*

Show the cover of *An Extraordinary Egg* and read the title and author's name aloud. Explain that *extraordinary* means *unusual* or *not regular.* Explain that this is a story about three frogs: Jessica, Marilyn, and August. The frogs live on Pebble Island. (Check to make sure that students understand the words *pebble* and *island.*) One day Jessica discovers something extraordinary on the island. This is the story of what she finds.

Materials

- *An Extraordinary Egg* (pages 2–17)
- Scratch paper and a pencil
- "Resource Sheet for IDR Conferences" (BLM13), prepared ahead (to be used throughout the program)
- *Assessment Resource Book*

Being a Writer™ **Teacher**
You may either have the students work with their *Being a Writer* partner or assign them a different partner for the *Making Meaning* lessons.

Note

You may want to explain to your English Language Learners that when you *wonder* about something, you *want to know more* about it.

 Introduce and Model Wondering

Remind the students that this year they have practiced visualizing, or picturing in their minds, what is happening in a story. Explain that another thing good readers do is wonder, or have questions in mind, as they hear or read a story.

Show the cover of *An Extraordinary Egg,* reread the title, and wonder aloud about the story. (You might say, "I wonder what will be different or special about this egg. I wonder if it really is an egg.")

 Have the students use "Think, Pair, Share" to first think about and then discuss:

Q *What do you wonder about this story?*

Have two or three students share their ideas with the class.

> **Students might say:**
> "I wonder what is inside the egg."
> "I wonder if that is an egg or a big rock."
> "I wonder why the egg is so big."

Tell the students that you will stop during the reading and partners will talk about the story and what they are wondering. Tell the students you will read the first part of the story today and finish reading the story tomorrow.

 Read *An Extraordinary Egg* Aloud and Stop and Wonder

Read pages 3–17 of *An Extraordinary Egg* aloud, showing the illustrations and stopping as described on the next page.

Suggested Vocabulary

pebble: small stone or rock (p. 3)

island: land surrounded by water (p. 3)

wonder: curiosity (p. 5)

were never impressed: didn't think much of it (p. 5)

mound: pile (p. 6; refer to the illustration on pp. 6–7)

triumphantly: proudly (p. 10)

astonished: surprised (p. 10)

amazement: surprise (p. 12)

a commotion: lots of noise and activity (p. 17)

ELL Vocabulary

English Language Learners may benefit from discussing additional vocabulary, including:

ordinary: not different or special (p. 5)

float: rest or lie on top of the water (p. 15)

paddle: move arms and legs in the water to swim (p. 15)

Read pages 3–5 and stop after:

p. 5 "But Marilyn and August were never impressed."

Ask:

Q *What do you know so far about the three frogs?*

 Have the students use "Turn to Your Partner" to discuss the question; then have two or three volunteers share what they know with the class.

Reread the last sentence on page 5 and continue reading. Stop after:

p. 6 "Even though it was almost as big as she was, Jessica decided to bring it home."

Ask:

Q *What do you wonder about the story up to this point?*

◀ **Teacher Note**

To maintain the flow of the read-aloud, have only two or three students share with the class at each stop. Hearing others' ideas gives the students examples of the kinds of things that can be wondered about as they hear a story.

Have the students use "Turn to Your Partner" to discuss the question; then have two or three volunteers share their ideas with the class. Ask the students to begin their sharing with the prompt "I wonder…." If the students have difficulty generating ideas, model one or two yourself. (For example, you might say, "I wonder if Jessica will be able to carry the big stone.")

CLASS PROGRESS ASSESSMENT

As partners talk, circulate and ask yourself:

Q *Are the students able to generate "I wonder" statements?*

Q *Are the statements relevant to the story?*

Record your observations on page 14 of the *Assessment Resource Book.*

Reread the last sentence on page 6, and continue reading to page 12. Stop after:

p. 12 "'Straight ahead!' the frogs cried out excitedly."

Ask:

Q *What has happened? What is surprising or funny about what has happened?*

 Have the students use "Turn to Your Partner" to discuss the questions; then have two or three volunteers share their ideas with the class.

Reread the last two paragraphs on page 12, and continue reading to page 17. Stop after:

p. 17 "August and Marilyn were frightened."

▶5 Discuss the Story and Wonder

Facilitate a whole-class discussion of the story. Ask:

Q *What has happened in this story so far? What do you think might happen next?*

Q *What do you wonder about the story?*

Review that good readers do lots of wondering as they hear and read stories. Tell the students that tomorrow they will hear the rest of the story and continue to practice wondering.

6 ▶ Reflect on Partner Work

Facilitate a brief discussion about how the students worked together today. Ask:

Q *How did things work for you and your new partner today?*

Students might say:

"When I was talking, my partner wasn't talking over my words."

"My partner talked loud so I could hear her."

"I didn't have to tell my partner to talk loud so that taught me to talk loud."

INDIVIDUALIZED DAILY READING

7 ▶ Use the "Resource Sheet for IDR Conferences" to Monitor Reading Levels and Understanding

During the next two weeks, you will use the questions on the "Resource Sheet for IDR Conferences" to guide your discussions with individual students. Select questions that are appropriate to your individual students' reading levels and interests and that are suited to the kind of material they are reading.

Have the students read independently for up to 20 minutes. Confer with several students during IDR today.

At the end of IDR, give the students a few minutes to share in pairs what they read. Circulate as the pairs share and note their conversations.

> **Teacher Note**
>
> On Day 3, you will remind the students of some of their "I wonder" statements from today's lesson. Jot down two or three statements on scratch paper to use as examples tomorrow. (See Day 3, Step 2 on page 166.)

Day 3

Materials

- *An Extraordinary Egg*
- Your notes of students' "I wonder" statements from Day 2
- "Resource Sheet for IDR Conferences"

Teacher Note ▶

If the students have difficulty recalling the events in the story, reread the first part of the book.

Note

You may want to remind the students that when they *wonder* about a story they *have questions in mind* or *ask themselves what more they want to know* about the story.

Read-aloud/Strategy Lesson

In this lesson, the students:

- *Retell* part of a story
- *Wonder* about a story read aloud
- Refer to the story to support their thinking
- Read independently for up to 20 minutes
- Share ideas with one another

▶1 Retell the First Part of *An Extraordinary Egg*

Have partners sit together. Review the first part of *An Extraordinary Egg* by having the students retell it. Use the illustrations on pages 2–17 to help the students remember the story. Begin the retelling yourself by showing the illustrations on pages 2–3 and telling what the pictures show. (You might say, "This is a story about some frogs who live on Pebble Island.") Then call on volunteers to retell as you show the remaining illustrations.

▶2 Review Wondering

Remind the students that as they listened to the first part of the story they wondered about it. Review that wondering is something good readers do to help them understand and enjoy stories. Use your notes from Day 2 to review some of the students' "I wonder" statements.

Tell the students that today you will read the rest of *An Extraordinary Egg* aloud. As before, you will stop during the reading and ask partners to talk about the story. Ask the students to think about what they wonder as they listen.

3 **Read the Rest of *An Extraordinary Egg* Aloud**

Reread page 17, and then read the rest of the story aloud, showing the illustrations and stopping as described below.

Suggested Vocabulary

inseparable: always together (p. 20)
monument: sculpture (p. 23)

ELL Vocabulary

English Language Learners may benefit from discussing additional vocabulary, including:

rescuer: person who saves someone or something (p. 20)
alligator: large reptile with strong jaws and very sharp teeth (p. 30; refer to the illustration)

Read pages 19–26 and stop after:

p. 26   "They walked under the warm sun and the cool moon, and then..."

Ask:

Q *What happens in the part of the story you just heard?*

 Have the students use "Turn to Your Partner" to discuss the question; then have one or two volunteers share their ideas with the class. Reread the last sentence on page 26, and continue reading to the end of the story.

4 **Discuss the Story and Wonder**

Facilitate a whole-class discussion about the story using questions such as:

Q *Why do you think the alligator saves Jessica?*

Q *Why do you think the frogs call the alligator a chicken?*

FACILITATION TIP

During this unit, we invite you to focus on **pacing** whole-class discussions so that they are lively and focused. A class discussion should be long enough to allow thinking and sharing, but short enough to sustain the attention of all the students. Good pacing during a discussion requires careful observation of all the students—not just those responding—and the timely use of pacing techniques such as:

* Use wait-time before calling on anyone to respond.

* Call on only a few students to respond to a question, even if others have their hands up.

* If many students want to respond, use "Turn to Your Partner" to give partners an opportunity to share with each other. Then call on two or three students to share with the whole class.

* If a discussion goes off topic, restate the question.

Grade One | **167**

Show the illustration on page 20. Remind the students that Jessica likes to wonder and that good readers wonder, too. Ask:

Q *What do you wonder about this story?*

 Have the students use "Turn to Your Partner" to discuss what they wonder. Then have one or two students share what they are wondering with the class. Ask the students to begin their sharing with the prompt "I wonder...."

Tell the students that they will have more opportunities to wonder about a story in the next lesson.

INDIVIDUALIZED DAILY READING

 5 Monitor the Students' Reading Levels and Understanding

Have the students read independently for up to 20 minutes.

Use the questions on the "Resource Sheet for IDR Conferences" to monitor whether the students are reading books at appropriate reading levels and whether they are making sense of what they read.

If time permits at the end of IDR, ask a few students who have finished their books to share them with the class. Have each student read the title of the book aloud. Then have the student retell the story. Prompt the students with questions such as:

Q *What happens first in your story?*

Q *Then what happens?*

Q *How does the story end?*

 ELL Note

Before the students begin IDR, tell your English Language Learners that you may ask them to retell what they read and remind them that when they retell a story, they say in their own words what happened. After IDR, support any student who retells his story by providing prompts for sequencing the events of the story such as, "First...," "Then...," and "At the end...."

EXTENSION

Read and Compare Other Stories by Leo Lionni

In Unit 1, Week 4, the students heard *It's Mine!* by Leo Lionni. Review *It's Mine!* and have the students talk about and compare *It's Mine!* and *An Extraordinary Egg*. Read other stories by Leo Lionni—some of these are *Inch by Inch, Frederick, Swimmy,* and *Alexander and the Wind-Up Mouse.* Have the students discuss similarities and differences in the stories.

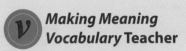

Making Meaning Vocabulary Teacher

Next week you will revisit *An Extraordinary Egg* to teach Vocabulary Week 15.

Week 2

Overview

UNIT 5: WONDERING
Fiction and Narrative Nonfiction

George Washington and the General's Dog
by Frank Murphy, illustrated by Richard Walz
(Random House, 2002)

George Washington's love of animals leads him to return a dog belonging to the general of the English army in the midst of the American Revolution.

ALTERNATIVE BOOKS

The Statue of Liberty by Lucille Recht Penner

Jackie Robinson and the Story of All-Black Baseball
by Jim O'Connor

Comprehension Focus

• Students *wonder* to help them understand a nonfiction story.

• Students read independently.

Social Development Focus

• Students relate the value of responsibility to their behavior.

• Students develop the group skill of sharing ideas with one another.

• Students have a check-in class meeting.

**Making Meaning
Vocabulary Teacher**

If you are teaching Developmental
Studies Center's *Making Meaning
Vocabulary* program, teach
Vocabulary Week 15 this week.
For more information, see the
*Making Meaning Vocabulary
Teacher's Manual.*

Day 1

Materials

- *George Washington and the General's Dog* (pages 5–29)
- Scratch paper and a pencil
- "Resource Sheet for IDR Conferences"

ELL Note

You may need to explain to your English Language Learners who George Washington was, when he lived, and the role he played in American history.

Read-aloud/Strategy Practice

In this lesson, the students:

- *Wonder* about a story read aloud
- Refer to the story to support their thinking
- Read independently for up to 20 minutes
- Share ideas with one another

1 ▶ Talk About Sharing Ideas

Have partners sit together. Explain that today you will read another story aloud and they will talk about the story with in pairs. Remind them that they will be responsible for both thinking on their own and sharing with their partners. Ask:

Q *What did you and your partner do the last time you worked together to make sure you both shared your ideas?*

Tell the students that you will check in with them about how they shared ideas at the end of the lesson.

2 ▶ Introduce *George Washington and the General's Dog* and Wonder About the Story

Show the cover of *George Washington and the General's Dog* and read aloud the title and the name of the author and illustrator. Tell the students that this book is a biography of George Washington, the first president of the United States. A biography is a book about a real person's life. This biography tells us about how much George Washington loved animals.

 Have students use "Turn to Your Partner" to discuss:

Q *What do you wonder about* George Washington and the General's Dog *before you hear the story?*

Students might say:

"I wonder if that's George Washington's dog on the cover."

"I wonder what happens to the dog."

"I wonder if George Washington's dog was in the army."

Tell the students that you will stop during the reading and ask partners to talk about the story and what they are wondering. Tell the students you will read the first part of the story today and finish reading the story tomorrow.

 ## Read *George Washington and the General's Dog* Aloud and Stop and Wonder

Read pages 5–29 of *George Washington and the General's Dog* aloud, showing the illustrations and stopping as described below.

Suggested Vocabulary

heroes: brave people (p. 5)
colonists: people who lived in America a long time ago (p. 17)
general: leader of an army (p. 19)
George's troops: the men who fought along with George (p. 27)

ELL Vocabulary

English Language Learners may benefit from discussing additional vocabulary, including:

spoiled his dogs: didn't make rules for them (p. 14)
supplies: things the soldiers needed to fight the war (p. 22)

ELL

Read pages 5–11 aloud, and stop after:

p. 11 "But he spent the most time with his dogs."

As a class briefly discuss the following questions:

Q *What do you know about George Washington so far?*

Q *What do you wonder about George Washington?*

As the students share their thinking, have them use the prompt, "I wonder…."

Teacher Note

If the students have difficulty generating ideas, model one or two statements, for example, "I wonder how he became president of the United States."

Students might say:

"I wonder how he learned to ride a horse so well."

"I wonder why he likes animals so much."

"I wonder what games he plays with the dogs."

Reread the last sentence on page 11, and continue reading to page 19. Stop after.

> **p. 19** "Sweetlips was right beside him."

Ask and briefly discuss:

Q *What have you found out about George Washington so far?*

Reread page 19 and continue reading to page 29. Stop after:

> **p. 29** "George bent down and patted the dog's head."

4▶ Discuss What the Students Wondered

 Use "Think, Pair, Share" to have the students think about and discuss:

Q *What do you wonder about what you have heard so far?*

Students might say:

"I wonder who the dog belongs to."

"I wonder if the dog was scared."

"I wonder who will win the war."

Teacher Note ▶

Circulate as the students share their thinking with their partners. Notice whether the students are thinking of ideas easily or are having difficulty wondering about the story. Also notice whether they are sharing ideas.

After the partners share, have a few volunteers share their thinking with the class. Remind them to use the "I wonder" prompt to begin their sharing.

Teacher Note ▶

In preparation for tomorrow's lesson, jot down two or three of the students' statements on scratch paper to help you remember them. (See Day 2, Step 1 on page 176.)

Tell the students that they will continue to wonder and talk about the story in the next lesson.

Reflect on the Partner Work

Briefly share your own observations of what is going well as partners work together. Then ask:

Q *What problems did you and your partner have working together today?*

Q *What might you do differently the next time you work together?*

INDIVIDUALIZED DAILY READING

 Monitor the Students' Reading Levels and Understanding

Have the students read independently for up to 20 minutes.

Continue to use the "Resource Sheet for IDR Conferences" to monitor whether the students are reading books at appropriate reading levels and whether they are making sense of what they read.

If time permits at the end of IDR, give each student a few minutes to read a page from her book to her partner and tell her partner about the book. Circulate as the pairs share and note their conversations.

Day 2

Materials

- *George Washington and the General's Dog* (pages 28–47)
- Your notes of students' "I wonder" statements from Day 1
- (Optional) Chart paper and a marker
- *Assessment Resource Book*
- "Resource Sheet for IDR Conferences"

Read-aloud/Strategy Practice

In this lesson, the students:

- *Wonder* about a story
- Refer to the story to support their thinking
- Read independently for up to 20 minutes
- Share ideas with one another

1▶ Review *George Washington and the General's Dog* and the Students' "I Wonder" Statements

Have partners sit together. Remind the students that in the last lesson they heard the first part of *George Washington and the General's Dog*. Ask:

Q *What is this story about so far?*

Teacher Note ▶

If the students have difficulty recalling the events in the story, reread the first part of the book.

As the students recall the story, support their thinking by showing the illustrations or rereading.

Review that as they listened to the first part of *George Washington and the General's Dog* they wondered about the story. Use your notes to remind the students of some of their "I wonder" statements. Explain that today you will read the rest of the story, and partners will talk about the story and what they wonder.

Teacher Note ▶

You may want to write two or three of the students' "I wonder" statements on chart paper or the board and ask them to listen to hear if what they are wondering about is discussed in the story.

2▶ Read the Rest of *George Washington and the General's Dog* Aloud and Stop and Wonder

Reread pages 28–29; then read the rest of the story aloud, stopping as described on the next page.

Suggested Vocabulary

respected: had a good opinion of (p. 37)

elected: chose (p. 45)

ELL Vocabulary

English Language Learners may benefit from discussing additional vocabulary, including:

George couldn't believe his eyes: George was very surprised (p. 31)

enemy: person in the other army (p. 31)

Word about the dog spread through the camp: All of George's soldiers heard about the dog (p. 33)

master: owner (p. 33)

battlefield: place where the two armies fought (p. 34)

honor George: show George how much they liked and respected him (p. 40)

Stop after:

p. 35   "They gave him back to General Howe."

 Have the students use "Think, Pair, Share" to think about and discuss the following question. Then have one or two volunteers share their thinking with the class.

Q   *What do you wonder now?*

Reread page 35 and continue reading to the end of the book.

CLASS PROGRESS ASSESSMENT

As partners talk, circulate and ask yourself:

Q   *Are the students able to generate "I wonder" statements?*

Q   *Are the statements relevant to the story?*

Record your observations on page 15 of the *Assessment Resource Book.*

FACILITATION TIP
This week continue to focus on **pacing** class discussions so that they are long enough to allow thinking and sharing but short enough to sustain the students' attention. See page 167 for a list of specific techniques.

3 ▶ **Discuss the Story as a Class**

Facilitate a whole-class discussion using questions such as:

Q *What did you find out about George Washington?*

Q *Why do you think George Washington gave the dog back to General Howe?*

Students might say:

"George Washington was a general and fought in a war."

"He was the first president."

"George knew that General Howe would be sad if he lost his dog."

Remind the students that wondering about a story helps them understand it. Explain that they will have more opportunities to wonder about stories in the coming weeks.

INDIVIDUALIZED DAILY READING

ELL Note

Before IDR, preview the questions you will ask at the end of independent reading. Ask your English Language Learners to pay attention to what they wonder as they read and what is especially interesting in their reading.

4 ▶ **Monitor the Students' Reading Levels and Understanding**

Have the students read independently for up to 20 minutes. Continue to use the "Resource Sheet for IDR Conferences" to monitor whether the students are reading books at appropriate reading levels and whether they are making sense of what they read.

 At the end of IDR, ask the students to think about what they read today. First in pairs, and then as a class, discuss:

Q *What do you still wonder about your story?*

Q *What was interesting about the book you read today?*

Day 3

Independent Reading/ Class Meeting

In this lesson, the students:

- Practice the procedure for Individualized Daily Reading
- Read independently for up to 20 minutes
- Share their thinking with one another
- Have a check-in class meeting

1 Discuss Procedures for Independent Reading

Have partners sit together. Remind them that they have been focusing on reading books at just the right reading level. Have the students use "Think, Pair, Share" to discuss:

Q *If you were to tell someone about what we do during independent reading time, what would you say?*

Have a few volunteers share their ideas with the whole class.

2 Select Books and Read Independently

Have the students select their books and read silently for up to 20 minutes. Stop them after 10 minutes to talk briefly with their partners about what they are reading. As they read, monitor individual students to make sure they are reading books at appropriate reading levels.

Materials

- Books of various genres at appropriate levels for independent reading
- "Class Meeting Ground Rules" chart
- Scratch paper and a pencil

 Note

Support your English Language Learners by providing a prompt for their response such as "During independent reading we...."

Teacher Note

To get a sense of whether the students are reading appropriate texts, you might ask questions such as:

Q *Tell me what is happening in your book so far.*

Q *What is confusing to you?*

Q (Point to a challenging word.) *What do you think this word means?*

Class Meeting Ground Rules

- one person talks at a time
- listen to one another

Teacher Note ▶

In the time period following a class meeting, it is important to hold the students accountable for things they agree to work on during the meeting. Use your notes to regularly remind the students and to check in with them about how they are doing.

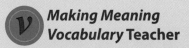

Making Meaning Vocabulary Teacher

Next week you will revisit *George Washington and the General's Dog* to teach Vocabulary Week 16.

3 **Have a Brief Check-in Class Meeting**

At the end of the independent reading, explain that the students will have a brief class meeting to check in on how they are getting along during independent reading time. Review the procedure for coming to a class meeting and have them move with their partners into a circle. Review the "Class Meeting Ground Rules" and then ask:

Q *How do you think our class has been doing during independent reading?*

Q *What have you been doing to help make independent reading go well?*

Q *What do you think we might want to work on to make independent reading go more smoothly?*

As the students share their thinking, jot down a few notes for yourself to remind the students of what they want to work on during upcoming independent reading times.

Briefly discuss how the students did following the "Class Meeting Ground Rules" and adjourn the meeting.

UNIT 5: WONDERING

Fiction and Narrative Nonfiction

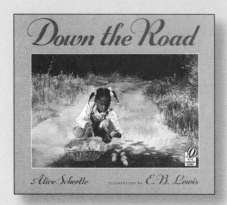

Down the Road
by Alice Schertle, illustrated by E. B. Lewis
(Voyager, 2000)

Hetty is allowed to walk to town all by herself for the first time.

ALTERNATIVE BOOKS

Hazel's Amazing Mother by Rosemary Wells
Dear Juno by Soyung Pak

Comprehension Focus

• Students use *wondering* to help them understand a story.

• Students *visualize* to understand and enjoy a story.

• Students use the sequence of events to *retell* a story.

• Students read independently.

Social Development Focus

• Students relate the value of responsibility to their behavior.

• Students develop the group skill of sharing ideas with one another.

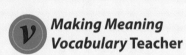

Making Meaning
***Vocabulary* Teacher**

If you are teaching Developmental Studies Center's *Making Meaning Vocabulary* program, teach Vocabulary Week 16 this week. For more information, see the *Making Meaning Vocabulary Teacher's Manual.*

DO AHEAD

• Make multiple copies of the "IDR Conference Notes" from the blackline master on page BLM14. This week you will begin using these to document individual students' growth in their independent reading. You will continue to use these sheets throughout the program. (For more about documenting IDR, see page xxvi.)

• Make copies of the Unit 5 Parent Letter (BLM5) to send home with the students on the last day of the unit.

Day 1

Materials

- *Down the Road* (pages 4–18)
- "What Good Readers Do" chart and a marker
- "IDR Conference Notes" record sheets, prepared ahead

What Good
Readers Do

- make connections to
  our lives

- wonder about stories

Read-aloud/Strategy Practice

In this lesson, the students:

- *Wonder* about a story read aloud
- Refer to the story to support their thinking
- Read independently for up to 20 minutes
- Share ideas with one another

▶1 Review Wondering and Add to the "What Good Readers Do" Chart

Have partners sit together. Remind the students that they have been listening to and wondering about stories.

Refer to the "What Good Readers Do" chart and read the strategies listed on it. Remind the students that this year they have been learning what good readers do to help them understand the stories that they hear and read. Write *wonder about stories* on the chart, and explain that this is what they have been practicing in the last few lessons.

Explain that today they will have another chance to wonder before, during, and after the story.

▶2 Introduce *Down the Road*

Show the cover of *Down the Road* and read the title and the author's and illustrator's names aloud. Tell the students that this is a story about a girl named Hetty and her mother and father. Open the book to the title page and show the students the title page and facing page. Explain that Hetty and her parents live in the country, and that this is a picture of where they live.

Tell the students that in this story Hetty's parents want eggs for breakfast, but they are too busy to go to the store. They decide to let Hetty go to the store by herself to get the eggs.

Ask:

Q *After hearing a little about the story and seeing the two illustrations, what do you wonder about this book?*

Students might say:

"I wonder how old Hetty is."

"I wonder if any eggs will break."

Have two or three students share their "I wonder" statements.

Explain that you will read the story aloud and stop during the reading to have partners talk about the story and what they are wondering. Explain that you will read part of the story today. They will hear the rest of the story in the next lesson.

 Read *Down the Road* Aloud and Stop and Wonder

Read pages 4–18 of *Down the Road* aloud, showing the illustrations and stopping as described on the next page.

Suggested Vocabulary

mended: fixed (p. 4)
one dozen: twelve (p. 6)
dillydally: waste time (p. 6)
meadow: field of grass (p. 12)
emporium: store selling many kinds of things (p. 15)
dry goods: items made from cloth or fabric (p. 15)
bolts of fabric: rolls of cloth (p. 17)

ELL Vocabulary

English Language Learners may benefit from discussing additional vocabulary, including:

chimney: opening on the top of a building that carries out smoke from a fireplace or furnace (p. 4)

shed: small building used for storage (p. 4; refer to the illustration on p. 5)

smoothest: most even and flat (p. 10)

pond: body of water smaller than a lake (p. 10)

pigtails: braided hair (p. 10; refer to the illustration)

stream: body of moving water that is smaller than a river (p. 12; refer to the illustration)

wobbles: moves unsteadily from side to side (p. 18)

Stop after:

> **p. 6**   "'Don't dillydally,' said Mama."

Ask:

Q *What have you learned about Hetty and her family so far?*

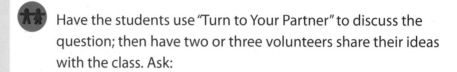 Have the students use "Turn to Your Partner" to discuss the question; then have two or three volunteers share their ideas with the class. Ask:

Q *What does Papa mean when he asks Hetty to get "twelve big beauties"?*

Have one or two students share their ideas with the class. Reread the last sentence on page 6, and continue reading to page 10. Stop after:

> **p. 10**   *"When this basket is full of eggs,* thought Hetty, *I'll walk my smoothest so they won't roll around and break."*

Ask:

Q *What is Hetty thinking as she walks to the store?*

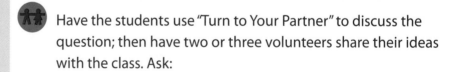 Have the students use "Turn to Your Partner" to discuss the question; then have two or three volunteers share their ideas with the class. Ask:

Q *What do you wonder about the story?*

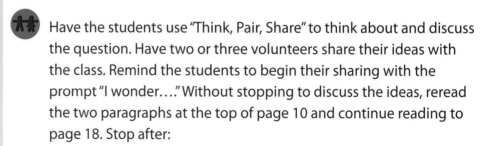 Have the students use "Think, Pair, Share" to think about and discuss the question. Have two or three volunteers share their ideas with the class. Remind the students to begin their sharing with the prompt "I wonder…." Without stopping to discuss the ideas, reread the two paragraphs at the top of page 10 and continue reading to page 18. Stop after:

> **p. 18**   *"No use taking a chance,* thought Hetty."

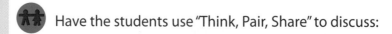 Have the students use "Think, Pair, Share" to discuss:

Q *What do you wonder about?*

Students might say:

"I wonder if she will break the eggs and have to buy more."

"I wonder if her mom and dad will be proud of her."

Have two or three students share their thinking.

 Discuss the Story as a Class

Facilitate a whole-class discussion of the story, using questions such as:

Q *Hetty is given the first grown-up job of her life. What is the job?*

Q *How do you think Hetty is doing so far?*

Tell the students that they will have a chance to hear the rest of the story in the next lesson and that they will discuss some of the things they wondered as they listened today.

INDIVIDUALIZED DAILY READING

 Start Using the "IDR Conference Notes" Record Sheet to Document Conferences

Tell the students that starting this week during IDR, you will spend more time conferring, or talking with them one-on-one, about their books so that you can help them become better readers. Tell the students that they will continue to choose books they can read and enjoy. During the conference, you will have each student read part of his book and talk about what he has read.

Before conducting the first IDR conference, facilitate a brief discussion about the importance of everyone reading quietly and independently while you meet with each student.

Have the students read books at their appropriate reading levels independently for up to 20 minutes.

FACILITATION TIP

Reflect on your experience over the past three weeks with **pacing** class discussions. Do the pacing techniques feel comfortable and natural? Do you find yourself using them throughout the school day? What effect has your focus on pacing had on the students' participation in discussions? We encourage you to continue to focus on pacing class discussions during the remainder of the school year.

Teacher Note

This week you will use the "IDR Conference Notes" to conduct and document individual student conferences. Each conference should last approximately 5 minutes. Conferences with struggling students may be more frequent or last longer.

Note

When conferring with students with limited English proficiency, pay close attention to nonverbal evidence of comprehension, such as pointing to characters in story illustrations or acting out story events. During the conference, you may wish to provide students with a chance to draw to demonstrate comprehension.

Select a student and have him bring a book he can read to the conference. Use the questions on the "IDR Conference Notes" to guide your conference. Jot down the student's responses as well as any other notes that you think are important (for example, "reads fluently and with understanding" or "does not have a strategy for attacking an unfamiliar word").

During the conferences you document, it is important that the students are reading books at appropriate levels. If you begin a conference and find that the student is not in an appropriate book, stop documenting the conference and help the student find a different book. Then return to document an IDR conference with the student another day.

Stop between conferences to circulate among and check in with the students.

At the end of independent reading, facilitate a brief discussion about how IDR went. Ask and briefly discuss questions such as:

Q *What went well during independent reading today?*

Q *What might we do differently next time to make sure IDR goes well?*

> **Students might say:**
>
> "I picked two books at the beginning of reading time so I didn't have time to bother anyone."
>
> "After a while I had trouble reading because people were talking and not reading. Next time people need to be quiet during reading time."

Day 2

Strategy Practice

In this lesson, the students:

- *Retell* the first part of a story
- *Wonder* about the story
- Refer to the story to support their thinking
- Read independently for up to 20 minutes
- Share their ideas with one another

▶ 1 Retell the First Part of *Down the Road*

Have partners sit together. Show the cover of *Down the Road* and remind the students that in the previous lesson they wondered about the first part of the story. Explain that today they will have a chance to hear the rest of the story.

Review the first part of *Down the Road* by having the students retell the story using the illustrations. Begin the retelling yourself by showing the illustration on pages 4–5 and telling what they show. (For example, you might say, "Hetty lives with her Mama and Papa in a house in the country.") Call on volunteers to continue the retelling, using the illustrations on pages 6–19.

▶ 2 Read the Rest of *Down the Road* Aloud and Stop and Wonder

Reread page 18; then read pages 21–36 aloud, showing the illustrations and stopping as described on the next page.

Materials

- *Down the Road*
- Scratch paper and a pencil
- *Assessment Resource Book*
- "IDR Conference Notes" record sheets

Suggested Vocabulary

obstacles: things that get in the way (p. 24)

foxtails: weeds that stick to clothes (p. 26)

nudged: gave a small push (p. 30)

magpie: noisy black and white bird (p. 32)

Note

You may want to have your English Language Learners briefly act out these words as you define them.

ELL Vocabulary

English Language Learners may benefit from discussing additional vocabulary, including:

stumbled: almost fell down (p. 22; refer to the illustration)

examined: looked closely at (p. 23; refer to the illustration)

sob: crying sound (p. 30)

Stop after:

> **p. 23** "She wiped each egg off on her shirt and put them all back inside."

Ask:

Q *What do you wonder about the story now?*

 Have the students use "Think, Pair, Share" to think about and discuss the question. After the partners share, have two or three volunteers share their ideas with the class. Remind the students to begin their sharing with the prompt "I wonder…."

CLASS PROGRESS ASSESSMENT

Circulate as the students talk. Ask yourself:

Q *Do the students support their thinking by referring to the text?*

Q *Did the students generate a variety of "I wonder" statements?*

Record your observations on page 16 of the *Assessment Resource Book.*

Reread the last paragraph on page 23 and continue reading. Stop after:

> **p. 29** "And there she sat, just thinking, and feeling sad, and not wanting to go home."

Ask:

Q *What happens in the part of the story you just heard?*

Have the students use "Turn to Your Partner" to discuss the question; then have two or three volunteers share their thinking with the class. Ask:

Q *What do you wonder?*

 Have the students use "Think, Pair, Share" to think about and discuss the question.

> ***Students might say:***
>
> "I wonder if Hetty will go back to the store for more eggs."
>
> "I wonder if her mom and dad will come looking for her."
>
> "I wonder if her mom and dad will get mad at her when they find out."

After pairs share, have two or three volunteers share their ideas with the class. Without stopping to discuss the ideas, reread page 29 and continue reading to the end of the story. Ask:

Q *What do you still wonder?*

 Use "Think, Pair, Share" to have the students first think about, and then discuss, the question. Then have two or three students share their thinking with the class.

▶3 Discuss "I Wonder" Statements as a Class

Explain that sometimes what they wonder about is discussed in the story, and sometimes it isn't. Select two of the students' "I wonder" statements about *Down the Road*. Facilitate a whole-class discussion of the statements by asking:

Q *Do you think the story talks about this "I wonder" statement?*

Q (If yes) *What part of the story talks about this?*

Q (If no) *Why do you think that?*

Remind the students that wondering is something readers do to think more deeply about a story. Tell them that they will continue to practice wondering about stories they hear and read independently in the coming weeks.

◀ **Teacher Note**

As you circulate among the students, jot down some of their "I wonder" statements to use during the class discussion following the read-aloud. (See Step 3.)

INDIVIDUALIZED DAILY READING

 Use the "IDR Conference Notes" Record Sheet to Document Conferences

Have the students read books at their appropriate reading levels independently for up to 20 minutes.

Continue to monitor the students' reading, using the "IDR Conference Notes" record sheet to record your observations.

Stop between conferences to circulate among and check in with the students.

At the end of independent reading, facilitate a brief discussion about how IDR conference time went. Have a few students share their reading with the class.

Day 3

Strategy Practice

In this lesson, the students:

- *Visualize* to enjoy and understand a story
- Draw their mental images
- Read independently for up to 20 minutes
- Share ideas with one another

1 ▶ Review Visualizing

Have partners sit together. Show the cover of *Down the Road* and review that the students heard the story and wondered about it. Explain that today the students will visualize, or picture in their minds, parts of the story that you will reread aloud. Then they will use "Think, Pair, Share" to talk with their partners about the pictures they have in mind. Ask:

Q *What is important to remember when using "Think, Pair, Share"?*

Q *Why is it important not to talk during the thinking time?*

Have a few volunteers share their ideas.

2 ▶ Reread Two Passages and Visualize

Introduce the first reading by telling the students that it is from the beginning of the story, when Hetty is walking to the store to get the eggs. Explain that you will read the part of the story aloud twice, and that you would like the students to close their eyes as they listen and make a mental picture of how Hetty is moving as she walks to the store.

Read page 10 aloud twice, pausing between the readings.

Materials

- *Down the Road* (pages 10, 27–28, and 32–33)
- Markers or crayons
- A sheet of drawing paper for each student
- "IDR Conference Notes" record sheets
- Unit 5 Parent Letter (BLM5)

 Note

English Language Learners may benefit from hearing and discussing pages 10, 27–28, and 32–33 before you read these pages to the whole class.

Have the students use "Think, Pair, Share" to discuss the pictures in their minds. After a moment, ask the class:

Q *What did you picture in your mind?*

Q *Which words helped you get the picture?*

Q *How do you imagine Hetty feels?*

Introduce the next reading by telling the students that it comes later in the story, when Hetty is reaching for apples on the tree. Read page 27 and the first word on page 28 aloud twice.

 Follow the same procedure as before to have the students discuss their visualizations in pairs and as a class.

3 ▶ **Reread Pages 32–33, Visualize, and Draw Mental Images**

Explain that you will read another part of *Down the Road,* and ask the students to picture the reading in their minds. They will draw their mental images and will share their pictures in pairs.

Introduce the reading by telling the students it is at the end of the story, when Mama finds Hetty and Papa sitting in the apple tree. Read pages 32–33 aloud twice, pausing between the readings.

Teacher Note

As the students draw, circulate ▶ among them and notice whether their drawings are relevant to the story. Also notice which story details they include (for example, the apple cores under the tree or Hetty's and Papa's sticky chins).

 Have the students use "Think, Pair, Share" to discuss their mental images. Then distribute a sheet of drawing paper to each student. Ask each student to draw a picture of her mental image and write a sentence about it. Later, partners will share their work.

4 ▶ **Share the Drawings**

Have partners share their drawings. Then facilitate a whole-class discussion using questions such as:

Q *What did you picture?*

Q *What did you write about your drawing?*

Teacher Note

This is the last week of Unit 5. You will need to reassign partners for Unit 6.

INDIVIDUALIZED DAILY READING

5 ## Document IDR Conferences/Have Students Discuss Wondering

Remind the students that they have been wondering about stories read aloud. Have each student look at the cover of the book she is reading and wonder quietly. Then have a few students share what they wonder with the class. Ask the students to notice what they wonder as they read their book today.

Have the students read for up to 20 minutes, and continue to use the "IDR Conference Notes" to conduct and document individual conferences.

At the end of independent reading, have the students talk about what they read and what they wondered in pairs or with the class. Circulate as the students share. Stop and ask questions such as:

Q *What was your story about?*

Q *What do you wonder about your story?*

◀ **Teacher Note**

If necessary, review the procedures for reading conferences.

 **Parent Letter**

Send home with each student the Parent Letter for this unit (see "Do Ahead," page 183). Periodically, have a few students share with the class what they are reading at home.

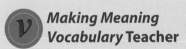 ***Making Meaning Vocabulary* Teacher**

Next week you will revisit *Down the Road* to teach Vocabulary Week 17.

Unit 6

Making Connections

EXPOSITORY NONFICTION

During this unit, the students explore the difference between fiction and nonfiction and identify what they learn from nonfiction. They make text-to-self connections and use schema to make sense of nonfiction. They also informally explore expository text features and visualize to make sense of texts. During IDR, the students share with their partners what they read independently. Socially, they share their ideas with one another, and they participate in a class meeting to discuss their independent reading time.

Week 1 *Hearing* by Sharon Gordon

Week 2 *A Good Night's Sleep* by Allan Fowler

Week 3 *Dinosaur Babies* by Lucille Recht Penner

Week 1

Overview

UNIT 6: MAKING CONNECTIONS
Expository Nonfiction

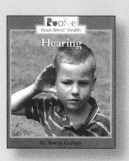

Hearing
by Sharon Gordon
(Children's Press, 2001)

This book explains how people hear sounds.

ALTERNATIVE BOOKS

Your Senses by Helen Frost

Smelling by Sharon Gordon

Comprehension Focus

- Students explore the difference between fiction and nonfiction.

- Students *use schema* to help them understand nonfiction.

- Students *make text-to-self connections*.

- Students identify what they learn from nonfiction.

- Students read independently.

Social Development Focus

- Students share ideas with one another.

- Students participate in a class meeting to discuss their independent reading time.

DO AHEAD

- Prior to Day 1, decide how you will randomly assign partners to work together during the unit.

- Collect a variety of nonfiction texts for the students to read and explore. (See "About Nonfiction: Making Connections" on page 200.)

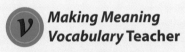

Making Meaning
Vocabulary Teacher

If you are teaching Developmental Studies Center's *Making Meaning Vocabulary* program, teach Vocabulary Week 17 this week. For more information, see the *Making Meaning Vocabulary Teacher's Manual*.

Day 1

Materials

- *Hearing*
- Variety of fiction books
- Variety of nonfiction books
- Nonfiction books at appropriate reading levels for independent reading
- "IDR Conference Notes" record sheets

Being a Writer™ **Teacher**

You can either have the students work with their *Being a Writer* partner or assign them a different partner for the *Making Meaning* lessons.

Read-aloud

In this lesson, the students:

- Begin working with new partners
- Explore the difference between fiction and nonfiction
- *Make text-to-self connections*
- Read independently for up to 20 minutes
- Share their thinking

About Nonfiction: Making Connections

The purpose of this unit and the two that follow is to introduce the students to nonfiction text and to help them make sense of nonfiction using the reading comprehension strategies they have learned in earlier units. These strategies include *making connections* to information the students already know, *wondering* or asking questions about topics they read about, and *visualizing* what authors describe. The nonfiction books in Unit 6 provide information for the students to learn, but the unit's primary goal is for the students to use comprehension strategies to make sense of what they read, rather than to recall the many facts presented in the books.

In this and the next two units, the students informally compare nonfiction and fiction and explore some of the features of expository text, such as photographs, chapter titles, tables of contents, maps, glossaries, timelines, and indexes. If possible, provide a variety of nonfiction books at various reading levels for the students to read independently. For information about Developmental Studies Center's Individualized Reading Libraries, see page xxvii and visit Developmental Studies Center's website at devstu.org.

1 Pair Students and Get Ready to Work Together

Randomly assign new partners and have them sit together. Tell the students that they will work with their new partners for the next few weeks. To help the new partners get to know each other, ask them to tell each other one thing they like about working in pairs. Explain that the students should listen carefully to their partners, because you will be asking them to share what their partners say with the class. Give the students a few minutes to share; then have a few students briefly share what their partners said.

Remind the students that today they will be responsible for both thinking on their own and sharing with a partner. Explain that at the end of the lesson, they will have opportunities to talk about how their partner work is going.

 Introduce Nonfiction

Show a variety of fiction stories that the students have heard, and remind them that they have heard several books about imaginary people and events. These books have characters and tell a story with a beginning, middle, and end. (For example, in *Curious George Goes to an Ice Cream Shop* there is an imaginary monkey who gets into trouble at an ice cream shop.) Make-believe stories are called fiction. Write *fiction: make-believe stories* on the board. Ask and briefly discuss:

Q *What other fiction books have you read?*

Show a variety of nonfiction books and explain that these are books about real people, animals, or places. They are called nonfiction. Write *nonfiction: books about real things* on the board. Ask and briefly discuss:

Q *What other nonfiction books have you read?*

Explain that for the next few weeks the students will hear, read, and explore nonfiction.

 Introduce *Hearing*

Show the cover of *Hearing* and read the title and author's name aloud. Explain that this is a nonfiction book about how people hear sounds.

Ask the students to close their eyes and listen quietly to the sounds in the room. After a few moments, ask:

Q *What sounds did you hear?*

Q *What are other sounds you might hear at school? At home?*

◀ **Teacher Note**

You may want to show the students these nonfiction books from previous units and remind the students that they heard and talked about the books *Where Do I Live?* (Unit 1) and *George Washington and the General's Dog* (Unit 5). You may also want to show magazines, newspapers, and other informational texts and point out that these are also examples of nonfiction.

Note

The many facts and other information found in expository books make the books especially challenging for English Language Learners. You may want to preview each book in this unit with the students by reading it aloud to them a few times prior to reading the book aloud to the class.

4 ▶ Read *Hearing* Aloud

Explain that you will read the book aloud and ask the students to think about what they learn about how people hear sounds. Tell them you will stop during the reading to have them talk with their partners about what they are learning.

Read *Hearing* aloud, showing the photographs and stopping as described below.

Suggested Vocabulary

outer ear: part of your ear on the outside of your head (p. 8; refer to the illustrations on pp. 8–9)

inner ear: part of your ear inside your head that you can't see (p. 15)

cup your hands: make your hands into the shape of a cup (p. 16; refer to the illustration)

ELL Vocabulary

English Language Learners may benefit from discussing additional vocabulary, including:

tube: shape like a straw (p. 12)

soft: quiet (p. 16)

Stop after:

> **p. 7** "This helps you hear things all around you."

Teacher Note ▶

The students will not share with the whole class at each stop. This maintains the flow of the story and cultivates the habit of relying on a partner, rather than depending on the teacher or the whole class, to confirm or support one's thinking.

 Have the students use "Turn to Your Partner" to talk about what they have learned so far from the book. Tell them that later they will have a chance to share with the whole class.

 At each of the following stops, have the students use "Turn to Your Partner" to talk about what they have learned so far:

> **p. 11** "It *catches* the sounds around you."
>
> **p. 15** "That is how you hear things."
>
> **p. 19** "Here comes the fire engine!"

Continue reading to the end of the book.

Discuss the Reading as a Whole Class

Ask and briefly discuss:

Q *What is one thing you learned from this book?*

As volunteers share, show the corresponding pages to the class and ask follow-up questions, such as:

Q *[Joey] learned that [having ears on the side of your head helps you hear things all around you]. What else did you learn about [how your ears help you hear]?*

Q *[Teneca] learned that [the part of your ear you can see is called your outer ear]. What else did you learn about [the different parts of your ear]?*

Explain that in the next lesson the students will hear the book again and talk about different sounds they hear every day.

 Reflect on Working with a New Partner

Ask:

Q *What is one thing you like about working with your new partner?*

Share your observations of the students' interactions, without using names. (For example, you might say, "I noticed that partners helped each other remember information" or "I heard some students ask their partners to please talk a little more loudly so they could understand them.") Also point out any problems you observed and ask the students to suggest solutions.

INDIVIDUALIZED DAILY READING

> **Read to Partners/Document IDR Conferences**

Tell the students that today each student will read independently and then partners will talk about a favorite part of their books. Ask each student to think as she reads independently about which part she would like to read to her partner.

FACILITATION TIP

During this unit, we encourage you to **avoid repeating or paraphrasing** students' responses. Repeating what students say when they speak too softly or paraphrasing them when they don't speak clearly teaches the students to listen to you but not to one another. Help the students learn to take responsibility by asking one another to speak up or by asking a question if they don't understand what a classmate has said.

ELL Note

When conferring with students with limited English proficiency, pay close attention to nonverbal evidence of comprehension, such as pointing to animals, objects, or people in photographs and illustrations or acting out information. During the conference, you may wish to provide the students with a chance to draw to demonstrate comprehension.

Have the students read for up to 20 minutes. Use the "IDR Conference Notes" record sheet to conduct and document individual conferences.

At the end of independent reading, ask a student to model being your partner. Hold your book between you and your partner, say the name of your book, and read aloud the part you chose. Then switch roles with your partner.

 Ask each student to find the parts she wanted to read and take turns reading aloud in pairs.

EXTENSION

Find Real-world Examples of Nonfiction Text

Take the class on a walking field trip around the school or the neighborhood to look for examples of nonfiction text. As you or the students notice these examples, stop to read some of them aloud. (For example, you might see nonfiction books in the school library, textbooks, street signs, posters, newsletters, and flyers.)

At the end of the walk, list on a sheet of chart paper the various examples of nonfiction text you and the students saw. Discuss the kinds of information that each item communicates. (For example, you might say, "The poster we saw in the third-grade classroom tells people about healthy foods to eat.")

Throughout Unit 6, encourage the students to be on the lookout—both in and out of school—for more examples of nonfiction text to add to your class list.

Day 2

Strategy Practice

In this lesson, the students:

- *Make text-to-self connections*
- Identify what they learn from a nonfiction text
- Read independently for up to 20 minutes
- Share their thinking

 Review Nonfiction

Have partners sit together. Show the cover of *Hearing* and remind the students that this is a nonfiction book. Ask:

Q *What do you know now about nonfiction?*

If necessary, remind the students that nonfiction books give true information about things like people, places, and animals. Many nonfiction books, like this one, have photographs as well as drawings. Show the picture on page 10, and have the students describe what the photographs tell them about how people hear.

Tell the students that today you will reread the book and show the pictures again to help them remember more information about how people hear.

 Reread *Hearing* Aloud

Reread pages 3–8, 11–17, and 18–29 aloud, stopping after each section to ask and discuss:

Q *What is one thing you remember from the part I just read?*

As the students offer ideas, be ready to refer to the text or show photographs to confirm their thinking.

Materials

- *Hearing*
- *Assessment Resource Book*
- "IDR Conference Notes" record sheets

 Note

You might prompt the students to begin their response by saying, "I remember…."

Discuss Text-to-self Connections

Ask and briefly discuss:

Q *What are some different kinds of sounds we read about in the last part of the book?*

As volunteers share, show the corresponding pages to the class, and ask follow-up questions such as:

Q *[Jasmin] remembered that the book talks about [whistling sounds]. What [whistling sounds] have you heard?*

Q *[Theodore] said the sound of [his] brother watching TV wakes him up in the morning. What sounds wake you up?*

 Have the students use "Turn to Your Partner" to discuss the following questions; then have one or two students share with the class.

Q *What sounds do you like? Why?*

Q *What sounds do you dislike? Why?*

> **CLASS PROGRESS ASSESSMENT**
>
> As the students contribute to the discussions, ask yourself:
>
> **Q** *Are the students able to make text-to-self connections?*
>
> **Q** *Do the students easily share their ideas with their partners?*
>
> Record your observations on page 17 of the *Assessment Resource Book.*

Explain to the students that as they heard the book *Hearing* read aloud they made connections to the sounds they know and like. Remind them that *making connections* is a strategy good readers use to help them understand and enjoy what they read. Explain that in the coming weeks the students will continue to hear nonfiction texts and make connections.

INDIVIDUALIZED DAILY READING

 Read to Partners/Document IDR Conferences

Have the students read for up to 20 minutes. Continue to use the "IDR Conference Notes" record sheet to conduct and document individual conferences.

 At the end of independent reading, have each student read a favorite part of his book to his partner.

After partners share, facilitate a whole-class discussion using questions such as:

Q *What do you like about reading to your partner? What do you like about listening to your partner read [her] book to you?*

Q *What did you do to show your partner you were listening?*

Q *What might you do to help your partner the next time you listen to [her] read?*

EXTENSIONS

Read Other Books About the Senses

Collect other books about the five senses to read aloud or to have available for the students to read or browse through. Have the students keep a record of what they learn about the senses.

Explore a Text Feature in *Hearing*

Show the diagram on page 14 of *Hearing*. Point out and read the labels aloud, and explain that this picture shows how sounds travel to the brain. Explain that sometimes nonfiction books include diagrams—or pictures—like this to help readers understand how something works or how something is put together. Explain that nonfiction books often include extra information, like diagrams, a contents page, or a "new words" page.

 Note

Some of your English Language Learners might benefit from reading books in their primary language. If possible, have these students share books with other students who speak and read the same language.

Day 3

Materials

- Space for the class to sit in a circle.
- "Class Meeting Ground Rules" chart
- "Reading Together" chart
- Scratch paper and a pencil
- "IDR Conference Notes" record sheets

Class Meeting

In this lesson, the students:

- Review ground rules and practice the procedure for a class meeting
- Analyze the ways they have been interacting
- Use *visualizing* to analyze their independent reading
- Read independently for up to 20 minutes
- Share their thinking

1 ▶ Get Ready for the Class Meeting

Have partners sit together. Explain that today the students will have a class meeting to talk about how they are working together during IDR. Before asking the students to move to the circle, have partners tell each other the procedure for coming to a class meeting. Then have one or two volunteers review the procedure for the class.

Have partners move to the circle and sit together.

2 ▶ Review the "Class Meeting Ground Rules"

Remind the students that the purpose of this class meeting is to check in on how they are helping one another when they read independently.

Refer to the "Class Meeting Ground Rules" chart and read and review the rules. Remind the students that these are the rules that you want them to follow during the meeting.

> Class Meeting
> Ground Rules
>
> - one person talks
>   at a time

3 Conduct the Class Meeting

On the board, write the steps that the students usually follow during IDR. For example:

1. *Choose a book.*

2. *Read to yourself.*

3. *Share with your partner.*

 Ask the students to close their eyes and visualize themselves doing each step of IDR. Have them use "Think, Pair, Share" to discuss:

Q *When you choose a book to read, what do you do?*

Students might say:

"I make sure I have a book that I can read so I don't have to stop and get another book."

"Sometimes I get more than one book to make sure I have a book I can read."

Q *What do you look like when you are reading to yourself? When you are sharing with your partner?*

Q *What might we want to work on to make IDR go better?*

Students might say:

"[Allan and I] think there aren't any problems when we talk to each other."

"Sometimes people talk too loud. That makes it hard to hear my partner."

"Maybe we can put up a 'be quiet' sign."

Encourage the students to keep their suggestions in mind during IDR, and tell them that you will check in with them to see how they are doing. Jot down some of the students' suggestions for yourself and remind them of these during IDR in the coming days.

Reflect and Close the Class Meeting

Facilitate a brief discussion about the class meeting by referring to the "Class Meeting Ground Rules" and "Reading Together" charts. Have the students briefly discuss the rules on the charts that helped them during today's class meeting.

 Have partners review the procedure for leaving the class meeting. Dismiss the students and have them move from the circle to their desks or tables.

INDIVIDUALIZED DAILY READING

 Share with Partners/Document IDR Conferences

Have the students read for up to 20 minutes. Continue to use the "IDR Conference Notes" record sheet to conduct and document individual conferences.

 At the end of independent reading, have each student tell her partner about a favorite part of her book. Explain that you will ask the students to share with the class what their partners said.

After partners share, facilitate a whole-class discussion using questions such as:

Q *What was your partner's favorite part of their book?*

Q *How did you and your partner work together? What might you do the same or differently the next time you work together?*

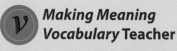

Making Meaning
Vocabulary Teacher

Next week you will revisit *Hearing* to teach Vocabulary Week 18.

Week 2

Overview

UNIT 6: MAKING CONNECTIONS
Expository Nonfiction

A Good Night's Sleep
by Allan Fowler
(Children's Press, 1996)

Readers learn about sleep and why it is important for humans and animals alike.

ALTERNATIVE BOOKS

Sleep Is for Everyone by Paul Showers

Sniffles, Sneezes, Hiccups, and Coughs by Penny Durant

Comprehension Focus

• Students *make text-to-self connections*.

• Students *use schema* to help them understand nonfiction.

• Students identify what they learn from nonfiction.

• Students read independently.

Social Development Focus

• Students share ideas with one another.

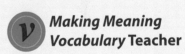

Making Meaning
Vocabulary Teacher

If you are teaching Developmental Studies Center's *Making Meaning Vocabulary* program, teach Vocabulary Week 18 this week. For more information, see the *Making Meaning Vocabulary Teacher's Manual*.

Day 1

Materials

*   *A Good Night's Sleep*

Read-aloud

In this lesson, the students:

*   *Make text-to-self connections*
*   Identify what they learn from a nonfiction text
*   Read independently for up to 20 minutes
*   Share their thinking

1▶ Gather and Review Nonfiction

Have partners sit together. Review that last week the students heard the nonfiction book *Hearing* and talked about what they learned from the book. Explain that during today's lesson they will hear and discuss another nonfiction book.

Ask and briefly discuss:

Q *What makes nonfiction books different from fiction books?*

2▶ Introduce *A Good Night's Sleep*

Show the cover of *A Good Night's Sleep* and read the title and author's name aloud. Explain that this is a nonfiction book about sleep and why sleep is important.

Ask and briefly discuss:

Q *Why is it important to get a good night's sleep?*

Q *How do you feel in the morning when you get a good night's sleep? When you don't?*

Read Part of *A Good Night's Sleep* Aloud

Explain that during today's lesson the students will hear the first part of the book. Tell them you will stop during the reading to have them talk in pairs about what they are learning.

Read pages 3–19 of *A Good Night's Sleep* aloud, showing the photographs and stopping as described below.

> **Suggested Vocabulary**
>
> **doze off:** fall asleep (p. 8)
> **fortunately:** luckily (p. 19)
>
> **ELL Vocabulary**
>
> English Language Learners may benefit from discussing additional vocabulary, including:
>
> **keep your mind on:** think about (p. 7)
> **snore:** breathe loudly while sleeping (p. 13)
> **fool you:** trick you (p. 17)
> **pleasant:** nice (p. 19)

Stop after:

> **p. 8**　"and you'd doze off during the day."

 Have the students use "Turn to Your Partner" to talk about what they have learned so far.

Without sharing as a class, continue reading to the following stop:

> **p. 13**　"Many people talk in their sleep—or snore."

 Have the students use "Turn to Your Partner" to talk about what they learned in the part they just heard.

Read to the end of page 19. Explain to the students that they will hear the rest of the book tomorrow.

FACILITATION TIP

This week continue to **avoid repeating or paraphrasing** the students' responses. Help them to learn to participate responsibly in class discussions by asking one another to speak up or by asking a question if they don't understand what a classmate has said.

4 ▶ **Discuss the Reading as a Whole Class**

Ask and briefly discuss:

Q *What did you find out about dreams in the part you just heard?*

As volunteers share, show the corresponding pages to the class to help the students remember what they heard.

> *Students might say:*
>
> "People dream every night."
>
> "Dreams can scare you."
>
> "Sometimes dreams don't make sense."
>
> "You can only remember a dream if you wake up right after it or in the middle of it."

 Use "Turn to Your Partner" to have the students discuss the following question; then have several volunteers students share with the class.

Q *What are some dreams you've had that you remember?*

Review that today the students used what they already knew about sleep to help them understand a nonfiction book about sleep. Explain that in the next lesson they will hear the rest of the book and talk about it.

5 ▶ **Reflect on Working Together**

Ask and briefly discuss:

Q *What went well with your partner today?*

Q *What did you do to make sure both of you had a chance to share your thinking?*

INDIVIDUALIZED DAILY READING

 Identify Something Learned

Explain that at the end of independent reading today partners will share something they learned from their nonfiction books.

Have the students independently read nonfiction books for up to 20 minutes. As they read, circulate among them. Stop and ask individual students questions such as:

Q *What is your book about?*

Q *What is something you learned about [turtles]?*

Q *Have you ever seen [turtles]? What were they like?*

Q *What do you want to share with your partner?*

 At the end of independent reading, have partners share what they learned with each other.

 Note

Your English Language Learners will benefit from rehearsing what they would like to share with their partners prior to working in pairs.

Day 2

Materials

- *A Good Night's Sleep*
- *Assessment Resource Book*

Read-aloud

In this lesson, the students:

- *Make text-to-self connections*
- Identify what they learn from a nonfiction text
- Read independently for up to 20 minutes
- Share their thinking

1 **Review and Introduce the Second Part of *A Good Night's Sleep***

Have partners sit together. Show the cover of *A Good Night's Sleep* and remind the students that yesterday they heard the first part of the book. Ask the following question and be ready to reread the first part of the book if the students have difficulty remembering what they heard.

Q *What did you find out about sleep in the first part of the book?*

Have a few volunteers share what they remember.

Explain that today the students will hear the second part of *A Good Night's Sleep*. Explain that the part of the book they will hear today is about how animals sleep.

Ask and discuss the following question:

Q *When have you seen an animal sleeping? Tell us about it.*

Point out that the students shared what they already know about animals sleeping. Ask them to listen for new information about how animals sleep.

ELL Note

You might prompt the students to begin their response by saying, "I found out…."

Teacher Note

If the students have difficulty answering this question, support their thinking by asking additional questions, such as:

Q *What kind of animal was it?*

Q *What did the [dog] look like when it was sleeping?*

Q *How did you know it was asleep?*

2 Read the Second Part of *A Good Night's Sleep* Aloud

Read aloud, beginning on page 20 and continuing to the end of the book.

Suggested Vocabulary

mammals: animals that have live babies and feed them milk—like dogs, horses, and mice (p. 20)

stored: kept (p. 27)

ELL Vocabulary

English Language Learners may benefit from discussing additional vocabulary, including:

scientists: people who study things in nature (p. 22)

 Have the students use "Turn to Your Partner" to discuss the following question; then have a few volunteers share with the class.

Q *What did you find out in the part you just heard?*

As the students offer ideas, be ready to reread parts of the text or show photographs to confirm their thinking. If necessary, prompt them with questions such as:

Q *What is something else you learned about [animals that hibernate]?*

Q *[Jared] said [he] remembers hearing about how [fish] sleep. What other animals did you hear about? What did you find out about how [cows] sleep?*

Q *[Olivia] was surprised that [some animals sleep during the day instead of at night]. What else did you find out that surprised you?*

CLASS PROGRESS ASSESSMENT

As the students contribute to the discussions, ask yourself:

Q *Are the students able to remember the facts they hear?*

Q *Are the students able to make connections to the text?*

Q *Do the students listen carefully and share their ideas with their partners and the class?*

Record your observations on page 18 of the *Assessment Resource Book*.

3 ▶ **Reflect on Sharing Ideas**

Ask and briefly discuss:

Q *What helped you listen well today?*

Briefly share your observations of what is going well and what the students might want to work on the next time they work in pairs.

INDIVIDUALIZED DAILY READING

4 ▶ **Identify Something Learned**

Explain that at the end of independent reading today partners will share something they learned from their nonfiction books.

Have the students read nonfiction books independently for up to 20 minutes. As they read, circulate among them. Stop and ask individual students questions such as:

Q *What is your book about?*

Q *What is something you learned about [horses]?*

Q *Have you ever seen [horses]? What were they like?*

Q *What do you want to share with your partner?*

 At the end of independent reading, have partners share what they learned with each other.

EXTENSION

Compare Fiction and Nonfiction

Read aloud a fiction book about sleep or dreaming, and have the students compare the story to *A Good Night's Sleep*. Some fiction possibilities are *Where the Wild Things Are* by Maurice Sendak, *Time to Sleep* by Denise Fleming, *Sleep, Black Bear, Sleep* by Jane Yolen, and *In the Night Kitchen* by Maurice Sendak.

Day 3

Materials

- *A Good Night's Sleep*

Strategy Lesson

In this lesson, the students:

- *Make text-to-self connections*
- Identify what they learn from a nonfiction text
- Read independently for up to 20 minutes
- Share their thinking

1▶ Review Making Connections

Have partners sit together. Show the cover of *A Good Night's Sleep* and review that the students have been making connections to the information in the book. Explain that today you will reread parts of *A Good Night's Sleep* aloud and make more connections to the text.

2▶ Reread Sections of *A Good Night's Sleep* and Make Connections

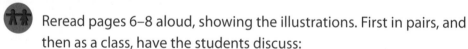 Reread pages 6–8 aloud, showing the illustrations. First in pairs, and then as a class, have the students discuss:

Q *When have you not gotten enough sleep? How did you feel?*

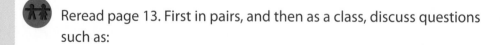 Reread page 13. First in pairs, and then as a class, discuss questions such as:

Q *Have you ever walked in your sleep? Tell us about it.*

Q *When have you heard someone snore?*

Remind the students that they have been making connections to nonfiction books. Explain that making connections with nonfiction books can help them understand the information in a book.

Reflect on Reading Nonfiction Texts

Facilitate a brief discussion about reading nonfiction texts. Remind the students that they have read two nonfiction books, *Hearing* and *A Good Night's Sleep.* Ask:

Q *How is a nonfiction book different from a fiction story?*

Q *What other topics would you like to read about?*

Tell the students that in the coming weeks they will hear and read more nonfiction books.

 ## Reflect on Partner Work

Facilitate a brief discussion about how the students worked together today. Ask:

Q *What did you like about working with your partner?*

Have partners tell each other one thing they liked about working together.

INDIVIDUALIZED DAILY READING

 ## Identify Something Learned

Explain that at the end of independent reading today, partners will share something they learned from their nonfiction book.

 Have the students independently read nonfiction books for up to 20 minutes. At the end of independent reading, have the students ask their partners about their books. The students might ask questions such as:

Q *What is your book about?*

Q *What is something you learned about [life on a farm]?*

Q *What do you like about the book you are reading?*

 ELL Note

Before the students begin to read independently, preview the questions you will have partners ask each other later. Before partners question each other, you might ask a volunteer to help you model asking questions.

 ***Making Meaning Vocabulary* Teacher**

Next week you will revisit *A Good Night's Sleep* to teach Vocabulary Week 19.

UNIT 6: MAKING CONNECTIONS
Expository Nonfiction

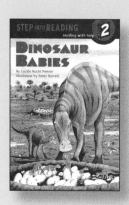

Dinosaur Babies
by Lucille Recht Penner, illustrated by Peter Barrett
(Random House, 1991)

Readers learn what life might have been like for baby dinosaurs.

ALTERNATIVE BOOKS

Snakes! by Lisa Jo Rudy

Penguin by DK Publishing

Comprehension Focus

- Students *make text-to-self connections*.

- Students *use schema* to help them understand nonfiction.

- Students identify what they learn from nonfiction.

- Students read independently.

Social Development Focus

- Students share ideas with one another.

DO AHEAD

- Make copies of the Unit 6 Parent Letter (BLM6) to send home with the students on the last day of the unit.

***Making Meaning
Vocabulary* Teacher**

If you are teaching Developmental
Studies Center's *Making
Meaning Vocabulary* program,
teach Vocabulary Week 19 this
week. For more information,
see the *Making Meaning
Vocabulary Teacher's Manual.*

Day 1

Read-aloud

Materials

- *Dinosaur Babies*
- *Hearing* (from Week 1)
- *A Good Night's Sleep* (from Week 2)

In this lesson, the students:

- *Make text-to-self connections*
- *Use schema* to help them understand nonfiction
- Identify what they learn from a nonfiction text
- Share their thinking
- Read independently for up to 20 minutes

1 ▶ **Review Nonfiction and Informally Make Connections**

Have partners sit together. Review that in the last few weeks the students have been reading nonfiction books, or books about true things.

Ask:

Q *What do you know about nonfiction books?*

Have a few volunteers share.

Show *Hearing* and *A Good Night's Sleep* and point out that these are both nonfiction books about people. Remind the students that nonfiction books can also be about animals or other real things in the world. Explain that today the students will hear a nonfiction book about dinosaurs.

 Use "Turn to Your Partner" to have the students discuss:

Q *What do you think you know about dinosaurs?*

Have a few volunteers share their thinking with the class.

ELL Note

Consider showing your students pictures of dinosaurs before asking this question.

2 ▶ Introduce *Dinosaur Babies*

Show the cover of *Dinosaur Babies* and read the title and author's name aloud. Explain that this is a nonfiction book about baby dinosaurs. Refer to the cover illustration and explain that nonfiction books about dinosaurs often have illustrations instead of photographs because no dinosaurs are alive today.

3 ▶ Read Part of *Dinosaur Babies* Aloud

Explain that today the students will hear the first part of the book and you will stop during the reading to have them talk with their partners about what they are learning.

Read pages 3–17 of *Dinosaur Babies* aloud, showing the illustrations and stopping as described below. At each stop, use "Turn to Your Partner" to have the students discuss what they learned in the part they heard.

> **ELL Vocabulary**
>
> English Language Learners may benefit from discussing the following vocabulary:
>
> **dinosaur hunters:** people who dig in the ground to look for dinosaur bones (p. 6)
>
> **kept them away:** stopped them from coming close (p. 12)
>
> **cracked:** broke (p. 14)
>
> **human babies:** babies people have (p. 17)

Stop after:

p. 9   "The biggest was about the size of a football!"

p. 13   "They breathed through tiny holes in the eggshells."

Reread page 13 and continue reading to the end of page 17.

4 ▶ Discuss the Reading

Use "Turn to Your Partner" to have the students discuss:

Q   *What other animals do you know of that come from eggs?*

Q *What other baby animals do you know about that wait for their mothers to feed them?*

As volunteers share, show the corresponding pages to the class to help the students remember what they heard.

Use "Turn to Your Partner" to have the students discuss the following question; then have several volunteers share with the class.

Q *What is something you know about dinosaurs that isn't in the book?*

Explain that in the next lesson the students will hear the rest of the book and talk about it.

5 ▶ Reflect on Working Together

Ask and briefly discuss:

Q *What is one thing your partner did today that helped you share your thinking?*

INDIVIDUALIZED DAILY READING

6 ▶ Share Reading with Partners

Have the students read nonfiction books for up to 20 minutes.

At the end of independent reading, explain that this week partners will ask one another questions about their nonfiction books. Model asking a student the following questions:

Q *What is your book about?*

Q *What do you like about the book you are reading?*

Ask partners to take turns asking one another questions like the two you modeled. As partners work, circulate and observe the students. Help individual students as necessary.

Day 2

Read-aloud/Strategy Lesson

Materials

- *Dinosaur Babies*

In this lesson, the students:

- *Make text-to-self connections*
- *Use schema* to help them understand nonfiction
- Identify what they learn from a nonfiction text
- Read independently for up to 20 minutes
- Share their thinking

1 Review and Introduce the Second Part of
Dinosaur Babies

Have partners sit together. Show the cover of *Dinosaur Babies* and review that yesterday the students heard the first part of the book. Ask and briefly discuss:

Q *What is one thing you remember finding out about baby dinosaurs?*

◀ **Teacher Note**

If the students have trouble recalling what they learned, prompt their thinking by paging through the first part of the book and showing the illustrations.

Students might say:

"Some dinosaur eggs are as big as a football."

"Dinosaur babies have a lot of teeth."

"The mothers build nests for the eggs."

Have a few volunteers share what they remember.

Explain that today the students will hear the second part of *Dinosaur Babies*. You will stop during the reading so that partners can talk about what they are learning.

▶ 2 Read the Second Part of *Dinosaur Babies* Aloud

Read aloud beginning on page 18, showing the illustrations and stopping as described below. At each stop, use "Turn to Your Partner" to have the students discuss what they learned in the part they heard.

> **Suggested Vocabulary**
>
> **herds:** big groups of animals that live together (p. 23)
>
> **ELL Vocabulary**
>
> English Language Learners may benefit from discussing additional vocabulary, including:
>
> **enemies:** other animals who want to hurt them (p. 20)
> **guarded:** kept safe (p. 25)

Stop after:

p. 20 "They could only hide."

p. 27 "The dinosaurs walked and ate and slept together."

Reread pages 26–27 and continue reading to the end of the book.

▶ 3 Discuss the Reading

Use "Turn to Your Partner" to have the students discuss:

Q *What did you find out in the part of the book you heard today?*

As volunteers share, ask follow-up questions such as:

Q *[Cheyenne] said [she] learned that [some dinosaurs lived in herds and they all slept together]. What else did you find out about [dinosaurs that lived in herds]?*

Q *[Christian] said [he] found out that [it wasn't safe for baby dinosaurs to be alone]. Why wasn't it safe for baby dinosaurs to be alone?*

Make Connections to the Reading

Review that in the past few weeks, the students have been making connections to their own lives to help them understand nonfiction books. Explain that one way readers make connections to nonfiction books is to think about what they already know.

Explain that you will reread a part of the book about baby dinosaurs growing up and then have partners talk about what else they know about what happens to baby animals as they grow up.

 Reread pages 28–29 aloud. Use "Think, Pair, Share" to have the students think about and discuss:

Q *The part you just heard is about what happens to baby dinosaurs as they grow up. What happens to other baby animals as they grow up?*

After several moments, have volunteers share what they talked about.

> **Students might say:**
>
> "A caterpillar turns into a butterfly."
>
> "When animals grow up, they get bigger and they eat more."
>
> "Baby ducks get new feathers when they get bigger."
>
> "When they get older, they learn how to live by themselves."

Review that today the students made connections by thinking about what they already know about baby animals. Explain that tomorrow the students will hear other parts of the book again and talk with their partners about what they already know.

 ## Reflect on Sharing Ideas

Ask and briefly discuss:

Q *What is one thing you did today to help your partner share [his] thinking?*

Briefly share your observations of what is going well and what the students might want to work on the next time they work in pairs.

◀ **Teacher Note**

Circulate as partners share. If the students are having trouble coming up with ideas, support them by asking questions, such as:

Q *What baby animals have you seen in real life, on TV, or in books?*

Q *When a [puppy] gets older, what happens to it?*

Q *What makes a [dog] different from a [puppy]?*

Q *What else happens to a [tadpole] when it grows into a [frog]?*

INDIVIDUALIZED DAILY READING

6 ▸ ## Share Reading with Partners/Document IDR Conferences

Have the students read nonfiction books for up to 20 minutes. Continue to monitor the students' reading, using the "IDR Conference Notes" record sheet to record your observations.

At the end of independent reading, remind the students that this week partners are asking one another questions about their nonfiction books. Model asking a student the following questions:

Q *What is your book about?*

Q *What do you like about the book you are reading?*

Q *What did you learn about [tigers]?*

 Ask partners to take turns asking one another questions like the three you modeled. As partners work, circulate and observe the students. Help individual students as necessary.

EXTENSION

Read Other Books About Animal Babies

Collect other books about animal babies to read aloud or to have available for the students to read or browse through. Have the students keep a record of what they learn about different kinds of animal babies.

ELL Note

You may want to write these questions on the board to provide additional support to your English Language Learners.

Day 3

Guided Strategy Practice

In this lesson, the students:

- *Make text-to-self connections*
- *Use schema* to help them understand nonfiction
- Identify what they learn from a nonfiction text
- Read independently for up to 20 minutes
- Share their thinking

1 Review the "What Good Readers Do" Chart and Making Connections

Have partners sit together. Review that the "What Good Readers Do" chart reminds the students of things they can do to enjoy and understand what they read. Briefly review the strategies *retell*, *make connections to our lives*, and *wonder about stories*.

Show *Hearing* and *A Good Night's Sleep* and review that the students made connections to their own lives to help them understand these nonfiction books. Show the cover of *Dinosaur Babies* and review that yesterday the students made connections to the book by thinking about what they already know about baby animals. Explain that today they will hear parts of *Dinosaur Babies* again and make more connections to the information in the book.

2 Reread Sections of *Dinosaur Babies* and Make Connections

Reread pages 10–15 aloud, showing the illustrations. Encourage the students to listen for what they find out about how dinosaur mothers take care of their babies. After the reading, ask:

Q *What is one thing dinosaur mothers do to take care of their babies?*

Have several volunteers share.

Materials

- *Dinosaur Babies*
- "What Good Readers Do" chart
- *Hearing* (from Week 1)
- *A Good Night's Sleep* (from Week 2)
- *Assessment Resource Book*
- Unit 6 Parent Letter (BLM6)

> *What Good Readers Do*
>
> - make connections to our lives

Use "Think, Pair, Share" to have the students think about and discuss:

Q *What do other animal mothers do to take care of their babies?*

Circulate as pairs share. If students are having difficulty coming up with ideas, stimulate their thinking by asking questions such as:

Q *What baby animals have you seen or read about? What do [mother dogs] do to feed their [puppies]?*

Q *You said [bears] take good care of their babies. What do [mother bears] do to make sure their babies are safe?*

Have volunteers share what they talked about.

CLASS PROGRESS ASSESSMENT

As the students work in pairs and contribute to the discussions, ask yourself:

Q *Are the students able to use schema to generate ideas that connect to the text?*

Q *Do the students listen carefully and share their ideas with their partners and the class?*

Record your observations on page 19 of the *Assessment Resource Book*.

Reread pages 18–19. As a class, discuss questions such as:

Q *What other animals eat plants? What does a [panda bear] eat?*

Q *What other animals eat animals? What do [lions] eat?*

Review that today the students made connections to the nonfiction book *Dinosaur Babies* by thinking about what they know about other animals. Remind them that making connections to nonfiction books helps readers understand what they are learning. Encourage them to continue making connections in their own reading.

Reflect on Partner Work

Facilitate a brief discussion about how the students worked together today. Briefly discuss as a class:

Q *What went well with your partner today?*

Explain that next week the students will work with new partners.

Q *What is one thing you can do to work well with your next partner?*

Teacher Note

This is the last week in Unit 6. You will reassign partners for Unit 7.

INDIVIDUALIZED DAILY READING

Share Reading with Partners/Document IDR Conferences

Have the students read nonfiction books for up to 20 minutes. Continue to monitor the students' reading, using the "IDR Conference Notes" record sheet to record your observations.

At the end of independent reading, have the partners ask one another questions about the nonfiction books they are reading. The students might ask questions such as:

Q *What is your book about?*

Q *What do you like about the book you are reading?*

Q *What did you learn about [the moon]?*

As partners work, circulate and observe the students. Help individual students as necessary.

 Parent Letter

Send home with each student the Parent Letter for this unit (see "Do Ahead," page 225). Periodically, have a few students share with the class what they are reading at home.

 ***Making Meaning* Vocabulary Teacher**

Next week you will revisit *Dinosaur Babies* to teach Vocabulary Week 20.

Unit 7

Wondering

EXPOSITORY NONFICTION

During this unit, the students continue to identify what they learn from nonfiction. They use the comprehension strategy of wondering to help them to make sense of nonfiction. They also informally explore expository text features and visualize to make sense of texts. During IDR, the students read nonfiction books independently and practice monitoring their own reading. Socially, they share their partners' thinking during whole-class discussions and reflect on how they are taking responsibility for their behavior.

Week 1 *A Kangaroo Joey Grows Up* by Joan Hewett

Week 2 *A Harbor Seal Pup Grows Up* by Joan Hewett

Week 3 *Throw Your Tooth on the Roof* by Selby B. Beeler
            A Look at Teeth by Allan Fowler

Week 1 Overview

UNIT 7: WONDERING
Expository Nonfiction

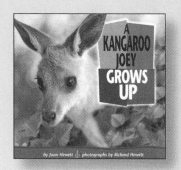

A Kangaroo Joey Grows Up
by Joan Hewett, photographs by Richard Hewett
(First Avenue Editions, 2002)

Kipper, a kangaroo joey, grows up and becomes independent.

ALTERNATIVE BOOKS

The Emperor's Egg by Martin Jenkins
A Koala Joey Grows Up by Joan Hewett

Comprehension Focus

- Students use *wondering* to help them understand nonfiction.

- Students identify what they learn from nonfiction.

- Students informally *explore text features* of expository nonfiction.

- Students read independently.

Social Development Focus

- Students share their partners' thinking with the class.

- Students relate the value of responsibility to their behavior.

DO AHEAD

- Prior to Day 1, decide how you will randomly assign partners to work together during the unit.

- Collect nonfiction books at various reading levels for independent reading (see Day 3).

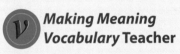

Making Meaning
Vocabulary Teacher

If you are teaching Developmental Studies Center's *Making Meaning Vocabulary* program, teach Vocabulary Week 20 this week. For more information, see the *Making Meaning Vocabulary Teacher's Manual.*

Day 1

Materials

- *A Kangaroo Joey Grows Up* (pages 3–19)
- Scratch paper and a pencil

Being a Writer™ **Teacher**

You can either have the students work with their *Being a Writer* partner or assign them a different partner for the *Making Meaning* lessons.

Teacher Note ▶

If the students have difficulty answering this question, suggest some ideas like those in the "Students might say" note.

 Note

English Language Learners will benefit from previewing the photographs and hearing the story prior to the lesson.

Read-aloud

In this lesson, the students:

- Use *wondering* to help them understand nonfiction
- Identify what they learn from a nonfiction text
- Read independently for up to 20 minutes
- Share their partners' thinking
- Relate the value of responsibility to their behavior

1 ▶ Pair Students and Get Ready to Work Together

Randomly assign new partners and have them sit together. Explain that for the next few weeks you will be asking the students to share their partners' thinking with the class.

Ask and briefly discuss:

Q *What will you have to do to be ready to share your partner's thinking with the class?*

Students might say:

"I will have to listen carefully when my partner is talking."

"I might have to ask her a question to make sure I understood her."

"I might repeat what my partner said to check to make sure I got it right."

2 ▶ Introduce *A Kangaroo Joey Grows Up*

Remind the students that they have been listening to and discussing nonfiction books. Review with the students that nonfiction books are books about real things.

Explain that today they will hear and discuss the first part of another nonfiction book. Show the cover of *A Kangaroo Joey Grows Up* and read the title and the names of the author and photographer aloud. Explain that this book is about a baby kangaroo. Point out that *joey* means "baby kangaroo," just as *puppy* means "baby dog." The joey in the story is named Kipper.

Ask and briefly discuss:

Q *What do you think you already know about kangaroos?*

Explain that Kipper, the baby kangaroo in the story, lives on a nature preserve in Australia. Point out that on a nature preserve, animals are protected from hunters and they live as they would live in the wild.

◀ **Teacher Note**
You may wish to use a world map to show the students where Australia is located.

 Read the First Two Chapters Aloud

Explain that you will read the first part of *A Kangaroo Joey Grows Up* aloud. Ask the students to listen and think about what they learn about the kangaroo. Point out that some of the information might surprise them or be new. Explain that you will stop during the reading to give partners a chance to talk.

Read pages 3–19 of *A Kangaroo Joey Grows Up* aloud, following the procedure described below.

Suggested Vocabulary

pouch: part of a female kangaroo's body that is like a pocket (p. 3)
kidney bean: small bean (p. 5; show the size of a bean with your fingers)
is curious: wants to find out or learn (p. 8)
springs: jumps (p. 13)
lickety-split: very fast (p. 15)

ELL Vocabulary

English Language Learners may benefit from discussing additional vocabulary, including:

peeks out: looks out (p. 7)
somersaults: rolls in a complete circle (p. 14)
front-row seat: (idiom) place that he can see well from (p. 19)

Point out that sometimes nonfiction books are divided into chapters or sections. Open the book to page 3 and read the chapter title aloud. Explain that a title lets you know what information is in the chapter (for example, this chapter, "In His Mother's Pouch," tells what happens when a joey is born).

Read pages 3–9 aloud, showing the photographs as you read. Stop after:

    p. 9   "Kipper sees other kangaroos!"

 Remind the students that this chapter is called "In His Mother's Pouch." Have them use "Turn to Your Partner" to discuss:

Q *What did you learn about Kipper in his mother's pouch?*

Without stopping to discuss the question as a class, show page 10, read the chapter title aloud, and continue reading to page 19. Stop after:

    p. 19   "She can hop all day without stopping."

 Ask, and have the students use "Turn to Your Partner" to discuss:

Q *What did you learn about how Kipper learns to hop?*

 Discuss What the Students Learned and Wonder

Tell the students that you will ask a question and they will talk in pairs about it. Explain that later you will ask the students to share their partners' thinking with the class, so it is important to listen carefully. Have the students use "Turn to Your Partner" to discuss:

Q *What did you learn today about kangaroos that surprised you?*

Have a few volunteers share their partners' thinking with the class.

Point out that the students have learned some interesting information about kangaroos. Explain that, often, learning new information from nonfiction books causes more questions to come into readers' minds. Ask:

Q *What are some things you are wondering about kangaroos?*

As the students share, jot down some of their questions for yourself on a piece of scratch paper. Tell the students that some of their questions may be answered in the next lesson, when they will hear the second half of *A Kangaroo Joey Grows Up.*

Teacher Note ▶

As partners talk, circulate and notice whether they are talking about examples from the book. If necessary to keep them focused, remind them to think about what they are learning from the book.

FACILITATION TIP

During this unit, we invite you to practice **responding neutrally** with interest during class discussions. To respond neutrally means to refrain from overtly praising (e.g., "Great idea" or "Good job") or criticizing (e.g., "That's wrong") the students' responses. Although it may feel more natural to avoid criticism rather than praise, research shows that both kinds of response encourage students to look to you, rather than themselves, for validation. To build the students' intrinsic motivation, try responding with genuine curiosity and interest (e.g., "Interesting—say more about that") while avoiding statements that communicate judgment, whether positive or negative.

5 ▶ **Reflect on Sharing Their Partners' Thinking**

Review that the students shared their partners' thinking about something surprising they learned today about kangaroos. Ask and briefly discuss:

Q *What did you have to do to be ready to share your partner's thinking with the class?*

Consider sharing your observations of the students' behaviors.

Teacher Note

Avoid using names when sharing your observations, for example, "I noticed partners looking directly at each other while they were talking" or "I heard some students repeating their partners' thinking to make sure they understood before sharing with the class."

INDIVIDUALIZED DAILY READING

6 ▶ **Read Independently**

Have the students independently read nonfiction books for up to 20 minutes. As the students read, circulate among them and monitor whether they are reading books at appropriate reading levels. Ask individual students to read a part of their book to you and explain what they have read. If a book seems too difficult or too easy for a student, help her select a more appropriate book.

At the end of independent reading, give the students time to share with the whole class what they read. Help the students reflect on their independent reading time by asking questions such as:

Q *What did you do to take responsibility for yourself during independent reading?*

Q *What do you think is working well during independent reading? What do you want to do differently during independent reading next time?*

ELL Note

Some of your English Language Leaners may benefit from reading books written in their primary language.

EXTENSIONS

Read "More About Kangaroos"

Explain that the last section of *A Kangaroo Joey Grows Up* gives more information about kangaroos. Read the title "More About Kangaroos" and read aloud or paraphrase pages 30–31, stopping periodically to have the students talk about what they are learning.

Compare Fiction and Nonfiction

Read a fiction story about kangaroos and have the students compare the story with *A Kangaroo Joey Grows Up*. Some fiction possibilities are *Katy No-Pocket* by Emmy Payne, *Marsupial Sue* by John Lithgow, *Norma Jean, Jumping Bean* by Joanna Cole, and *Snap* by Marcia K. Vaughn.

Day 2

Strategy Lesson

Materials

- *A Kangaroo Joey Grows Up*
- Your jotted notes from Day 1

In this lesson, the students:

- Identify what they learn from a nonfiction text
- Use *wondering* to help them understand nonfiction
- Read independently for up to 20 minutes
- Share their partners' thinking
- Relate the value of responsibility to their behavior

▶1 Review the First Half of *A Kangaroo Joey Grows Up*

Remind the students that in the previous lesson they listened to two chapters of a story about a kangaroo joey growing up. Leaf through pages 2–19, reading the chapter titles aloud. Ask:

Q *What did Kipper do in the first part of the book?*

Have a few students share what they remember.

▶2 Read the Second Half of the Book Aloud

Tell the students that you will read the rest of *A Kangaroo Joey Grows Up* aloud. Ask them to listen to find out what Kipper will do now that he is a little older. Read aloud pages 20–29 today, showing the photographs and following the procedure described on the next page.

Suggested Vocabulary

grazing: eating grass (p. 20)

ELL Vocabulary

English Language Learners may benefit from discussing additional vocabulary, including:

leafy trees: trees with many leaves (p. 23)

dives: jumps headfirst (p. 24)

nap: rest during the day; sleep (p. 25)

tags along: follows (p. 27)

Show the photo on page 20, read the chapter title aloud, and explain that "Kangaroos Abound" means that there are lots of kangaroos around. Read to page 25. Stop after:

> **p. 25** "They take a long nap."

 Have the students use "Turn to Your Partner" to discuss:

Q *What do Kipper and his mother do in the chapter I just read?*

Without stopping to discuss as a class, show the photo on page 26, read the chapter title, and continue reading to page 29. Stop after:

> **p. 29** "The kangaroo joey has grown up."

 Have the students use "Turn to Your Partner" to discuss:

Q *What does Kipper do now that he has grown up?*

▶3 Discuss What the Students Learned and Wonder

 Facilitate a brief discussion about the second half of the story. Have the students use "Turn to Your Partner" to discuss the following questions. Ask the students to be ready to share their partners' thinking during the whole-class discussion.

Q *What does "he can live on his own" mean?*

Q *What was the most surprising or interesting thing that you learned today about kangaroos?*

Have a few volunteers share their partners' thinking.

Teacher Note ▶

If possible, discuss at least one question that was addressed in the book and one that was not.

Use the notes you jotted down for yourself on Day 1 to remind the students of some of their questions. Ask:

Q *Yesterday you wondered [what happens when the joey gets too big to fit in his mother's pouch]. What did we find out about that?*

Q *Now that we've finished the book, what are you still wondering about kangaroos?*

Q *How could we find answers to some of those questions?*

If necessary, explain that the students could read other books or magazines, watch a television program on kangaroos, or talk to a person who knows about kangaroos, like a zookeeper or veterinarian.

4 Reflect on Sharing Their Partners' Thinking

Review that the students shared their partners' thinking about the most surprising or interesting thing they learned today about kangaroos. Ask and briefly discuss:

Q *What did you have to do to be ready to share your partner's thinking with the class?*

Explain that the students will have more opportunities to share their partners' thinking with the class in the next few days. Tell the students that in the coming weeks they will hear and read more nonfiction books.

INDIVIDUALIZED DAILY READING

5 Read Independently and Share Books

Have the students independently read nonfiction books for up to 20 minutes. Explain that at the end of IDR today each student will show a picture or photograph from the book he is reading to his partner and talk about it.

As the students read, circulate among them. Stop and ask individual students to talk about the photograph or picture they will share in pairs. Ask questions such as:

Q *What is your book about?*

Q *Which picture are you going to share with your partner? Tell me about it.*

At the end of independent reading, have partners share their books and a picture or photograph with each other.

Teacher Note ▶

Before starting this activity, write the following main events on sentence strips. If possible, include a picture clue for each event:

- The joey is the size of a bean and lives in his mother's pouch.
- The joey begins to look like a kangaroo.
- The joey peeks out of the pouch.
- The joey stands up for the first time.
- The joey eats grass.
- The joey cannot fit in his mother's pouch.
- The joey can live on his own.

EXTENSIONS

Create a Timeline of a Joey's Development

Point to the timeline on the top of pages 30–31 of *A Kangaroo Joey Grows Up* and explain that this is a line that gives information about a joey's life from birth until he can live on his own. Draw this timeline showing the ages of the kangaroo joey on a long sheet of butcher paper and post it where everyone can see it. Do not fill in the events below the line.

Explain that you have written the important events in Kipper's life on sentence strips. With the students, read the sentence on each strip. Place the strips randomly in a pocket chart. First in pairs, and then as a class, discuss:

Q *Which event do you think comes first? Why do you think this?*

Once the students reach agreement, have a student tape the strip on the timeline under the appropriate age label. Continue this procedure to order the remaining strips, and then reread passages or show illustrations from the book to check the order of events.

Read More About Kangaroos

Continue to explore the subject of kangaroos by reading aloud more nonfiction books about kangaroos. Ask the students to pay attention to questions about kangaroos that come into their minds as they listen. Stop periodically during the reading to have the students share what they are wondering. Some choices are *The Secret World of Kangaroos* by Malcom Penny, *Kangaroos Have Joeys* by Emily J. Dolbear and E. Russell Primm, *True Kangaroos (Animals of the Rain Forest)* by Chuck Miller, and *The Wonder of Kangaroos (Animal Wonders)* by Patricia Lantier-Sampson and Judith Logan Lehne.

Day 3

Independent Strategy Practice

In this lesson, the students:

* Read nonfiction books independently
* Identify what they learn from a nonfiction text
* Relate the value of responsibility to their behavior

1 Review Nonfiction Topics

Remind the students that they have heard and read stories about real people, places, and animals. Ask:

Q *What have you read about in nonfiction books during IDR recently?*

Students might say:

"I read a book about robots. It was funny."

"I read a book about cats. One cat looked like my cat."

"I read a book about rocks. There were cool pictures."

Explain that today the students will continue to read nonfiction.

2 Review Identifying One Thing You Learned

Explain that today each student will read the nonfiction book she chose. Then the students will each choose one thing they learn from their reading and share that information in pairs.

Use *A Kangaroo Joey Grows Up* to model. Ask:

Q *What is one thing you learned from this book about a kangaroo joey?*

Have one or two students volunteer ideas (for example, "A kangaroo joey is the size of a bean when it is born"). Model finding one of the facts they mention in the book. Read the information aloud and place a self-stick note in the margin of the page.

Materials

* *A Kangaroo Joey Grows Up*
* Nonfiction texts at appropriate levels for independent reading
* A small self-stick note for each student
* *Assessment Resource Book*

Teacher Note

Have the students select their independent reading books before starting the lesson.

Explain that the students will read to themselves for a short time. Then you will stop them and ask them to choose one interesting thing they learned from their reading. They will mark that page with a self-stick note.

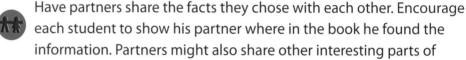

Read Nonfiction Books Independently

Distribute a self-stick note to each student. Have the students read independently for 5 minutes. Stop them and ask them to reread the pages they just read and think about something interesting they learned from the book. Have them each mark that page with a self-stick note.

Teacher Note ▶

Note challenging vocabulary in the students' independent reading books and have brief discussions with individual students to help them define the terms as they read. In some cases, you may want to have the students read the text with you.

Share Facts from Nonfiction Books

 Have partners share the facts they chose with each other. Encourage each student to show his partner where in the book he found the information. Partners might also share other interesting parts of their books.

CLASS PROGRESS ASSESSMENT

As the partners discuss their ideas, circulate among them and ask yourself:

Q *Are the students comprehending what they read?*

Q *Are they finding factual information?*

Record your observations on page 20 of the *Assessment Resource Book*.

Ask and have the students use "Turn to Your Partner" to discuss:

Q *What do you like about your book? Would you recommend this book to your partner to read? Why or why not?*

Students might say:

"I would recommend this book to my partner because it's about cats and she loves cats."

"I wouldn't recommend this book to my partner because it doesn't have many pictures."

"This book has lots of facts about sharks. I think my partner would be interested in it."

Have a few volunteers share with the class whether they would recommend their book to their partner and why or why not.

 Reflect on Working Together

 Have the students use "Think, Pair, Share" to discuss:

Q *When your partner was sharing a fact from [her] book with you, what did you do to act responsibly?*

Share some of your observations of partners' interactions during the lesson. If the students had any difficulties acting responsibly as they listened to each other, have them think about and discuss what they might do to avoid those difficulties next time.

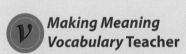

Making Meaning
Vocabulary Teacher

Next week you will revisit *A Kangaroo Joey Grows Up* to teach Vocabulary Week 21.

Week 2

Overview

UNIT 7: WONDERING
Expository Nonfiction

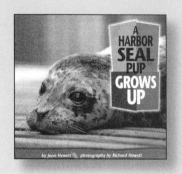

A Harbor Seal Pup Grows Up
by Joan Hewett, photographs by Richard Hewett
(First Avenue Editions, 2002)

A harbor seal pup is rescued and released back to the ocean.

ALTERNATIVE BOOKS

Penguin Chick by Betty Tatham

A Salamander's Life by John Himmelman

Comprehension Focus

- Students use *wondering* to help them understand nonfiction.

- Students identify what they learn from nonfiction texts.

- Students informally *explore text features* of expository nonfiction.

- Students read independently.

Social Development Focus

- Students share their partners' thinking with the class.

- Students relate the value of responsibility to their behavior.

DO AHEAD

- Collect nonfiction books at various reading levels for independent reading (see Day 3).

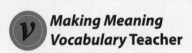

**Making Meaning
Vocabulary Teacher**

If you are teaching Developmental Studies Center's *Making Meaning Vocabulary* program, teach Vocabulary Week 21 this week. For more information, see the *Making Meaning Vocabulary Teacher's Manual.*

Day 1

Materials

- *A Harbor Seal Pup Grows Up* (pages 3–17)
- Scratch paper and a pencil
- "IDR Conference Notes" record sheets

ELL Note

English Language Learners will benefit from previewing the photographs and hearing the story prior to the lesson.

Read-aloud/Strategy Lesson

In this lesson, the students:

- Use *wondering* to help them understand nonfiction
- Identify what they learn from a nonfiction text
- Read independently for up to 20 minutes
- Share their partners' thinking
- Relate the value of responsibility to their behavior

 Get Ready to Work Together

Gather the class with partners sitting together. Explain that during today's lesson they will hear the first part of another nonfiction book and talk in pairs about it.

Remind the students that they have been sharing their partners' thinking with the class. Explain that they will have more opportunities to share their partners' thinking this week.

 Introduce *A Harbor Seal Pup Grows Up*

Show the cover of the book and read the title and the names of the author and photographer aloud. Explain that this is another story about how an animal grows up. It was written by the same author as *A Kangaroo Joey Grows Up*. Read the summary on the back cover of the book. Ask and briefly discuss:

Q *What do you think you know about harbor seals?*

Explain that Sidney, the harbor seal in the story, was born on land near the ocean, in a place where harbor seal mothers come to give birth and nurse their pups.

Read the First Half of the Book Aloud

Explain that you will read the first part of *A Harbor Seal Pup Grows Up* aloud. Ask the students to listen and think about what they learn about the harbor seal. Point out that some of the information might surprise them or be new. Explain that you will stop during the reading to give partners a chance to talk.

Read aloud pages 3–17 of *A Harbor Seal Pup Grows Up* today, following the procedure described below.

> **Suggested Vocabulary**
>
> **nursed back to health:** cared for when unwell (p. 10)
>
> **sea mammal center:** place that takes care of animals such as seals until they can be returned to the wild (p. 10)

Review that sometimes nonfiction books are divided into chapters or sections. Open the book to page 3 and read the chapter title aloud. Review that a title lets you know what information is in the chapter (for example, this chapter, "By the Ocean," describes Sidney's first weeks of life at the edge of the ocean).

Read pages 3–9 aloud, showing the photographs as you read. Stop after:

> **p. 9** "Sidney is rescued."

 Remind the students that this chapter is called "By the Ocean." Have them use "Turn to Your Partner" to discuss:

Q *What did you learn about Sidney during her first weeks of life?*

Without stopping to discuss the question as a class, show page 10, read the chapter title aloud, and continue reading to page 17. Stop after:

> **p. 17** "Sidney is small for her age."

 Ask and have the students use "Turn to Your Partner" to discuss:

Q *What did you learn about how Sidney is nursed back to health?*

Teacher Note

As partners talk, circulate and notice whether they are talking about examples from the book. If necessary to keep them focused, remind them to think about what they are learning from the book.

4 ▶ **Discuss What the Students Learned and Wonder**

Tell the students that you will ask a question and the students will talk in pairs about it. Explain that later you will ask the students to share their partners' thinking with the class, so it is important to listen carefully. Have the students use "Turn to Your Partner" to discuss:

Q *What did you learn today about harbor seals that surprised you?*

Have a few volunteers share their partners' thinking with the class.

Point out that the students have learned some interesting information about harbor seals. Remind the students that, often, learning new information from nonfiction books causes more questions to come into readers' minds. Ask:

Q *What are some things you are wondering about harbor seals?*

As the students share, jot down some of their questions for yourself on a sheet of scratch paper. Tell the students that some of their questions may be answered in the next lesson when they will hear the second half of *A Harbor Seal Pup Grows Up*.

5 ▶ **Reflect on Sharing Their Partners' Thinking**

Review that the students shared their partners' thinking about something surprising they learned today about harbor seals. Ask and briefly discuss:

Q *What did you do to make sure you understood your partner's thinking?*

INDIVIDUALIZED DAILY READING

6 ▶ **Read Independently/Document IDR Conferences**

Have the students independently read nonfiction books for up to 20 minutes. As the students read, circulate among them and monitor whether they are reading books at appropriate reading levels. Ask individual students to read part of the book to you and explain what they have read. If a book seems too difficult or too easy for a student, help her select a more appropriate book. Continue to use the "IDR Conference Notes" record sheet to conduct and document individual conferences.

At the end of independent reading, facilitate a whole-class discussion by asking questions such as:

Q *What is something you learned today from your reading?*

Q *What is something you are wondering?*

Q *What is one thing you did today to take responsibility for yourself during independent reading?*

EXTENSION

Read More About Seals

Continue to explore the subject of seals by reading aloud books such as the ones listed here. Stop periodically as you read the books to have the students share what they are wondering. Some choices are *A Seal Called Andre: The Two Worlds of a Maine Harbor Seal* by Harry Goodridge and Lew Dietz, *Seals* by Emily Rose Townsend, *Seals* by Charles Rotter, and *Baby Seal* by Aubrey Lang.

Day 2

Materials

- *A Harbor Seal Pup Grows Up* (pages 18–29)
- Your jotted notes from Day 1

Strategy Lesson

In this lesson, the students:

- Identify what they learn from a nonfiction text
- Use *wondering* to help them understand nonfiction
- Read independently for up to 20 minutes
- Share their partners' thinking
- Relate the value of responsibility to their behavior

1 ▶ Review the First Half of *A Harbor Seal Pup Grows Up*

Remind the students that in the previous lesson they listened to the first part of a story about a harbor seal pup growing up. Leaf through pages 2–17, reading the chapter titles aloud. Ask:

Q *What happens to Sidney before the scientists rescue her?*

Q *What do the scientists do to help Sidney get healthy again?*

Have a few students share what they remember.

2 ▶ Read the Second Half of the Book Aloud

Tell the students that you will read the rest of *A Harbor Seal Pup Grows Up* aloud. Ask them to listen to find out what will happen to Sidney next. Read pages 18–29, showing the photographs and following the procedure described below.

Read to page 25. Stop after:

p. 25 "Sidney is ready to be on her own."

Have the students use "Turn to Your Partner" to discuss:

Q *What happens to Sidney in the part I just read? Why is she ready to be on her own now?*

Without stopping to discuss as a class, show the photo on page 26, read the chapter title, and continue reading to page 29. Stop after:

> **p. 29** "Sidney will grow up in her ocean home."

 Have the students use "Turn to Your Partner" to discuss:

Q *How do the scientists return Sidney to her ocean home? What will happen to her now?*

 ## Discuss What the Students Learned and Wonder

Tell the students that you will ask a question and they will talk in pairs about it. Explain that later you will ask them to share their partners' thinking with the class, so it is important to listen carefully. Have the students use "Turn to Your Partner" to discuss:

Q *What was the most surprising or interesting thing that you learned today about harbor seals?*

Have a few volunteers share their partners' thinking.

Use the notes you jotted down for yourself on Day 1 to remind the students of some of their questions. Ask:

◀ **Teacher Note**

If possible, discuss at least one question that was addressed in the book and one that was not.

Q *Yesterday you wondered [whether Sidney would survive without her mother]. What did we find out about that?*

Q *Now that we've finished the book, what are you still wondering about harbor seals?*

Q *How could we find answers to some of those questions?*

If necessary, explain that the students could read other books or magazines, watch a television program on harbor seals, or talk to a person who knows about seals, like a zookeeper or veterinarian.

Reflect on Sharing Their Partners' Thinking

Review that the students shared their partners' thinking about the most surprising or interesting thing they learned today about harbor seals. Ask and briefly discuss:

Q *How did you and your partner do listening to each other today?*

Q *What problems did you have, if any? What can you do differently next time to avoid those problems?*

INDIVIDUALIZED DAILY READING

 Read Independently and Wonder

Have the students independently read nonfiction books for up to 20 minutes. Explain that at the end of IDR today they will each tell their partner about the book they are reading and what they are still wondering about.

As the students read, circulate among them. Stop and ask students to talk about the book they are reading and what they are wondering about. Ask questions such as:

Q *What is your book about?*

Q *What are you still wondering about?*

 At the end of independent reading, have partners share their books and what they are wondering about.

Help the students reflect on their independent reading by asking questions such as:

Q *What did you do to take responsibility for yourself during independent reading?*

ELL Note

These questions will help your English Language Learners rehearse what they will say to their partners.

EXTENSIONS

Read "More about Harbor Seals" and "Rescuing Orphaned Harbor Seal Pups"

Explain that the last section of *A Harbor Seal Pup Grows Up* gives more information about harbor seals. Read the title "More about Harbor Seals" and read aloud or paraphrase page 30, stopping periodically to have the students talk about what they are learning. Repeat this procedure for "Rescuing Orphaned Harbor Seal Pups" on page 31.

Create a Timeline of Events in the Harbor Seal Pup's Development

Point to the timeline on the top of pages 30–31 of *A Harbor Seal Pup Grows Up* and explain that this is a line that gives information about one harbor seal pup's life from birth until she can live on her own. Draw this timeline showing the ages of the harbor seal pup on a long sheet of butcher paper and post it where everyone can see it. Do not fill in the events below the line.

Explain that you have written the important events in Sidney's life on sentence strips. With the students, read the sentence on each strip. Place the strips randomly in a pocket chart. First in pairs, and then as a class, discuss:

Q *Which event do you think comes first? Why do you think this?*

Once the students reach agreement, have a student tape the strip on the timeline under the appropriate age label. Continue this procedure to order the remaining strips, and then reread passages or show illustrations from the book to check the order of events.

◀ **Teacher Note**

Before starting this activity, write the following main events on sentence strips. If possible, include a picture clue for each event:

- The harbor seal pup drinks her mother's milk.
- The harbor seal pup's mother goes into the ocean to fish.
- The harbor seal pup is rescued.
- The harbor seal pup learns to eat fish.
- The harbor seal pup is set free in the ocean.

Day 3

Materials

- *A Harbor Seal Pup Grows Up*
- Nonfiction texts at appropriate levels for independent reading
- A small self-stick note for each student
- *Assessment Resource Book*

Teacher Note

Have the students select their independent reading books before starting the lesson.

Independent Strategy Practice

In this lesson, the students:

- Read nonfiction books independently
- Identify what they learn from a nonfiction text
- Share their partners' thinking

1 Review Identifying One Thing You Learned

Remind the students that last week during independent reading they read a nonfiction book and chose one thing they learned to share in pairs. Explain that today the students will read nonfiction books and learn new facts. Then each student will choose one new thing he learned and share it with his partner.

Explain that the students will read to themselves for a short time. Then you will stop them and ask them to choose one thing they learned from their reading. They will mark that page with a self-stick note.

2 Read Nonfiction Books Independently

Distribute a self-stick note to each student. Have the students read independently for 5 minutes. Stop them and ask them to reread the pages they just read and each think about something they learned from the book that they think their partner might find interesting. Have them mark that page with a self-stick note.

3 Share Facts from Nonfiction Books

 Have partners share the facts they chose with each other. Encourage them to show one another where in their books they found the information. They might also share other interesting parts of their books.

CLASS PROGRESS ASSESSMENT

As the partners discuss their ideas, circulate among them and ask yourself:

Q *Are the students comprehending what they read?*

Q *Are they finding factual information?*

Record your observations on page 21 of the *Assessment Resource Book*.

Have the students use "Turn to Your Partner" to discuss the following question. Remind the students to be ready to share their partners' thinking.

Q *Would you recommend this book to your partner to read? Why or why not?*

Have a few volunteers share what their partners said.

Students might say:

"My partner said I might like his book because it has a lot of information about trucks."

"My partner said she doesn't like her book because she thinks spiders are creepy, but I might like it."

"My partner loved his book. He said I should read it if I want to learn about the desert."

 Reflect on Working with a Partner

Ask and briefly discuss:

Q *What did you need to do to make sure you and your partner worked well together?*

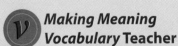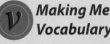

Making Meaning
***Vocabulary* Teacher**

Next week you will revisit *A Harbor Seal Pup Grows Up* to teach Vocabulary Week 22.

Week 3   Overview

UNIT 7: WONDERING
Expository Nonfiction

Throw Your Tooth on the Roof
by Selby B. Beeler, illustrated by G. Brian Karas
(Houghton Mifflin, 1998)

From this collection of tooth traditions, the students learn what children around the world do when a tooth falls out.

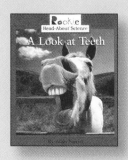

A Look at Teeth
by Allan Fowler (Children's Press, 1999)

This nonfiction book includes information and photographs about the importance of teeth and how teeth are used by various animals.

ALTERNATIVE BOOKS

Man on the Moon by Anastasia Suen

The Sun Is Always Shining Somewhere by Allan Fowler

Comprehension Focus

- Students use *wondering* to help them understand nonfiction.

- Students *visualize* to make sense of texts.

- Students identify what they learn from nonfiction.

- Students informally *explore text features* of expository nonfiction.

- Students read independently.

Social Development Focus

- Students share their partners' thinking with the class.

- Students relate the value of responsibility to their behavior.

DO AHEAD

- Prepare the "Thinking About My Reading" chart for independent reading (see Day 1, Step 5 on page 268).

- Make copies of the Unit 7 Parent Letter (BLM7) to send home with the students on the last day of the unit.

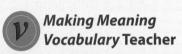

Making Meaning Vocabulary Teacher

If you are teaching Developmental Studies Center's *Making Meaning Vocabulary* program, teach Vocabulary Week 22 this week. For more information, see the *Making Meaning Vocabulary Teacher's Manual.*

Read-aloud

Materials

- *Throw Your Tooth on the Roof*
- "What Good Readers Do" chart
- "Thinking About My Reading" chart, prepared ahead

> **What Good Readers Do**
>
> - make connections to our lives

In this lesson, the students:

- *Use schema* to help them understand nonfiction
- *Visualize* to make sense of the text
- Identify what they learn from a nonfiction text
- Read independently for up to 20 minutes
- Share their partners' thinking
- Relate the value of responsibility to their behavior

1 Review Visualizing

Gather the class with partners sitting together. Refer to the "What Good Readers Do" chart and briefly review the items on it. Focus on visualizing. Ask:

Q *What do you do when you visualize something from a book?*

Have a few students share their ideas. Remind them that they have been listening to and reading nonfiction stories. Tell them that today you will read another nonfiction book and they will have a chance to visualize some of the things described in the book.

2 Introduce *Throw Your Tooth on the Roof*

Show the cover of *Throw Your Tooth on the Roof* and read aloud the title, subtitle, and names of the author and illustrator. Read the sentences on the back cover aloud. Ask:

Q *If one of your teeth falls out, what do you do with it?*

Tell the students that traditions, or customs, are special ways of doing things. People follow traditions over and over again. Explain that families, countries, and cultures have different traditions (for example, many families follow the tradition of putting candles on birthday cakes; another tradition in the United States is eating turkey on Thanksgiving Day).

Have a few students share their "tooth traditions." Point out that today's book tells what children from many different countries do when their teeth fall out.

ELL Note

Consider asking any student who grew up in another country to share a tradition from that country.

▶3 Read *Throw Your Tooth on the Roof* Aloud and Visualize

Tell the students that you will read parts of the book without showing the pictures. Ask them to close their eyes and use the author's words to create a mental picture of each "tooth tradition." Explain that you will read each part twice before asking them to describe the picture that came to mind.

Read aloud passages from *Throw Your Tooth on the Roof* as described below. Before reading about each tradition, use the map on pages 4–5 to point out the country where children practice these customs.

Read the paragraph on page 6 headed "United States" aloud twice. Pause between readings to give the students a chance to think about their mental images. After the second reading, have them use "Turn to Your Partner" to describe their mental pictures to one another. Then have a few volunteers share their visualizations with the class.

ELL Note

The sections of the book used in the lesson have been chosen based on the variety of traditions described. You might want to choose other excerpts based on your students' cultural backgrounds.

If necessary, prompt the students with questions such as:

Q *What do children in the United States do with their teeth after they fall out?*

Q *What pictures came into your mind as you listened?*

Repeat this procedure with one or more of the following excerpts:

p. 10 Argentina

p. 12 Cameroon

p. 19 Russia

p. 23 Vietnam

FACILITATION TIP

Reflect on your experience over the past three weeks with **responding neutrally** with interest during class discussions. Does this practice feel natural to you? Are you integrating it into class discussions throughout the school day? What effect is it having on the students? We encourage you to continue to try this practice and reflect on the students' responses as you facilitate class discussions in the future.

4 ▶ Discuss the Reading

 Have the students use "Turn to Your Partner" to discuss the following question. Ask the students to be ready to share their partners' thinking.

Q *What tradition did you like? Why did you like that one?*

Have a few volunteers share their partners' thinking with the class.

Point out that at the back of the book there is more information about teeth. Show the diagram on page 29 and explain that this picture shows what the inside of a tooth looks like.

Then show the diagram on page 31 and explain that this picture shows all the different kinds of teeth that adults have. Some are the right shape for cutting food and others are just right for chewing.

Explain that in the next lesson you will read another book about teeth.

INDIVIDUALIZED DAILY READING

5 ▶ Introduce Self-monitoring

Explain that today you will stop the students during their independent reading and have them think about how well they are understanding their reading. Tell them that good readers pause while reading to think about what they are reading and how well they are understanding. Direct their attention to the following questions, which you have written on chart paper labeled "Thinking About My Reading."

- What is happening in my book?

- Do I understand what I am reading?

- Can I read most of the words?

Read each of the questions on the chart. Explain that these questions will help them know whether a book is right for them. When they do not understand, they need to reread. If they still don't understand, they may need to get a new book.

Have the students read independently for up to 20 minutes. Stop them at 5-minute intervals. Read the questions on the chart and have them think about each question.

As they read, circulate among them and ask individual students to read a selection aloud and tell you what it is about. If a student is struggling to understand the text, use the questions on the chart to help him be aware of his own comprehension.

At the end of independent reading, ask and briefly discuss:

Q *What did you decide about the book you are reading? Is it too hard or just right? How did you decide?*

Q *What did you do to take responsibility for yourself today?*

Save the "Thinking About My Reading" chart for use in future lessons.

EXTENSIONS

Read More from *Throw Your Tooth on the Roof*

Read and discuss other traditions from the book. Make the book available for students to read independently.

Act Out Some of the Traditions

Read a tradition aloud, and have partners first talk about and then act out the tradition. (One example that is suited for this activity is "Botswana: I throw my tooth on the roof and say, 'Mr. Moon, Mr. Moon, please bring me a new tooth.'" See page 12.)

ELL Note

This extension is especially helpful for your English Language Learners.

Visualize and Draw Traditions

Read a "tooth tradition" aloud and have the students visualize and discuss their mental images, and then individually draw what they visualized. Have partners share their drawings.

Day 2

Materials

- *A Look at Teeth* (pages 3–11)
- (Optional) *Throw Your Tooth on the Roof*
- *Assessment Resource Book*
- "Thinking About My Reading" chart

Read-aloud/Strategy Practice

In this lesson, the students:

- Use *wondering* to help them understand nonfiction
- Identify what they learn from a nonfiction text
- Read independently for up to 20 minutes
- Relate the value of responsibility to their behavior

1 ▶ Review Wondering and Asking Questions

Gather the class with partners sitting together. Remind the students that they have been listening to different nonfiction books read aloud and having opportunities to wonder about the information they are hearing. Explain that today they will continue to wonder and ask questions before, during, and after they hear a nonfiction story.

2 ▶ Introduce *A Look at Teeth* and Wonder

Remind the students that they listened to *Throw Your Tooth on the Roof,* a book about various traditions that children around the world follow when their teeth fall out. Tell them that the book they will hear today contains more information about people's and animals' teeth.

Show the cover of *A Look at Teeth* and read aloud the title and author's name. Have the students use "Turn to Your Partner" to discuss:

Teacher Note ▶

If the students have difficulty generating "I wonder" statements, model one or two (for example, "I wonder whether kittens and puppies lose their baby teeth like human children do").

Q *What are some things you wonder about people's or animals' teeth?*

Students might say:

"I wonder whether human teeth are cleaner than animal teeth."

"I wonder if animals' teeth are sharper than humans' teeth."

"I wonder if sharks lose their teeth."

Have one or two volunteers share their thinking with the class. Ask them to listen for information about their questions as you read the book aloud.

Read the First Part of *A Look at Teeth* Aloud

Read pages 3–11 of *A Look at Teeth* aloud today, showing the photographs and stopping as described below.

◀ **Teacher Note**

This book contains a lot of factual information, which the students might have difficulty tracking. In order to support them, structure the reading as described. This procedure is somewhat different from earlier read-alouds.

> **Suggested Vocabulary**
>
> **solid food:** food that is not very soft (p. 3)
> **mushy:** very soft (p. 5)
> **form:** grow (p. 9)
> **grind:** chew (p. 11)

Read the first sentence on page 3 aloud. Stop after:

> **p. 3** "Can you imagine eating without using your teeth?"

Ask the students to pause and try to imagine it. Have a few students share their ideas. Then reread the sentence and continue reading. Stop after:

> **p. 4** "Try saying the word 'teeth' without touching your teeth with your tongue."

Have the students try this and say if they were able to do it. Then reread pages 3–4 and continue reading. Stop after:

> **p. 8** "You may already be losing those milk teeth."

Ask:

Q *What have you learned about people's teeth so far?*

Have a few students share what they learned. Reread page 8 and continue reading. Stop after:

> **p. 9** "Your last four teeth—called wisdom teeth—will probably grow in by the time you are 21 years old."

 Ask and have the students use "Turn to Your Partner" to discuss:

Q *This book gives a lot of information about teeth. What are you wondering now about children's or grownups' teeth?*

Without stopping to discuss the students' questions, reread the last sentence on page 9 and continue reading. Stop after:

p. 11 "Your flatter back teeth are used to grind food."

Discuss as a class:

Q *What have you learned about the different kinds of teeth you have?*

CLASS PROGRESS ASSESSMENT

As you listen to individual students, ask yourself:

Q *Are the students able to describe what they learn from the text?*

Q *Are their ideas connected to the text?*

Record your observations on page 22 of the *Assessment Resource Book.*

Ask each student to feel her front and back teeth with her tongue. Have a few students describe the shapes they feel.

Teacher Note

At this point you may wish to show the diagram on page 31 of *Throw Your Tooth on the Roof* if you haven't already done so. The students may be interested to learn that their four pointed canine teeth are named after the teeth of dogs and wolves.

 Discuss What the Students Learned and Wonder

Facilitate a brief class discussion by asking:

Q *What did you learn about people's teeth today that surprised you?*

Q *You have learned many facts about people's teeth. What are you still wondering about your teeth?*

Explain that in the next lesson the students will hear about animals' teeth. As a preview, show page 31 of *A Look at Teeth* and ask the students to name some of the animals whose teeth they will learn about when you read the rest of the book.

 Reflect on Partner Work

Ask and briefly discuss:

Q *What did you do today that helped you and your partner during "Turn to Your Partner"?*

INDIVIDUALIZED DAILY READING

 6 ## Practice Self-monitoring

Have the students read independently for up to 20 minutes.

Stop them at 5-minute intervals. Read the questions on the "Thinking About My Reading" chart and have them think about each question.

As they read, circulate among them and ask individual students to read a selection aloud and tell you what it is about.

At the end of independent reading, ask and briefly discuss:

Q *If you do not understand something you just read, what might you do?*

Q *If you do not know a lot of words in the book you are reading, what should you do?*

Q *What do you think is working well during independent reading? What do you think the class needs to work on to help independent reading go more smoothly? What will you do to help make that happen?*

> *Thinking About My Reading*
>
> *- What is happening in my book?*

EXTENSION

Read About and Discuss Other Parts of the Human Body

Read and discuss books about other parts of the human body. Some possible texts are *How Does Your Heart Work?* and *How Do Your Lungs Work?* by Don L. Curry, and *Tiny Life in Your Body* by Christine Taylor-Butler.

Day 3

Materials

- *A Look at Teeth* (pages 12–31)
- "Thinking About My Reading" chart
- Unit 7 Parent Letter (BLM7)

Read-aloud/Strategy Practice

In this lesson, the students:

- Use *wondering* to help them understand nonfiction
- Identify what they learn from a nonfiction text
- Read independently for up to 20 minutes
- Relate the value of responsibility to their behavior

▶**1** ## Introduce the Second Part of *A Look at Teeth* and Wonder

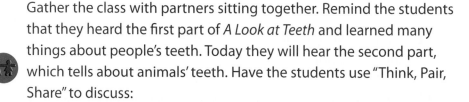

Gather the class with partners sitting together. Remind the students that they heard the first part of *A Look at Teeth* and learned many things about people's teeth. Today they will hear the second part, which tells about animals' teeth. Have the students use "Think, Pair, Share" to discuss:

Q *What do you wonder about animals' teeth?*

Have one or two volunteers share their thinking with the class. Ask them to listen for information about their questions as you read the book aloud.

▶**2** ## Read the Second Part of *A Look at Teeth* Aloud

Read pages 12–29 aloud, showing the photographs. At each of the following stopping points, facilitate a brief whole-class discussion about what the students learned from listening to those pages. As the students respond, be prepared to reread the text or show photographs again to support their thinking.

Stop after:

p. 15 "Horses can grind hay with their flatter back teeth."

p. 19 "Walruses have very long tusks."

p. 25 "That's why it's important to take care of them."

Finally, reread pages 24–25 and continue reading through page 29. Ask and have the students use "Think, Pair, Share" to discuss:

Q *What do you think the author of this book wants children to do, and why?*

Have one or two volunteers share their thinking with the class.

 ## 3 ▶ Use "Words You Know" to Discuss the Book and Wonder

Show pages 30–31 and explain that nonfiction books sometimes include pages like these that help readers understand the meanings of words in the book. Read some of the words aloud and show and describe the photos that accompany the words.

Review that the students have heard two books about teeth, *Throw Your Tooth on the Roof* and *A Look at Teeth.* Ask:

Q *Now that you have learned some new things about teeth from these two books, what are you still wondering about teeth?*

Explain that it is natural for readers to have more and more questions about a topic as they learn about that topic from books. Encourage the students to keep thinking about the questions they have as they read nonfiction books independently.

4 ▶ Reflect on Working Together

Review that the students have been taking responsibility for their behavior and have been sharing their partners' thinking during class discussions. Ask and briefly discuss:

Q *What did you have to do to make sure you understood your partner's thinking?*

Q *[Liza said that she had to listen very carefully to her partner.] What else did you do to make sure you understood your partner's thinking?*

Q *What did you do to act in a responsible way this week?*

Teacher Note

This is the last week of Unit 7. You will reassign partners for Unit 8.

Thinking About My Reading

- What is happening in my book?

Remind the students to keep these things in mind, and encourage them to continue to listen carefully and to take responsibility for their behavior in the coming weeks.

INDIVIDUALIZED DAILY READING

5 ▸ Practice Self-monitoring

Have the students read nonfiction independently for up to 20 minutes.

Stop them at 5-minute intervals. Read the questions on the "Thinking About My Reading" chart and have them think about each question.

As they read, circulate among them and ask individual students to read a selection aloud and tell you what it is about.

At the end of independent reading, ask and briefly discuss:

Q *What did you find out about your reading by using the questions on the chart?*

Q *What do you want to continue to do to help independent reading go smoothly?*

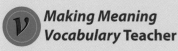

Parent Letter

Send home with each student the Parent Letter for this unit (see "Do Ahead," page 265). Periodically, have a few students share with the class what they are reading at home.

Making Meaning Vocabulary Teacher

Next week you will revisit *A Look at Teeth* to teach Vocabulary Week 23.

Unit 8

Exploring Text Features

EXPOSITORY NONFICTION

During this unit, the students continue to identify what they learn from nonfiction. They explore expository text features and continue to make connections, visualize, and wonder to make sense of texts. During IDR, the students use comprehension strategies to make sense of nonfiction books. Socially, they relate the values of respect and responsibility to their behavior and they continue to share their partners' thinking during whole-class discussions.

Week 1 *Raptors!* by Lisa McCourt

Week 2 *A Day in the Life of a Garbage Collector* by Nate LeBoutillier

Week 3 *An Elephant Grows Up* by Anastasia Suen

Week 1

Overview

UNIT 8: EXPLORING TEXT FEATURES
Expository Nonfiction

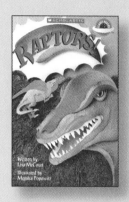

Raptors!
by Lisa McCourt, illustrated by Monika Popowitz
(Troll, 1998)

This is a nonfiction book about raptors, the fiercest of all dinosaurs.

ALTERNATIVE BOOKS

Are You a Snail? by Judy Allen

Gentle Giant Octopus by Karen Wallace

Comprehension Focus

- Students identify what they learn from nonfiction texts.

- Students *visualize* to make sense of the texts.

- Students *use schema* and *wondering* to help them understand the texts.

- Students *explore text features* of expository nonfiction.

- Students read independently.

Social Development Focus

- Students relate the values of caring and respect to their behavior.

DO AHEAD

- Prior to Day 1, decide how you will randomly assign partners to work together during the unit.

- Prior to Day 2, make a transparency of the "Index from *Raptors!*" (BLM10).

- Prior to Day 3, prepare to model by selecting something you learned from and wonder about *A Look at Teeth* (see Step 2 on page 290).

- Collect nonfiction books at various reading levels for independent reading throughout this unit.

Making Meaning
***Vocabulary* Teacher**

If you are teaching Developmental Studies Center's *Making Meaning Vocabulary* program, teach Vocabulary Week 23 this week. For more information, see the *Making Meaning Vocabulary Teacher's Manual.*

Read-aloud/Strategy Lesson

In this lesson, the students:

- *Use schema* to help them understand nonfiction
- Use *wondering/questioning* to help them understand nonfiction
- Identify what they learn from a nonfiction text
- Read independently for up to 20 minutes
- Act in a caring and respectful way

Materials

- *Raptors!*
- "Thinking About My Reading" chart

1 ▶ Pair Students and Get Ready to Work Together

Randomly assign new partners and have them sit together. Explain that for the next few weeks you will be asking the students to think about how they can show their partner respect and caring.

Ask and briefly discuss:

Q *How can you show your partner that you care about and respect [his] thinking?*

Students might say:

"I will let my partner finish talking before I start to talk."

"If I don't agree with her, I won't say, 'You're wrong.' I will say, 'I don't agree; let's ask the teacher to read that part again.'"

"I will repeat the question for my partner when she doesn't understand or remember it."

***Being a* Writer™ Teacher**

You can either have the students work with their *Being a Writer* partner or assign them a different partner for the *Making Meaning* lessons.

Teacher Note ▶

If the students have difficulty answering this question, suggest some ideas like those in the "Students might say" note.

Share Background Knowledge About Dinosaurs

Tell the students that today you will read a nonfiction book about a kind of dinosaur called *raptors*. Ask:

Q *What do you think you know about dinosaurs?*

 Have the students use "Turn to Your Partner" to discuss the question. If the students have heard or read about raptors, ask:

Q *How do you think raptors were different from other kinds of dinosaurs?*

 Introduce *Raptors!* and Wonder

Show the cover of *Raptors!,* read the title and the author's and illustrator's names aloud, and show the students a few of the illustrations. Point out that the illustrator used paper cutouts to create the pictures.

 Have the students use "Think, Pair, Share" to discuss:

Q *What do you wonder about raptor dinosaurs?*

Have two or three volunteers share their ideas with the class. Remind them to begin with "I wonder" as they share.

> **Students might say:**
>
> "I wonder how big they are."
>
> "[Shawna] and I wonder if they are mean."
>
> "I wonder if raptors eat eggs, plants, or meat."

 Read *Raptors!* Aloud

Explain that you will read the book aloud, stopping for the students to talk about what they are learning. At the end of the reading they will talk about what they still wonder about raptors and dinosaurs.

 Note

English Language Learners will benefit from previewing the book and hearing it read aloud prior to the lesson.

Read *Raptors!* aloud, showing the illustrations and following the procedure described below.

> **Suggested Vocabulary**
>
> **fierce:** violent or dangerous (p. 3)
>
> **pounced:** jumped [on its prey] (p. 7)
>
> **slash:** cut (p. 7)
>
> **prey:** animal that is hunted for food (p. 7)
>
> **cunning:** very smart and sneaky (p. 14)
>
> **predators:** animals that hunt other animals (p. 14)
>
> **packs:** groups (p. 14)
>
> **ferocious:** very fierce (p. 18)
>
> **Gobi Desert:** desert in Mongolia and China (p. 18)
>
> **blended in with their surroundings:** looked a lot like the land and plants around them and made the dinosaurs harder to see (p. 25)
>
> **mates:** animals' male or female partners (p. 25)
>
> **become extinct:** stop living on Earth; die out (p. 28)
>
> **terrifying:** frightening; very scary (p. 31)

Read pages 3–7 aloud, showing the illustrations as you read. Stop after:

> **p. 7** "When a raptor pounced, it used these horrible claws to slash at its prey."

 Have the students use "Turn to Your Partner" to discuss:

Q *What did you learn about raptors in this part of the book?*

Without stopping to discuss the question as a class, reread the sentence on page 7 and continue reading to page 18. Stop after:

> **p. 18** "A raptor skeleton and a Protoceratops skeleton were discovered lying side by side in the sand."

 Ask and have the students use "Turn to Your Partner" to discuss:

Q *What other information have you learned about raptors?*

Teacher Note ▶

As partners talk, circulate and notice whether they are talking about examples from the book. If necessary to keep them focused, remind them to think about what they are learning from the book.

Use the same procedure at the following stop:

> **p. 28**   "…they were one of the very last kinds of dinosaurs to become extinct."

Read to the end of the book.

5 Discuss What the Students Learned and Wonder

 Tell the students that you will ask a question and the students will talk in pairs about it. Explain that later you will ask the students to share their thinking with the class. Have the students use "Turn to Your Partner" to discuss:

Q   *What did you learn today about raptors from this book?*

Have a few volunteers share their thinking with the class.

Point out that the author raises some questions about dinosaurs at the end of the book (for example, "What happened to all the dinosaurs?"). Then ask:

Q   *What are some things you are wondering about raptors and about dinosaurs?*

Have a few volunteers share their thinking with the class.

6 Reflect on Working Together

Ask and briefly discuss:

Q   *How did you show your partner your cared about [her] ideas?*

Q   *What did you enjoy about working with your partner today? Why did that make you feel good?*

Consider sharing your observations of the students' behaviors.

FACILITATION TIP

During this unit, we invite you to continue practicing **responding neutrally** with interest during class discussions. This week, continue to respond neutrally by refraining from overtly praising or criticizing the students' responses. Try responding neutrally by nodding, asking them to say more about their thinking, or asking other students to respond.

Teacher Note

Avoid using names when sharing your observations. For example, you might say, "I noticed students waiting for their partners to finish talking" or "I heard some students thanking their partners because they helped them remember what they had learned about raptors and dinosaurs."

INDIVIDUALIZED DAILY READING

7 ▶ Practice Self-monitoring

Have the students read independently for up to 20 minutes in nonfiction books.

Stop the students at 5-minute intervals to read the questions on the "Thinking About My Reading" chart. As you read each question, ask the students to think about the question.

As they read, circulate among the students and ask individuals to read a selection aloud and tell you what it is about.

At the end of independent reading, ask and briefly discuss:

Q *If you did not understand something you read, what did you do? How did that help you understand?*

Q *What do you think is working well during independent reading? What do you want to do differently next time?*

EXTENSION

Read More About Dinosaurs

Continue to explore the topic of dinosaurs by reading aloud other nonfiction books about dinosaurs. Ask the students to pay attention to questions they have as they listen. Stop periodically during the reading to have the students share what they are learning and wondering. Book choices include *Digging Up Dinosaurs, Dinosaur Bones,* and *Dinosaurs Are Different,* all by Aliki; *What Happened to the Dinosaurs?* by Franklin M. Branley; and *Dinosaurs: The Biggest, Baddest, Strangest, Fastest* by Howard Zimmerman and George Olshevsky.

---

*Thinking About
My Reading*

- *What is happening in my book?*

- *Do I understand what I am reading?*

- *Can I read most of the words?*

Day 2

Read-aloud/Strategy Practice

In this lesson, the students:

- Identify what they learn from a nonfiction text
- *Visualize* to help them understand nonfiction
- Explore expository text features
- Use what they learned to draw and label a raptor
- Read independently for up to 20 minutes
- Act in a caring and respectful way

1 Review *Raptors!* and Explore the Index

Show the book and review that the students heard *Raptors!* and shared what they learned and wondered. Show the index on page 32 of *Raptors!* and explain that an index is found at the back of many nonfiction books. Tell the students that sometimes a reader uses an index to find a topic quickly without having to look through the whole book. Explain that using the index also is a good way to review what you have learned.

Use the "Index from *Raptors!*" transparency to point out that the index lists important words and topics and tells the reader on which pages the words or topics can be found. Read the word *claws* aloud and point out that information about claws can be found on pages 5 and 7. Ask:

Q *What do you remember about raptors' claws?*

Have a few volunteers share.

Turn to pages 5 and 7 and read the information aloud.

Repeat this procedure with one or two other examples. Then invite the students to participate by asking:

Q *What other topics are listed in this index?*

Q *Where would I find information about the hunting habits of raptors?*

Materials

- *Raptors!*
- "Index from *Raptors!*" transparency (BLM10)
- Chart paper and a marker
- *Throw Your Tooth on the Roof* (from Unit 7, Week 3)
- Sheet of drawing paper for each student
- Markers or crayons
- *Assessment Resource Book*

Reread *Raptors!* Aloud

Explain that you will reread the book today and that you would like the students to pay close attention to the parts of the book that describe how raptors might have looked.

Reread the book slowly and clearly, without stopping.

3 ▶ Discuss and List Raptors' Characteristics

Point out that scientists are not sure what raptors looked like. Ask:

Q *After hearing this book, what do you think raptors might have looked like?*

Students might say:

"I don't think that the raptors had feathers."

"I think raptors were the same color as the ground or the trees so their prey couldn't see them."

Teacher Note ▶

If the students have difficulty answering this question, suggest some ideas like those in the "Students might say" note.

List the students' ideas on the chart paper (for example, smaller than other dinosaurs, sharp teeth, big claws, scary eyes, long fingers, bright colors).

4 ▶ Briefly Model Creating a Labeled Drawing

Show the diagram on page 31 of *Throw Your Tooth on the Roof*. Remind the students that some nonfiction books include labeled pictures like this one. Point out that each label names a part of what is pictured in the drawing. A line or arrow connects each label with the part it names.

Explain that today each student will create a labeled picture of a raptor based on what he heard in the book. Briefly model creating a labeled drawing by sketching a child's face on the board or on chart paper and labeling its parts.

 Visualize, Draw, and Label a Raptor

Distribute a sheet of drawing paper to each student and explain that they will use information they learned from the story to visualize, or picture in their minds, how raptors looked. Then they will draw a raptor and name its parts.

Before the students begin drawing, have them close their eyes and visualize as you read aloud the list of raptor characteristics the class compiled in Step 3. Then have each student draw what she visualized and label the drawing.

6 Share and Discuss Drawings

Explain that partners will take turns showing each other their drawings and reading aloud the labels they wrote. Ask partners to tell each other how they used information from *Raptors!* to draw their picture. Remind the students to be caring and respectful as they view each other's work.

CLASS PROGRESS ASSESSMENT

As the students share their drawings, circulate among them and ask yourself:

Q *Do the students' labeled drawings show evidence that they understand the text?*

Q *Are they able to share their drawings in a caring and respectful way?*

Record your observations on page 23 of the *Assessment Resource Book.*

After partners share their drawings, have a few students tell the class what they liked about their partners' work.

INDIVIDUALIZED DAILY READING

7 Read Independently and Share Books

Make sure the students have a variety of nonfiction books to read today. Before the students begin to read independently, have them check to see if their book has an index. Remind the students that

ELL Note

This activity is especially helpful for your English Language Learners. It will help to reinforce the vocabulary they are learning.

not all books have an index. Have a few volunteers briefly share the information in their book's index with the class.

Have the students read independently for up to 20 minutes. Explain that at the end of IDR today they will each show their partner a picture or photograph from the book they are reading and talk about it.

As the students read, circulate among them. Stop and ask individual students to talk about the photograph or picture they will share in pairs. Ask questions such as:

Q *What is your book about?*

Q *Which picture are you going to share with your partner? Tell me about it.*

Q *Does your book have an index? If so, show me how you would use the index to find information in your book.*

At the end of independent reading, have the students share in pairs their books and a picture or photograph from the reading. Ask the students to tell their partners why they chose the picture or photograph.

EXTENSION

Compare Fiction and Nonfiction

Read fictional stories about dinosaurs and discuss the difference between nonfiction dinosaur books and fictional dinosaur stories. Some fiction stories about dinosaurs are *If the Dinosaurs Came Back* and *Dinosaur Cousins?* by Bernard Most, *Danny and the Dinosaur* by Syd Hoff, *If Dinosaurs Came to Town* by Dom Mansell, *The Dinosaur Who Lived in My Backyard* by B. G. Hennessy, and *Dinosaur Dream* by Dennis Nolan.

Day 3

Independent Strategy Practice

In this lesson, the students:

- Read nonfiction books independently
- Identify what they learn from nonfiction texts
- Use *wondering/questioning* to make sense of the nonfiction texts
- Write about what they wonder and learn from their nonfiction texts
- Share their thinking

1 Get Ready to Read Independently

Have partners sit together. Remind the students that they have read many nonfiction books during independent reading. Give students a few minutes to share in pairs the books they are going to read today. Ask:

Q *What topic is your partner reading about today?*

> ***Students might say:***
>
> "[Billy] is going to read a book about space."
>
> "[Samantha] is reading a book about big trucks because her dad drives a big truck."
>
> "[Carlotta] is reading a book about dinosaurs so she can learn more about them."

Explain that today they will continue to read nonfiction and write about something they learned and something they wondered.

2 Model Writing About a Nonfiction Book

Explain that today the students will read the nonfiction book they chose. Then they will write about something they learned and something they wondered.

Materials

- Nonfiction texts at appropriate levels for independent reading
- *A Look at Teeth* (from Unit 7, Week 3)
- Chart paper and a marker
- Writing paper for each student

Teacher Note

Have each student select his independent reading book before starting the lesson.

On a sheet of chart paper, model writing something you learned and wondered, using the book *A Look at Teeth*. Write the title of the book on a sheet of chart paper for all to see. Show the students a few of the photos in the book to refresh their memories; then ask:

Q *What did you learn about teeth from this book?*

Have one or two volunteers share; record their ideas on the chart paper. Ask:

Q *What are you wondering about teeth?*

Again, have one or two volunteers share; write their questions on the chart paper.

Distribute a sheet of writing paper to each student. Ask each student to write the title of her independent reading book on the writing paper.

Explain that the students will read by themselves for a short time. Then you will stop them and ask them to write about something they learned and something they are wondering about what they are reading.

▶3 Read Nonfiction Books Independently

Have the students read independently for 5 minutes. Stop them and ask them to reread the pages they just read and think about something interesting they learned from the book and something they are wondering about.

▶4 Write About What the Students Learned and Wondered

Have the students write about one thing they learned and one thing they are wondering about what they are reading.

ELL Note

Note challenging vocabulary and have brief discussions with individual students to help them with the vocabulary. In some cases, you may want to have a student read the text with you.

Teacher Note ▶

If several students struggle, you may need to model the writing process again. Have any student who is unable to read a nonfiction text write about *Raptors!* or another nonfiction text you read aloud previously.

5 Share Writing in Pairs

Have partners read to each other what they wrote. Encourage each student to show her partner where in the book she found the information. Partners might also show other interesting parts of their books.

6 Reflect on Working Together

Have the students use "Think, Pair, Share" to discuss:

Q *When your partner was sharing a fact from [his] book with you, how did you show respect for your partner?*

Q *What is one thing you liked about how you and your partner shared your writing with each other?*

Q *What would you do differently next time?*

Without saying names, share examples you observed of students working well together in pairs and as a class. Also describe any problems you noticed and invite the students to offer suggestions for solving such problems.

EXTENSION

Continue to Write About What They Learn and Wonder

Have the students periodically write about one fact they learned and one thing they wonder about from their independent reading or the read-alouds. Give the students time to share their writing with their partners and the class.

◀ **Teacher Note**

Circulate among the pairs and ask yourself questions such as:

- *Are both partners contributing to the discussion?*
- *Are both partners being respectful of each other?*

Note examples of what is working well to bring to the students' attention later.

***Making Meaning
Vocabulary* Teacher**

Next week you will revisit *Raptors!* to teach Vocabulary Week 24.

Week 2

Overview

UNIT 8: EXPLORING TEXT FEATURES
Expository Nonfiction

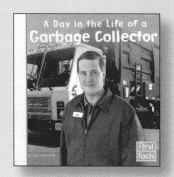

A Day in the Life of a Garbage Collector
by Nate LeBoutillier
(Capstone Press, 2005)

This book describes a garbage collector's day at work and what his job requires.

ALTERNATIVE BOOKS

A Day in the Life of a Doctor by Heather Adamson

I Drive a Garbage Truck by Sarah Bridges

Comprehension Focus

- Students *use schema* to help them understand nonfiction.

- Students use *wondering* to help them understand nonfiction.

- Students identify what they learn from nonfiction.

- Students *explore text features* in expository texts.

- Students read independently.

Social Development Focus

- Students relate the values of caring and respect to their behavior.

DO AHEAD

- Prior to Day 1, prepare a sheet of chart paper with the title "Nonfiction" (see Step 6 on page 297).

- Make a transparency of "Table of Contents from *A Day in the Life of a Garbage Collector*" (BLM11).

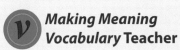

Making Meaning Vocabulary Teacher

If you are teaching Developmental Studies Center's *Making Meaning Vocabulary* program, teach Vocabulary Week 24 this week. For more information, see the *Making Meaning Vocabulary Teacher's Manual.*

Day 1

Read-aloud/Strategy Lesson

In this lesson, the students:

* *Use schema* to help them understand nonfiction
* Use *wondering* to help them understand nonfiction
* Identify what they learn from a nonfiction text
* Explore expository text features
* Read independently for up to 20 minutes
* Act in a caring and respectful way

1 ▶ Get Ready to Work Together

Have partners sit together. Explain that during today's lesson they will hear another nonfiction book and talk in pairs about it.

Remind the students to continue acting in a caring and respectful way with their partners and classmates. Without using names, share some of your observations of the students acting in caring and respectful ways with one another.

2 ▶ Introduce *A Day in the Life of a Garbage Collector*

Show the cover of the book and read the title and the name of the author aloud. Explain that this is a story about a garbage collector named Rick and his work. Read the first paragraph of the summary on the back cover of the book. Ask and briefly discuss:

Q *What do you know about garbage collectors?*

Have a few students share what they know.

3 ▶ Introduce the Table of Contents of *A Day in the Life of a Garbage Collector*

Show the students page 3, the table of contents, and tell them that before reading the book they will look at the table of contents.

Materials

* *A Day in the Life of a Garbage Collector* (pages 3–19)

* Transparency of "Table of Contents from *A Day in the Life of a Garbage Collector*" (BLM11)

* "Nonfiction" chart, prepared ahead, and a marker

ELL Note

English Language Learners will benefit from previewing the photographs and hearing the story read aloud prior to the lesson.

Explain that the table of contents is helpful because it lets readers know what information is in the book and where to find it.

Show the transparency of "Table of Contents from *A Day in the Life of a Garbage Collector*" and explain that this is the table of contents in *A Day in the Life of a Garbage Collector*. Point out that the table of contents lists the titles of the chapters in the book and the pages where the chapters start. Read the title of the first chapter aloud and point out that this chapter starts on page 4. Repeat the process with one or two more examples. Then ask:

Q *What do you think you might learn in this chapter?*

Have one or two students share.

Read the last six items in the table of contents and explain that these are sections found in the back of the book. Tell the students they will explore these sections tomorrow.

 Read the Book Aloud

Explain that you will read *A Day in the Life of a Garbage Collector* aloud. Tell the students that they will follow Rick, a garbage collector, as he goes about his job. Point out that this book has photographs of Rick doing his job. Ask the students to listen and think about what they learn about garbage collectors. Explain that you will stop during the reading to give partners a chance to talk.

Read pages 4–19 of *A Day in the Life of a Garbage Collector* aloud, following the procedure described on the next page.

Suggested Vocabulary

swipe: pull a plastic card through a machine that reads the information on the card (p. 4)

time card: card used to record the time workers start and end their workday (p. 4)

bin: large container or box for storing things (p. 10)

routes: ways to get from one place to another (p. 12)

holding area: place where things are kept until they can be moved (p. 16)

recycled: saved to be made into new things (p. 16)

landfill: place where garbage is buried (p. 16)

ELL Vocabulary

English Language Learners may benefit from discussing additional vocabulary, including:

paperwork: information that workers write about their job, such as what they did during the day (p. 4)

mechanics: people who fix machines (p. 15)

fuel: something that is used to give heat or energy, such as gasoline (p. 19)

Open the book to page 4. Read the chapter title aloud. Review that a title lets you know what information is in the chapter. (For example, this chapter, "When do garbage collectors start their days?" describes how and when Rick starts his day.)

Point to the clock and explain that this book has an illustration of a clock to show the time when Rick starts his day. For example, this clock shows 4:30 in the morning.

Point to the "Fun Fact!" and explain that the "Fun Fact!" gives them more information about garbage collection. Read the "Fun Fact!" aloud.

Read page 4 aloud, showing the photograph on page 5 as you read. Stop after:

> **p. 4** "He picks up his paperwork and swipes his time card to start the day."

 Remind the students that this chapter is called "When do garbage collectors start their days?" Have them use "Turn to Your Partner" to discuss:

Q *What did you learn about how Rick starts his day?*

Without stopping to discuss the question, show page 6, read the chapter title aloud, and continue reading. Stop after:

> **p. 6** "At the meetings, he learns how to keep himself and others safe on the job."

 Ask and have the students use "Turn to Your Partner" to discuss:

Q *What did you learn about how Rick learns about safety? Why is this important?*

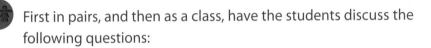 Use the same procedure for each of the following stops:

p. 9   "Garbage collectors also wear hard hats when they dump garbage."

p. 10   "This morning, he fills the tires with air."

p. 13   "The garbage is crushed to make room for more."

p. 15   "They can help by putting their garbage neatly into bags and cans."

p. 16   "At the landfill, the garbage will be covered with a layer of dirt."

p. 19   "Rick swipes his time card and goes home to rest for another day."

◀ **Teacher Note**

You may want to have fewer stops during the read-aloud and read two chapters followed by a brief discussion. If so, read each chapter title aloud prior to reading the chapter's text.

5 Discuss What the Students Learned

First in pairs, and then as a class, have the students discuss the following questions:

Q   *What happens during a garbage collector's day that surprises you?*

Q   *How can you help a garbage collector? Why is that important?*

Point out that the students have learned some interesting information about garbage collectors. Ask:

Q   *What are some things you are still wondering about garbage collectors?*

Q   *Where do you think you might find answers to these questions?*

FACILITATION TIP

Continue to focus on **responding neutrally** with interest during class discussions by refraining from overtly praising or criticizing the students' responses. Instead, build the students' intrinsic motivation by responding with genuine curiosity and interest, for example:

• *Say more about that.*

• *Explain your thinking further.*

• *Do you agree or disagree with [Martin]? Why?*

6 Introduce the "Nonfiction" Chart

Explain that the students have heard and read several nonfiction books over the past several weeks. Ask:

Q   *What is a nonfiction book? What do you like about reading nonfiction?*

Q   *What is one of your favorite topics to read about?*

Have a few students share their thinking.

Point to the "Nonfiction" chart and read the title aloud. Explain that nonfiction books can have special features. Explain that today you will start a chart that lists some of the special features in nonfiction books that help readers enjoy and understand the book. This chart will help them remember to look for these special features when they read independently.

Write *table of contents* on the chart and ask:

Q *How does the table of contents help you as a reader?*

Have a few students share.

Use *A Day in the Life of a Garbage Collector* to briefly point out that real-life photographs rather than drawings and the "Fun Facts!" boxes are other special features. Write these features on the chart.

Teacher Note

Save the "Nonfiction" chart for use throughout Unit 8.

Tell the students that they will add to the list as they find more special parts or features in books they read or hear read aloud.

INDIVIDUALIZED DAILY READING

 Read Independently/Document IDR Conferences

Have the students independently read nonfiction books at appropriate reading levels for up to 20 minutes. As the students read, circulate among them and monitor whether they are reading books at appropriate reading levels. Ask individual students to read part of their book to you and explain what they have read. If a book seems too difficult or too easy for a student, help him select a more appropriate book. Continue to use the "IDR Conference Notes" record sheet to conduct and document individual conferences. During individual conferences, encourage the students to think about the strategies they use to make sense of their reading.

At the end of independent reading, facilitate a whole-class discussion by asking and having students use "Turn to Your Partner" to discuss one or more of the following questions:

Q *What is something you learned today from your reading?*

Q *What are some strategies you used today during your reading?*

Q *What is something you do when you don't understand something you read?*

Q *What is one thing you did today to take responsibility for yourself during independent reading?*

EXTENSION

Create a Timeline of the Events in *A Day in the Life of a Garbage Collector*

Remind the students that they made a timeline of events in the book *A Harbor Seal Pup Grows Up.* Explain that today they will make a timeline about Rick's day as a garbage collector. Draw a timeline on a long sheet of butcher paper and post it where everyone can see it. Write the following times of day above the timeline: 4:30 in the morning, 6:30 in the morning, 7:00 in the morning, 1:30 in the afternoon, 2:00 in the afternoon. Do not fill in the events below the line.

Explain that you have written the important events in Rick's day on sentence strips. With the students, read each strip. Place the strips randomly in a pocket chart. First in pairs, and then as a class, have the students discuss:

Q *Which event do you think comes first? Why do you think this?*

Once the students reach agreement, have a student tape the strip on the timeline in the appropriate place. Continue this procedure to order the remaining strips; then reread passages or show illustrations from the book to check the order of events. Tell the students that timelines are another special feature in some nonfiction books. Write *timeline* on the "Nonfiction" chart.

◀ **Teacher Note**

Before starting this activity, write the following main events on sentence strips.

- Rick picks up his paperwork and swipes his time card.
- Rick checks the garbage truck.
- Rick drives the garbage truck on the route.
- Rick dumps the garbage at the holding area.
- Rick puts fuel in his truck for the next day.

Day 2

Materials

- *A Day in the Life of a Garbage Collector*
- "Nonfiction" chart and a marker
- Transparency of "Table of Contents from *A Day in the Life of a Garbage Collector*" (BLM11)

Strategy Lesson

In this lesson, the students:

- Identify what they learn from a nonfiction text
- Explore expository text features
- Read independently for up to 20 minutes
- Act in a caring and respectful way

1 ▶ **Review *A Day in the Life of a Garbage Collector* and Text Features**

Remind the students that yesterday they heard a book about a garbage collector's day. Leaf through pages 4–19, reading some of the chapter titles aloud. Ask:

Q *What did you learn about a garbage collector from this book?*

Have a few students share what they remember.

Refer to the "Nonfiction" chart and remind the students that yesterday they talked about some special features of nonfiction books. Briefly review the items listed on the chart. Explain that today you will read some other special features that are in *A Day in the Life of a Garbage Collector*.

2 ▶ **Introduce and Discuss "Equipment Photo Diagram"**

Show the "Table of Contents from *A Day in the Life of a Garbage Collector*" transparency and explain that the last six items in the table of contents are more special features that are found at the back of the book.

Read aloud the titles "Amazing but True!" and "Equipment Photo Diagram" in the table of contents and point out that they are found on page 20.

Read page 20 aloud without showing the picture. Have the students use "Turn to Your Partner" to discuss:

Q *What amazing fact did you learn? Do you think this is an amazing fact? Why?*

Show pages 20–21 and read the title "Equipment Photo Diagram" aloud. Explain that this is a photo of a garbage truck and other equipment a garbage collector uses. The labels identify important items in the photo. Remind the students that last week they each made a labeled drawing of a raptor. Give the students a few moments to look at the photo and the labels, and then ask:

Q *What did you learn from looking at the photo and reading the labels?*

Have a few students share their thinking.

Read aloud the information on the "Equipment Photo Diagram." Ask:

Q *What new information did you learn?*

Have a few students share their thinking.

3 ▸ Explore Additional Text Features

Tell the students that this book has more special features at the back. Show them the glossary on page 22 and read the title, "Glossary," aloud. Explain that a glossary lists and defines important words in the story. A glossary is like a dictionary because it gives a word and its meaning. Read aloud one or two of the words and their definitions.

◀ **Teacher Note**

As you discuss each of the text features, list them on the "Nonfiction" chart.

Show that on page 23 there is a list of books and an Internet site where readers can find out more about garbage collectors.

Show the index on page 24 and remind the students that they discussed the index in *Raptors!* Review that an index lists topics in the book and the pages where the topics can be found. Read a few of the topics listed in the index.

Explain to the students that not all nonfiction books have all of these special sections, but that it is important to notice them when they are in the students' books.

Reflect on Working Together

Ask and briefly discuss:

Q *What did you need to do to make sure you listened during the class discussions today?*

Q *What would you do differently next time?*

INDIVIDUALIZED DAILY READING

5 ▶ **Read Independently and Explore Special Features of Nonfiction**

Have the students independently read nonfiction books for up to 20 minutes. Explain that at the end of IDR today they will talk in pairs about the books they are reading and any special features in them. Review the features on the "Nonfiction" chart and ask the students to notice if some of these features are in their independent reading books. Point out that they might discover a feature that is not on the chart. Tell them that partners will share their reading and special features in their books at the end of independent reading.

As the students read, circulate among them. Stop and ask individual students to talk about the book they are reading and what they are noticing about the special features. Ask questions such as:

Q *What is your book about?*

Q *What is a feature in your book? What did you learn from this [photo]?*

Q *Read the [caption under this photo] to me. What did you learn?*

 At the end of independent reading, have partners share their books and any special features first with one another, and then with the whole class. If appropriate, add new features to the "Nonfiction" chart (for example, captions, maps, and graphs).

EXTENSION

Read and Share More Books in the Series "Community Helpers at Work"

Have partners continue to explore the subject of community helpers by reading books like the ones listed here. Have partners share what they know and what they wonder prior to reading the book. Some choices are *A Day in the Life of a Librarian, A Day in the Life of a Construction Worker, A Day in the Life of a Farmer,* and *A Day in the Life of a Zookeeper*. Have partners share their book with another pair.

Day 3

Materials

- Nonfiction texts at appropriate levels for independent reading
- "What Good Readers Do" chart
- "Nonfiction" chart and a marker
- Writing paper for each student
- *Assessment Resource Book*

Teacher Note

Have each student select her independent reading book before starting the lesson.

Independent Strategy Practice

In this lesson, the students:

- Read nonfiction books independently
- Explore expository text features
- Identify what they learn from a nonfiction text
- Use *wondering* to make sense of nonfiction text
- Write about what they learn and wonder from their nonfiction texts
- Share their thinking

1 ▶ Review What Good Readers Do

Have partners sit together. Display the "What Good Readers Do" chart and read the listed strategies aloud. Remind the students that they have been using some of the strategies—such as wondering, visualizing, and thinking about what they already know—to help them understand nonfiction books.

 Ask and have partners discuss:

Q *What strategies help you think about your reading? How does [wondering] help you?*

Have a few students share their thinking.

Refer to the "Nonfiction" chart and read the listed features aloud. Remind the students that they have been finding some of these features in their nonfiction books. Explain that taking time to look at and read or study these features, such as photos and labeled diagrams, helps them be better readers of nonfiction.

Review Writing About a Nonfiction Book

Remind the students that last week during independent reading they read a nonfiction book and wrote about what they learned and wondered about. Explain that they will repeat this activity with the nonfiction book they read today.

Distribute a sheet of writing paper to each student. Ask the students to each write the title of their independent reading book at the top of the sheet.

Explain that the students will read to themselves for a short time. Then you will stop them and ask them to write about something they learned from the book and something they wonder about the book's topic.

 Read Nonfiction Books Independently

Have the students read independently for 5–10 minutes. Stop them and ask them to reread the pages they just read and think about something they learned from the book and something they are wondering about.

 Write About What the Students Learned and Wonder

Have the students write about one thing they learned and one thing they are wondering about the topics of their books.

 Share Writing in Pairs

 Have partners read what they wrote to one another. Encourage each student to show his partner where in the book he found the information. Partners might also share other interesting features of their books.

◀ **Teacher Note**

If some students struggle, encourage them by reading the text aloud with them or using one of the nonfiction texts you read aloud during Unit 6 or 7. If necessary, assist them by recording their thinking and having them read it aloud to you.

CLASS PROGRESS ASSESSMENT

As the students discuss and share their writing and books, circulate among them and ask yourself:

Q *Do students' writings and discussions show evidence that they understand the text?*

Q *Do students' "wonderings" show evidence that they use the text to stimulate curiosity?*

Q *Are they beginning to use the features in their books to help them make sense of what they are reading?*

Record your observations on page 24 of the *Assessment Resource Book*.

Have a few volunteers share special features in their books. If appropriate, add new features to the "Nonfiction" chart.

 Reflect on Respecting Their Partners' Thinking

Ask and briefly discuss:

Q *How did you and your partner show respect for each other today?*

Q *What problems did you have, if any? What can you do differently next time to avoid those problems?*

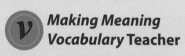

Making Meaning
Vocabulary Teacher

Next week you will revisit *A Day in the Life of a Garbage Collector* to teach Vocabulary Week 25.

Week 3

Overview

UNIT 8: EXPLORING TEXT FEATURES
Expository Nonfiction

An Elephant Grows Up
by Anastasia Suen, illustrated by Michael L. Denman
and William J. Huiett
(Picture Window Books, 2006)

This book tells the story of a baby elephant and her brother as they grow up in Africa.

ALTERNATIVE BOOKS

A Tiger Grows Up by Anastasia Suen

African Elephants by Shannon Knudson

Comprehension Focus

- Students *use schema* to help them understand nonfiction.

- Students use *wondering* to help them understand nonfiction.

- Students *visualize* to make sense of texts.

- Students identify what they learn from nonfiction.

- Students *explore text features* in expository nonfiction.

- Students read independently.

Social Development Focus

- Students relate the values of caring and respect to their behavior.

DO AHEAD

- Make copies of the Unit 8 Parent Letter (BLM8) to send home with the students on the last day of the unit.

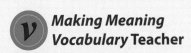

Making Meaning Vocabulary Teacher

If you are teaching Developmental Studies Center's *Making Meaning Vocabulary* program, teach Vocabulary Week 25 this week. For more information, see the *Making Meaning Vocabulary Teacher's Manual.*

Day 1

Materials

- *An Elephant Grows Up* (pages 3–15 and 23)
- "What Good Readers Do" chart
- "Nonfiction" chart and a marker

What Good
Readers Do

- make connections to our lives

Read-aloud

In this lesson, the students:

- *Use schema* to help them understand nonfiction
- *Visualize* to make sense of the text
- Identify what they learn from a nonfiction text
- Read independently for up to 20 minutes
- Act in a caring and respectful way
- Share their partners' thinking

▶1 Review What Good Readers Do and Discuss What They Know

Have partners sit together. Refer to the "What Good Readers Do" chart and briefly review the items on it.

Remind the students that they have been listening to and reading nonfiction stories. Tell them that today you will read another nonfiction book and they will have a chance to talk about what they already know and what they are wondering about the book's topic. They will also have a chance to visualize.

Tell the students that today's book is about elephants. Remind the students that one thing that good readers do when reading nonfiction is to think about what they already know about the book's topic. Have the students use "Think, Pair, Share" to discuss:

Q *What do you think you know about elephants?*

Have a few volunteers share with the class.

Introduce *An Elephant Grows Up*

Show the cover of *An Elephant Grows Up* and read the title and the author's and illustrators' names.

Tell the students that this is a story about a baby elephant that lives and grows up in Africa.

Show the map on page 23 and read the caption above the map. Show the students Africa and explain that the elephants in this story come from this country. Explain that sometimes books have maps to help the reader. Write *maps* on the "Nonfiction" chart.

Read the First Part of *An Elephant Grows Up* Aloud

Tell the students that today you will read the first part of the book. Tell them that you will stop during the reading for them to discuss what they are learning and to visualize.

Read the summary on page 3, and then read pages 4–15 of *An Elephant Grows Up* aloud, following the procedure described on the following page.

Suggested Vocabulary

calf: baby elephant (p. 4)

female: having to do with women or girls (p. 5)

male: having to do with men or boys (p. 5)

nuzzles up to: gently puts her face or head against (p. 7)

herd: large group of animals (p. 8)

roam: walk or travel about; wander (p. 8)

trunk: long nose (p. 13)

nurse: feed milk to (p. 14)

tusks: very long teeth that stick out from an animal's mouth (p. 15)

ELL Vocabulary

English Language Learners may benefit from discussing additional vocabulary, including:

gathering place: place where people or animals meet and get together (p. 12)

ELL Note

English Language Learners will benefit from previewing the pictures and hearing the story prior to the lesson.

Tell the students that the first part of the book describes a baby elephant when it is first born. Read pages 4–6 aloud, showing the pictures and reading the caption. Stop after:

p. 6 "She is already taller than your kitchen table!"

Ask the students to close their eyes and visualize the newborn elephant calf standing taller than their kitchen table.

Without stopping to discuss the students' visualizations, read the caption on page 7.

 Have the students use "Turn to Your Partner" to discuss:

Q *What have you learned about elephants so far?*

Without stopping to discuss the question as a class, reread the caption on page 7 and continue reading to page 12. Stop after:

p. 12 "They visit the water hole at least once a day."

 Have the students use "Turn to Your Partner" to discuss:

Q *What are some special things about elephants you are learning?*

Ask the students to visualize the herd of elephants walking to the gathering place.

Without stopping to discuss the question and what the students visualized, reread the sentence you stopped at on page 12 and continue reading to page 15. Stop after:

p. 15 "It's just like being right-handed or left-handed."

 Discuss What the Students Learned and Visualize

 Have the students use "Turn to Your Partner" to discuss the following question. Ask the students to be prepared to share their partners' thinking.

Q *What did you learn about elephants that surprised you?*

Have a few volunteers share their partners' thinking with the class.

Ask the students to close their eyes and visualize a favorite part of the story. Ask:

Q *What did you see in your mind?*

▶5 Reflect on Working with a Partner

Have the students reflect on their partner work. Ask:

Q *What went well when you talked with your partner today?*

Q *What might you and your partner do differently the next time you work together?*

Have a few students share their ideas with the class.

INDIVIDUALIZED DAILY READING

▶6 Read Independently/Document IDR Conferences

Have the students read independently for up to 20 minutes in nonfiction books at appropriate reading levels. As the students read, circulate among them and monitor whether they are reading books at appropriate reading levels. Ask different students to read part of their book to you and explain what they have read and use the "IDR Conference Notes" record sheet to record your observations. Encourage the students to talk about what is helping them understand what they are reading. Probe their thinking by asking questions such as:

Q *What idea on the "What Good Readers Do" chart have you used while reading this book?*

Q *If you don't understand something you read, what do you do? How does that help you?*

Q *If you think the book is too hard for you, what do you do to find another book?*

At the end of independent reading, facilitate a whole-class discussion by asking questions such as:

Q *What is something you learned today from your reading?*

Q *What is something you are wondering?*

Q *If you are having difficulty finding a book to read, what do you do so that you do not disturb others? How do you show respect for the other students' reading time?*

EXTENSIONS

Read and Discuss More About Elephants

Continue to explore the subject of elephants by reading aloud other nonfiction books about elephants. Ask the students to pay attention to what is helping them understand the book as they listen. Stop periodically during the reading to have the students share what strategies they are using (for example, wondering, making connections, visualizing). Some book choices are *African Elephants* by Roland Smith, *African Elephant: The World's Biggest Land Mammal* by Kristen Hall, *Biggest Animal on Land* by Allan Fowler, *Elephant* (Busy Baby Animal Series) by Jinny Johnson, *Elephants* by JoAnn Early Macken, *The Elephant Family Book* by Oria Douglas-Hamilton, *Elephants: Tusks & Trunks* by Adele D. Richardson, and *Wonder of Elephants* by Patricia Lantier-Sampon and Anthony D. Fredericks.

Compare Fiction and Nonfiction

Read fictional stories about elephants and discuss the difference between nonfiction elephant books and fictional elephant stories. Some fiction stories about elephants are *The Ant and the Elephant* by Bill Peet, *Elmer* by David McKee, *Five Minutes' Peace* by Jill Murphy, *The Last Wild Elephant* by Wendy Kerner, *The Story of Babar* by Jean de Brunhoff, and *Uncle Elephant* by Arnold Lobel.

Day 2

Read-aloud/Strategy Lesson

In this lesson, the students:

- Use *wondering* to help them understand nonfiction
- Identify what they learn from a nonfiction text
- Explore expository text features
- Read independently for up to 20 minutes
- Act in a caring and respectful way

Materials

- *An Elephant Grows Up* (pages 16–24)
- "Nonfiction" chart
- "What Good Readers Do" chart

1 ▶ Review the First Part of *An Elephant Grows Up* and Wonder

Have partners sit together. Remind the students that they heard the first part of *An Elephant Grows Up* and learned many things about African elephants. Today they will hear the second part of the story that tells them more about the elephants as they grow up. Have the students use "Think, Pair, Share" to discuss:

Q *What are some things you learned about African elephants?*

Have one or two volunteers share their thinking with the class.

Q *Now that you have learned some things about African elephants, what are some things you wonder?*

Students might say:

"I wonder how long elephants live."

"I wonder if elephants' tusks get shorter when they dig or do they grow all the time."

"I wonder if elephant families ever get back together."

Have one or two volunteers share their thinking with the class. Ask them to listen for information that might answer their questions.

Read the Second Part of *An Elephant Grows Up* Aloud

Read pages 16–21 aloud, showing the pictures.

> **Suggested Vocabulary**
>
> **bark:** outside covering of a tree trunk and branches (p. 17)
> **journey:** trip; story (p. 21)

At each of the following stopping points, facilitate a brief whole-class discussion about what the students have learned from listening to those pages. As the students respond, be prepared to reread the text or show the pictures again to support their thinking.

Stop after:

p. 18 "Most elephants keep growing until they are 30 or 40 years old!"

p. 21 "A mother elephant always watches over her calf to make sure all is well."

 Discuss What Students Learned and Wonder

Have partners use "Think, Pair, Share" to discuss the following questions:

Q *What are some things you still wonder about elephants?*

Q *What did you find to be the most surprising about elephants?*

Have one or two volunteers share their thinking with the class.

4 **Look at Other Text Features in *An Elephant Grows Up***

Refer to the "Nonfiction" chart and read and review the items listed on the chart. Explain that this book has many of these same features.

Show the "Elephant Diagram" on page 22 and explain that this is a diagram similar to the one in *A Day in the Life of a Garbage Collector.* Explain that this diagram has numbers rather than labels to describe

FACILITATION TIP

Reflect on your experience over the past three weeks with **responding neutrally** with interest during class discussions. Does this practice feel natural to you? Are you integrating it into class discussions throughout the school day? What effect is it having on the students? We encourage you to continue to use this practice and reflect on the students' responses as you facilitate class discussions.

the different parts. Point out that you need to read the information listed by the number. Read page 22 aloud.

Ask:

Q *What new information did you learn from this page?*

Leaf through pages 23–24, pointing out that this book also has a glossary, a list of more elephant books, website information, and an index.

5 Review Strategies the Students Used During the Read-aloud

Refer to the "What Good Readers Do" chart and have the students reflect on the strategies they used during the read-aloud. Remind them that they had opportunities to visualize a few parts of the story. Ask:

Q *How did visualizing the baby elephant help you enjoy and understand the story?*

Continue the discussion by asking one or more of the following questions:

Q *How did thinking about and discussing what you already know about elephants help you understand the reading? How did listening to what others know help you?*

Q *How did wondering help you think more about the book? What can you do to find out more about elephants?*

Q *What features in the book helped you understand and learn more about elephants?*

Students might say:

"I like to think about what I already know because it helps me think about the topic."

"I like to wonder because it makes me think more about what I want to know."

"Seeing the diagram helped me learn more about how the elephant looks."

◀ **Teacher Note**

If the students have difficulty generating ideas, mention one or two (for example, "I noticed that when you heard what other people knew about elephants it helped you remember some things").

Reflect on Partner Work

Ask and briefly discuss:

Q *In what ways were you respectful to your partner today during "Think, Pair, Share"?*

INDIVIDUALIZED DAILY READING

Read Independently/Document IDR Conferences

Have the students independently read nonfiction books at appropriate reading levels for up to 20 minutes. As the students read, circulate among them and monitor whether they are reading books at appropriate reading levels. Ask individual students to read part of their book to you and explain what they have read. Continue to use the "IDR Conference Notes" record sheet to conduct and document individual conferences. Encourage the students to talk about what is helping them understand what they are reading. Probe their thinking by asking questions such as:

Q *What idea on the "What Good Readers Do" chart have you used while reading this book?*

Q *If you don't understand something you read, what do you do? How does that help you?*

Q *If you think the book is too hard for you, what do you do to find another book?*

At the end of independent reading, facilitate a whole-class discussion by asking questions such as:

Q *What is something you learned today from your reading?*

Q *What did you do to help you understand what you are reading?*

Q *What features does your book have? What did you learn from looking at the [picture with labels]?*

EXTENSION

Conduct a Mini Research Project

Point out that the students have had many opportunities to read nonfiction. Have them use "Think, Pair, Share" to discuss topics that they would like to read about (for example, cars, space travel, or soccer). As a class, generate a list of topics. Have partners choose a topic to research, and then have pairs generate some things they wonder about their topic. Collect resources and have pairs conduct a mini research project. After the pairs have had sufficient time to read about their topic, have them share with the whole class what they learned.

Independent Strategy Practice

In this lesson, the students:

- Read nonfiction books independently
- *Explore text features* of expository texts
- Identify what they learn from a nonfiction text
- Act in a caring and respectful way
- Share their thinking

▶1 Get Ready to Read Independently

Have partners sit together. Remind the students that they have been hearing and reading stories about real people, places, and things. Ask:

Q *What nonfiction book have you enjoyed? Why did you like that book?*

Have a few students share their thinking.

Explain that today they will continue to read nonfiction. At the end of IDR they will share in pairs what they read. They will also have a chance to tell the class what they liked about the book.

▶2 Review Identifying One Thing You Learned

Explain that today the students will read independently, and then they will each choose one thing they learned from their reading and share that information in pairs. They will also look for special features in their book that they might want to share with their partner. They will mark these places in their book with self-stick notes in the margin of the page.

Explain that the students will read to themselves for a short time. Then you will stop them and ask them to choose one interesting

Materials

- Nonfiction texts at appropriate levels for independent reading
- Two self-stick notes for each student
- *Assessment Resource Book*
- Unit 8 Parent Letter (BLM8)

Teacher Note

Have each student select her independent reading book before starting the lesson.

Teacher Note ▶

If necessary, use *An Elephant Grows Up* to model finding a fact in the book and placing a self-stick note in the margin of the page. Use a second self-stick note to mark the margin of a page with a special feature, such as a map.

thing they learned from their reading. They will mark that page with a self-stick note.

Tell the students you will give them a second self-stick note to mark one special feature in their book.

Read Nonfiction Books Independently

Distribute two self-stick notes to each student. Have the students read independently for 5–10 minutes. Stop them and ask them to reread the pages they just read and think about something interesting they learned from the reading. Have them mark that page with a self-stick note.

Give the students a few more minutes to look through their books for special features. Have the students mark a page with a special feature with a self-stick note. Remind the students that not all books have special features.

Share Facts and Features from Nonfiction Books

Have the partners share with one another the facts and a feature they chose. Encourage each student to show his partner where in the book he found the information. Partners might also tell each other what they learned from the special features.

ELL Note

Note challenging vocabulary in the students' independent reading books and have brief discussions with individual students to help them define the terms as they read. In some cases, you may want to have the students read the text with you.

CLASS PROGRESS ASSESSMENT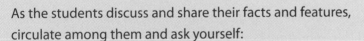

As the students discuss and share their facts and features, circulate among them and ask yourself:

Q *Do students' discussions show evidence that they understand the text?*

Q *Do students' discussions show evidence that they are beginning to use text features?*

Q *Are students respectful and caring to each other as they share their findings?*

Record your observations on page 25 of the *Assessment Resource Book*.

▶5 Discuss as a Class

Ask and briefly discuss:

Q *What do you like about your book? Would you recommend this book to the class to read? Why or why not?*

Students might say:

"I would recommend this book to anyone in the class who likes to read about zoo animals because it has lots of zoo animals and good photos."

"I wouldn't recommend this book because it has lots of big words and it was hard to read. I think it would be a good book for the teacher to read, not kids. I did like looking at the pictures."

"I would recommend this book because it was about volcanoes and it had lots of pictures and I learned a lot."

▶6 Reflect on Working Together

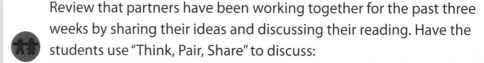

Review that partners have been working together for the past three weeks by sharing their ideas and discussing their reading. Have the students use "Think, Pair, Share" to discuss:

Q *When your partner was talking to you about [her] reading, how did you show [her] that you cared about [her] thinking?*

Q *What was one thing you did that showed respect for your partner?*

Continue the brief discussion by focusing on whole-class interactions. Ask:

Q *During whole-class discussions, how did you act respectfully? Why is this important?*

Share some of your observations of partner and class interactions during the lesson and unit. If the students had any difficulties acting responsibly, have them think about and discuss what they might do to avoid those difficulties next time.

Teacher Note

This is the last week of Unit 8. You will reassign partners for Unit 9.

 Parent Letter

Send home with each student the Parent Letter for this unit (see "Do Ahead," page 309). Periodically, have a few students share with the class what they are reading at home.

 ***Making Meaning Vocabulary* Teacher**

Next week you will revisit *An Elephant Grows Up* to teach Vocabulary Week 26.

Unit 9

Revisiting the Reading Life

During this unit, the students reflect on books they like and want to read. They think about the reading comprehension strategies they use to understand books, and they practice answering questions to understand stories. During IDR, students continue to practice self-monitoring, use the reading strategies, and reflect on how they use the strategies to help them understand their reading. Socially, they continue to develop the group skills of listening to one another and sharing their thinking. They also participate in a class meeting to discuss what they liked about working together in their reading community.

Week 1 *Julius* by Angela Johnson

Week 1

Overview

UNIT 9: REVISITING THE READING LIFE

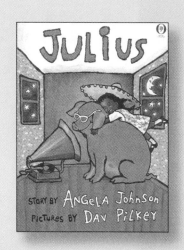

Julius
by Angela Johnson, illustrated by Dav Pilkey
(Orchard Books, 1993)

Maya's grandfather brings her a pig from Alaska and the two of them learn about fun and sharing.

ALTERNATIVE BOOKS

Nobody Likes Me! by Raoul Krischanitz

Friends by Helme Heine

Comprehension Focus

• Students answer questions to understand stories.

• Students reflect on books and stories they like and want to read.

• Students think about the reading comprehension strategies they use to understand books.

• Students read independently.

Social Development Focus

• Students analyze the effect of their behavior on others and on the group work.

• Students develop the group skills of listening to one another and sharing their ideas.

• Students participate in a class meeting to discuss what they liked about working together in their reading community.

DO AHEAD

• Prior to Day 1, decide how you will randomly assign partners to work together during the unit.

• Collect one book the students especially enjoyed from each unit in the *Making Meaning* program. These can include books listed as alternatives or other read-aloud books you used. (See Day 2, Step 1, on page 330.)

• Prepare a chart with the title "Books and Stories We Like" for Day 2.

• Make copies of the Unit 9 Parent Letter (BLM9) to send home with the students on the last day of the unit.

Making Meaning
Vocabulary Teacher

If you are teaching Developmental Studies Center's *Making Meaning Vocabulary* program, teach Vocabulary Week 26 this week. For more information, see the *Making Meaning Vocabulary Teacher's Manual.*

Day 1

Materials

- *Julius*
- Eight or more read-aloud books, one from each unit
- "What Good Readers Do" chart
- "Thinking About My Reading" chart

Read-aloud

In this lesson, the students:

- Begin working with new partners
- Hear and discuss a story
- Think about the reading comprehension strategies they use
- Read independently for up to 20 minutes
- Share ideas

About Reflection

The purpose of this unit is to help the students reflect on the reading work they have done in the *Making Meaning* program and the comprehension strategies they have learned to help them understand stories. This week they will think about the stories they like, and reflect on their partner work and their reading community.

Make all of the books used in the *Making Meaning* program as well as other books you read aloud available for Individualized Daily Reading and the lesson extensions. Select eight or more of these books to use for modeling in the first two lessons.

Prior to this week, have each student select a favorite book to share with the class. These might be books read or heard at school or home. The students will use these books during the lesson extensions.

Being a Writer™ **Teacher**

You can either have the students work with their *Being a Writer* partner or assign them a different partner for the *Making Meaning* lessons.

1 ▶ Pair Students and Get Ready to Work Together

Randomly assign partners and have them sit together. Tell the students that during this week they will think about books they like and their reading community. Today, they will talk about what strategies they learned to help them understand stories.

What Good Readers Do

- make connections to our lives

2 ▶ Review the "What Good Readers Do" Chart

Remind the students that they practiced several things this year that helped them understand stories. Refer to the "What Good Readers Do" chart and briefly review each strategy.

Tell the students that they will probably use some of these comprehension strategies as they listen to today's read-aloud.

 ## Introduce *Julius*

Show the cover of *Julius* and read the title and names of the author and illustrator aloud. Explain that this is a story about a girl named Maya and her pet pig, Julius. Remind the students that readers often look at the illustrations before reading a book to get to know the story. Show the cover again and leaf through the book showing a few of the illustrations. Ask:

Q *From the pictures on the cover and in the book, what are you wondering about the story?*

Have a few volunteers share their ideas with the class.

 ## Read *Julius* Aloud

Read the story aloud, showing the illustrations and stopping as described below.

Suggested Vocabulary

wintered: spent the winter (p. 4)

Alaska: one of the states in the United States where it is very cold (p. 4; refer to a map if possible)

did a polar bear imitation: acted like a polar bear (p. 8)

ELL Vocabulary

English Language Learners may benefit from discussing additional vocabulary, including:

crate: large, usually wooden box, used to carry or store things (p. 6; refer to the illustration)

slurped: drank or ate noisily (p. 12)

flour: ground wheat or other grain that is used for baking (p. 13; refer to the illustration)

Stop after:

    p. 7   "She'd always wanted one or the other."

Have the students use "Turn to Your Partner" to discuss:

Q *What do you think might be in the crate?*

Without sharing as a class, reread page 7 and continue reading to the next stop:

> **p. 17** "…and he'd always play records when everybody else wanted to read."

 Ask and have the students use "Turn to Your Partner" to discuss:

Q *What are some of the things that Julius does?*

Without sharing as a class, reread pages 16 and 17 and continue reading to the next stop:

> **p. 25** "Maya didn't think all the older brothers in the world could have taught her that."

 Ask and have the students use "Turn to Your Partner" to discuss:

Q *What are some things that Maya likes about Julius?*

Without sharing as a class, reread the last sentence on page 25, and continue reading to the end of the book.

▶5 Discuss the Story as a Class

Have the students discuss the following questions:

Q *What part of this story did you like? Why did you like that part?*

Q *What are some things that Julius and Maya like about each other?*

Q *What can we learn about being friends from this story?*

▶6 Reflect on Working Together

 Facilitate a brief discussion about how the students interacted during the read-aloud and discussion. Ask partners to tell each other one thing that they liked about how they worked together. Have a few students share their ideas with the class.

INDIVIDUALIZED DAILY READING

 ## Practice Self-monitoring

Direct the students' attention to the "Thinking About My Reading" chart and remind them that stopping and thinking about the questions on the chart helps them keep track of how well they are understanding their reading. Read the questions written on the chart and tell them that they will practice this procedure again today.

Have the students read independently and stop them at 5-minute intervals. Each time you stop, read the questions on the chart and have the students think about each question.

As the students read, circulate among them and ask individual students to tell you what their book is about. Encourage them to think about the questions on the chart.

At the end of independent reading, have the students share their reading with the class.

EXTENSIONS

Revisit Read-alouds

Give pairs time to read, retell, and talk about the books you have read aloud this year. Make time each day for partners to briefly share a book with each other or with another pair.

Visit the Community Library

If possible, arrange a visit to the community library. Check with the librarian about the procedure for obtaining a library card. Familiarize the students with the library, and encourage them to go to the library to borrow books to read during their summer break.

> *Thinking About*
> *My Reading*
>
> *- What is happening in*
> *my book?*

Day 2

Materials

- *Julius*
- Eight or more read-aloud books, one from each unit
- "Books and Stories We Like" chart, prepared ahead, and a marker
- A sheet of writing/drawing paper for each student
- Markers or crayons

Reflect on Reading Lives

In this lesson, the students:

- Discuss stories they like and want to read
- Read independently for up to 20 minutes
- Share ideas

▶ 1 Review Familiar Books

Have partners sit together. Tell them that today they will think about the kinds of stories they like and want to read.

Direct their attention to the books you have selected. Tell the students these are some of the books they heard or read this year. Remind them that some of these books are fiction (about imaginary people and events) and some are nonfiction (about real people, events, or things). Show examples of different types of fiction and nonfiction stories. If necessary, give a brief summary of each of the books you selected.

▶ 2 Discuss Favorite Stories

 Have the students use "Think, Pair, Share" to talk about the selected books and what kinds of books or stories they like. Ask:

Q *Which of these books did you enjoy the most? Why did you like that book?*

Q *What kinds of stories do you like to read? Why do you like to read these stories?*

Students might say:

"I like *Kangaroo Joey Grows Up* because the kangaroo is cute."

"I like *Really Big Cats* because I learned about big cats."

"I like books that rhyme."

As the students share their ideas, record the kinds of stories they like on the "Books and Stories We Like" chart (for example, rhyming stories, funny stories, books where I learn about things, or animal books).

Draw and Write About Favorite Books

Distribute a sheet of writing/drawing paper to each student. Explain that they will draw a picture and write about the books they like to read. Ask them to draw a picture of themselves reading a book that they like and write a sentence or two about the books they like to read. (For example, the students might draw a picture of a book with a dog and a cat if they like to read about animals.)

As the students work, circulate among them. Probe their thinking with questions such as:

Q *What kinds of stories do you like to listen to? Do you like books that are silly?*

Q *Do you like books about real things? What kinds of things do you want to learn about?*

Q *Where can you picture yourself reading?*

Share Pictures with a Partner and the Class

Explain that partners will share their pictures and what they wrote with one another. Tell the students to listen carefully to each other because they will be responsible for sharing their partners' ideas with the class.

After pairs have shared, facilitate a brief whole-class discussion, using the following questions:

Q *What do you like to read?*

Q *Where do you like to read?*

Q *What else do you want to tell us about your reading?*

Q *Do you and your partner like some of the same things about reading? What are they?*

Tell the students that in the next lesson they will talk about what they like about sharing books with the class.

INDIVIDUALIZED DAILY READING

▶ 5 Revisit the Students' Reading Lives

Have the students read independently for up to 20 minutes.

As the students read, circulate among them and talk to individual students about their reading lives. To guide your discussion, ask questions such as:

Q *What is one of your favorite books? Why do you like that book?*

Q *What kinds of books do you like to read? Do you prefer fiction or nonfiction books? Why?*

Q *What do you want to read this summer? What would you like to read next year?*

Q *What do you like about reading?*

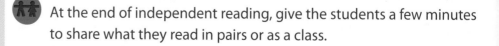 At the end of independent reading, give the students a few minutes to share what they read in pairs or as a class.

EXTENSIONS

Continue to Revisit Read-alouds

Give pairs time to read, retell, and talk about books you have read aloud this year. Make time each day for partners to briefly share a book with each other or with another pair.

Share Personal Favorites

Have the students share a favorite book from home or school with a partner or the class. Have them talk about why they like the book, share their favorite part, or show an illustration.

Day 3

Materials

- Space for the class to sit in a circle
- "Reading Together" chart
- A sheet of writing/drawing paper for each student
- Markers or crayons
- "Class Meeting Ground Rules" chart
- Unit 9 Parent Letter (BLM9)

Reading Together

- I will sit quietly on the rug.

Reflection and Class Meeting

In this lesson, the students:

- Reflect on and write about how they worked together
- Read independently for up to 20 minutes
- Share ideas
- Have a class meeting to discuss their reading community

▶ **1** **Get Ready to Work Together**

Have partners sit together. Remind the students that yesterday they talked about books they like. Today they will think about their reading community and talk and write about what they liked about sharing books with a partner and the class.

▶ **2** **Discuss the "Reading Together" Chart**

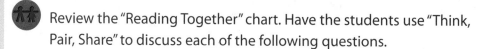 Review the "Reading Together" chart. Have the students use "Think, Pair, Share" to discuss each of the following questions.

Q *What is important to remember when working together?*

Q *What do you like best about working with a partner?*

▶ **3** **Draw and Write About Reading and Working Together**

Distribute a sheet of writing/drawing paper and markers or crayons to each student. Explain that the students will each draw a picture and write about what they liked about working in pairs and with their reading community. They will share their pictures and ideas later at a class meeting.

Have the students complete their drawings.

4▸ Gather for a Class Meeting

When most students have finished drawing and writing, have them bring their work to the circle for a class meeting. Have partners sit together and make sure the students can see one another.

Briefly review the "Class Meeting Ground Rules" chart.

5▸ Conduct the Class Meeting

Explain that the purpose of the class meeting is to talk about what they liked about working with a partner and their reading community.

 Have partners share what they drew and wrote. Remind them to listen carefully to each other because they will share their partners' ideas with the class.

After partners have shared, facilitate a whole-class discussion. Ask:

Q *What is something your partner liked about working with a partner?*

Q *What is something your partner liked about our reading community?*

> *Students might say:*
>
> "[Karl] wrote that he likes to talk to me because it helps him remember the story."
>
> "[Ashanti] likes when the class listens quietly to the story."

Q *What have you enjoyed about working with your partner? Tell your partner now.*

6▸ Reflect on the Class Meeting

Briefly discuss how the students followed the class meeting ground rules, adjourn the meeting and have the students return to their desks.

Teacher Note

You may want to hold the class meeting later in the day or on the following day.

◀ **Teacher Note**

You might want to share some of your personal observations about ways the students have changed or grown as members of the reading community over the year. (For example, you might say, "I remember how some of you only wanted to work with people you already knew in the beginning of the year. Now you seem more willing to work with people you don't know" or "I notice that both partners are talking about the story. In the beginning of the year, at times only one partner seemed to do most of the talking.")

INDIVIDUALIZED DAILY READING

 Revisit the Students' Reading Lives

Have the students read independently for up to 20 minutes.

As they read, circulate among them and talk to individual students about their reading lives. Ask question such as:

Q *What is one of your favorite books? Why do you like that book?*

Q *What kinds of books do you like to read? Do you prefer fiction or nonfiction books?*

EXTENSION

End-of-year "Book-sharing Party"

Have students share a favorite book from home or school in pairs or with the class. Have the students talk about why they like the book or their favorite part or show an illustration. Have the students display their books and give the students an opportunity to walk around and look at the books. At the end of the sharing time, briefly discuss which books the students might like to read over the summer. If possible, provide refreshments for the students to enjoy.

 **Parent Letter**

Send home with each student the Parent Letter for this unit (see "Do Ahead," page 325).

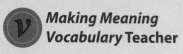 *Making Meaning Vocabulary* **Teacher**

Next week you will revisit *Julius* to teach Vocabulary Week 27.

Appendices

Grade 1

	Lesson	Title	Author	Form	Genre/Type
Unit 1	▶ Week 1	*Quick as a Cricket*	Audrey Wood	picture book	fiction
	▶ Week 2	*When I Was Little*	Jamie Lee Curtis	picture book	realistic fiction
	▶ Week 3	*Where Do I Live?*	Neil Chesanow	picture book	narrative nonfiction
	▶ Week 4	*It's Mine!*	Leo Lionni	picture book	fiction
Unit 2	▶ Week 1	*Matthew and Tilly*	Rebecca C. Jones	picture book	realistic fiction
	▶ Week 2	*McDuff and the Baby*	Rosemary Wells	picture book	fiction
	▶ Week 3	*Chrysanthemum*	Kevin Henkes	picture book	fiction
Unit 3	▶ Week 1	*Caps for Sale*	Esphyr Slobodkina	picture book	fiction
	▶ Week 2	*Curious George Goes to an Ice Cream Shop*	Margret Rey and Alan J. Shalleck (eds.)	picture book	fiction
	▶ Week 3	*Peter's Chair*	Ezra Jack Keats	picture book	realistic fiction
Unit 4	▶ Week 1	*Did You See What I Saw? Poems about School*: "School Bus" and "Sliding Board"	Kay Winters	poetry collection	poetry
		"The Balloon Man"	Dorothy Aldis	poem	poetry
	▶ Week 2	*In the Tall, Tall Grass*	Denise Fleming	picture book	fiction
	▶ Week 3	*Sheep Out to Eat*	Nancy Shaw	picture book	fiction
	▶ Week 4	*The Snowy Day*	Ezra Jack Keats	picture book	realistic fiction
Unit 5	▶ Week 1	*An Extraordinary Egg*	Leo Lionni	picture book	fiction
	▶ Week 2	*George Washington and the General's Dog*	Frank Murphy	picture book	narrative nonfiction
	▶ Week 3	*Down the Road*	Alice Schertle	picture book	realistic fiction
Unit 6	▶ Week 1	*Hearing*	Sharon Gordon	picture book	expository nonfiction
	▶ Week 2	*A Good Night's Sleep*	Allan Fowler	picture book	expository nonfiction
	▶ Week 3	*Dinosaur Babies*	Lucille Recht Penner	picture book	expository nonfiction
Unit 7	▶ Week 1	*A Kangaroo Joey Grows Up*	Joan Hewett	picture book	expository nonfiction
	▶ Week 2	*A Harbor Seal Pup Grows Up*	Joan Hewett	picture book	expository nonfiction
	▶ Week 3	*Throw Your Tooth on the Roof*	Selby B. Beeler	picture book	expository nonfiction
		A Look at Teeth	Allan Fowler	picture book	expository nonfiction
Unit 8	▶ Week 1	*Raptors!*	Lisa McCourt	picture book	expository nonfiction
	▶ Week 2	*A Day in the Life of a Garbage Collector*	Nate LeBoutillier	picture book	expository nonfiction
	▶ Week 3	*An Elephant Grows Up*	Anastasia Suen	picture book	expository nonfiction
Unit 9	▶ Week 1	*Julius*	Angela Johnson	picture book	fiction

Grade K

Brave Bear	Kathy Mallat
Building Beavers	Kathleen Martin-James
Cat's Colors	Jane Cabrera
"Charlie Needs a Cloak"	Tomie dePaola
Cookie's Week	Cindy Ward
A Day with a Doctor	Jan Kottke
A Day with a Mail Carrier	Jan Kottke
Flower Garden	Eve Bunting
Friends at School	Rochelle Bunnett
Getting Around By Plane	Cassie Mayer
Henry's Wrong Turn	Harriet M. Ziefert
I Want to Be a Vet	Dan Liebman
I Was So Mad	Mercer Mayer
If You Give a Mouse a Cookie	Laura Joffe Numeroff
Knowing about Noses	Allan Fowler
A Letter to Amy	Ezra Jack Keats
Maisy's Pool	Lucy Cousins
Moon	Melanie Mitchell
My Friends	Taro Gomi
Noisy Nora	Rosemary Wells
On the Go	Ann Morris
A Porcupine Named Fluffy	Helen Lester
Pumpkin Pumpkin	Jeanne Titherington
A Tiger Cub Grows Up	Joan Hewett
Tools	Ann Morris
When Sophie Gets Angry— Really, Really Angry…	Molly Bang
Whistle for Willie	Ezra Jack Keats

Grade 2

Alexander and the Terrible, Horrible, No Good, Very Bad Day	Judith Viorst
The Art Lesson	Tomie dePaola
Beatrix Potter	Alexandra Wallner
Bend and Stretch	Pamela Hill Nettleton
Big Al	Andrew Clements
Chester's Way	Kevin Henkes
Eat My Dust! Henry Ford's First Race	Monica Kulling
Erandi's Braids	Antonio Hernández Madrigal
Fathers, Mothers, Sisters, Brothers: A Collection of Family Poems	Mary Ann Hoberman
Fishes (A True Book)	Melissa Stewart
Galimoto	Karen Lynn Williams
The Ghost-Eye Tree	Bill Martin Jr. and John Archambault
The Incredible Painting of Felix Clousseau	Jon Agee
It Could Still Be a Worm	Allan Fowler
Jamaica Tag-Along	Juanita Havill
little blue and little yellow	Leo Lionni
McDuff Moves In	Rosemary Wells
Me First	Helen Lester
The Paper Crane	Molly Bang
The Paperboy	Dav Pilkey
Plants That Eat Animals	Allan Fowler
POP! A Book About Bubbles	Kimberly Brubaker Bradley
Poppleton	Cynthia Rylant
Poppleton and Friends	Cynthia Rylant
Sheila Rae, the Brave	Kevin Henkes
Snails	Monica Hughes
The Tale of Peter Rabbit	Beatrix Potter
A Tree Is Nice	Janice May Udry
What Mary Jo Shared	Janice May Udry

Grade 3

Alexander, Who's Not (Do you hear me? I mean it!) Going to Move	Judith Viorst
Aunt Flossie's Hats (and Crab Cakes Later)	Elizabeth Fitzgerald Howard
Boundless Grace	Mary Hoffman
Brave Harriet	Marissa Moss
Brave Irene	William Steig
Cherries and Cherry Pits	Vera B. Williams
City Green	DyAnne DiSalvo-Ryan
A Day's Work	Eve Bunting
Fables	Arnold Lobel
Flashy Fantastic Rain Forest Frogs	Dorothy Hinshaw Patent
The Girl Who Loved Wild Horses	Paul Goble
Have You Seen Bugs?	Joanne Oppenheim
Julius, the Baby of the World	Kevin Henkes
Keepers	Jeri Hanel Watts
Knots on a Counting Rope	Bill Martin Jr. and John Archambault
Lifetimes	David L. Rice
Mailing May	Michael O. Tunnell
The Man Who Walked Between the Towers	Mordicai Gerstein
Miss Nelson Is Missing!	Harry Allard and James Marshall
Morning Meals Around the World	Maryellen Gregoire
Officer Buckle and Gloria	Peggy Rathmann
The Paper Bag Princess	Robert Munsch
Reptiles	Melissa Stewart
The Spooky Tail of Prewitt Peacock	Bill Peet
What is a Bat?	Bobbie Kalman and Heather Levigne
Wilma Unlimited	Kathleen Krull

Grade 4

Amelia's Road	Linda Jacobs Altman
Animal Senses	Pamela Hickman
A Bad Case of Stripes	David Shannon
Basket Moon	Mary Lyn Ray
The Bat Boy & His Violin	Gavin Curtis
Chicken Sunday	Patricia Polacco
Coming to America	Betsy Maestro
Digging Up Tyrannosaurus Rex	John R. Horner and Don Lessem
Farm Workers Unite: The Great Grape Boycott	
Flight	Robert Burleigh
Hurricane	David Wiesner
In My Own Backyard	Judi Kurjian
Italian Americans	Carolyn P. Yoder
My Man Blue	Nikki Grimes
The Old Woman Who Named Things	Cynthia Rylant
Peppe the Lamplighter	Elisa Bartone
A Picture Book of Amelia Earhart	David A. Adler
A Picture Book of Harriet Tubman	David A. Adler
A Picture Book of Rosa Parks	David A. Adler
The Princess and the Pizza	Mary Jane and Herm Auch
Slinky Scaly Slithery Snakes	Dorothy Hinshaw Patent
Song and Dance Man	Karen Ackerman
Teammates	Peter Golenbock
Thunder Cake	Patricia Polacco

Grade 5

Big Cats	Seymour Simon
Chinese Americans	Tristan Boyer Binns
Earthquakes	Seymour Simon
Everybody Cooks Rice	Norah Dooley
Harry Houdini: Master of Magic	Robert Kraske
Heroes	Paul Dowswell
Hey World, Here I Am!	Jean Little
Letting Swift River Go	Jane Yolen
Life in the Rain Forests	Lucy Baker
The Lotus Seed	Sherry Garland
Richard Wright and the Library Card	William Miller
A River Ran Wild	Lynne Cherry
Something to Remember Me By	Susan V. Bosak
Star of Fear, Star of Hope	Jo Hoestlandt
The Summer My Father Was Ten	Pat Brisson
Survival and Loss: Native American Boarding Schools	
Uncle Jed's Barbershop	Margaree King Mitchell
The Van Gogh Cafe	Cynthia Rylant
Wildfires	Seymour Simon

Grade 6

America Street: A Multicultural Anthology of Stories	Anne Mazer, ed.
And Still the Turtle Watched	Sheila MacGill-Callahan
Asian Indian Americans	Carolyn P. Yoder
Baseball Saved Us	Ken Mochizuki
Chato's Kitchen	Gary Soto
Dear Benjamin Banneker	Andrea Davis Pinkney
Encounter	Jane Yolen
Every Living Thing	Cynthia Rylant
Life in the Oceans	Lucy Baker
New Kids in Town: Oral Histories of Immigrant Teens	Janet Bode
Out of This World: Science-Fiction Stories	Edward Blishen, ed.
Rosie the Riveter: Women in a Time of War	
The Strangest of Strange Unsolved Mysteries, Volume 2	Phyllis Raybin Emert
Train to Somewhere	Eve Bunting
Voices from the Fields	S. Beth Atkin
Volcano: The Eruption and Healing of Mount St. Helens	Patricia Lauber
Whales	Seymour Simon
Why Mosquitoes Buzz in People's Ears	Verna Aardema

Grade 7

Ancient Ones: The World of the Old-Growth Douglas Fir	Barbara Bash
Children of the Wild West	Russell Freedman
Death of the Iron Horse	Paul Goble
The Dream Keeper and Other Poems	Langston Hughes
Finding Our Way	René Saldaña, Jr.
the flag of childhood: poems from the middle east	Naomi Shahib Nye, ed.
The Friendship	Mildred D. Taylor
It's Our World, Too!	Phillip Hoose
The Land I Lost	Huynh Quang Nhuong
Life in the Woodlands	Roseanne Hooper
New and Selected Poems	Gary Soto
Only Passing Through: The Story of Sojourner Truth	Anne Rockwell
Roberto Clemente: Pride of the Pittsburgh Pirates	Jonah Winter
Shattered: Stories of Children and War	Jennifer Armstrong, ed.
Sports Stories	Alan Durant, ed.
The Village That Vanished	Ann Grifalconi
What If…? Amazing Stories	Monica Hughes, ed.
Wolves	Seymour Simon
The Wretched Stone	Chris Van Allsburg

Grade 8

the composition	Antonio Skármeta
The Giver	Lois Lowry
Immigrant Kids	Russell Freedman
In the Land of the Lawn Weenies	David Lubar
Life in the Polar Lands	Monica Byles
Nellie Bly: A Name to Be Reckoned With	Stephen Krensky
The People Could Fly	Virginia Hamilton
Satchel Paige	Lesa Cline-Ransome
Sharks	Seymour Simon
She Dared: True Stories of Heroines, Scoundrels, and Renegades	Ed Butts
When I Was Your Age: Original Stories About Growing Up, Volume One	Amy Ehrlich, ed.

Bibliography

Anderson, Richard C., Elfrieda H. Hiebert, Judith A. Scott, and Ian A. G. Wilkinson. *Becoming a Nation of Readers: The Report of the Commission on Reading*. Washington, DC: The National Institute of Education, 1985.

Anderson, Richard C., and P. David Pearson. "A Schema-Theoretic View of Basic Process in Reading Comprehension." In *Handbook of Reading Research*, P. David Pearson (ed.). New York: Longman, 1984.

Armbruster, Bonnie B., Fred Lehr, and Jean Osborn. *Put Reading First: The Research Building Blocks for Teaching Children to Read*. Jessup, MD: National Institute for Literacy, 2001.

Asher, James. "The Strategy of Total Physical Response: An Application to Learning Russian." *International Review of Applied Linguistics* 3 (1965): 291–300.

———. "Children's First Language as a Model for Second Language Learning." *Modern Language Journal* 56 (1972): 133–139.

Beck, Isabel L., and Margaret G. McKeown. "Text Talk: Capturing the Benefits of Read-Aloud Experiences for Young Children." *The Reading Teacher* 55:1 (2001): 10–19.

Beck, Isabel L., Margaret G. McKeown, and Linda Kucan. *Bringing Words to Life: Robust Vocabulary Instruction*. New York: Guilford Press (2002).

Block, C. C., and M. Pressley. *Comprehension Instruction: Research-Based Best Practices*. New York: Guilford Press, 2001.

Calkins, Lucy M. *The Art of Teaching Reading*. New York: Addison-Wesley Longman, 2001.

Contestable, Julie W., Shaila Regan, Susie Alldredge, Carol Westrich, and Laurel Robertson. *Number Power: A Cooperative Approach to Mathematics and Social Development Grades K–6*. Oakland, CA: Developmental Studies Center, 1999.

Cummins, James. "The Role of Primary Language Development in Promoting Educational Success for Language Minority Students." In *Schooling and Language Minority Students: A Theoretical Framework*. Los Angeles, CA: California State University, Evaluation, Dissemination, and Assessment Center, 1981.

Cunningham, Anne E., and Keith E. Stanovich. "What Reading Does for the Mind." *American Educator* Spring/Summer (1998): 8–15.

Developmental Studies Center. *Blueprints for a Collaborative Classroom*. Oakland, CA: Developmental Studies Center, 1997.

———. *Ways We Want Our Class to Be*. Oakland, CA: Developmental Studies Center, 1996.

DeVries, Rheta, and Betty Zan. *Moral Classrooms, Moral Children*. New York: Teachers' College Press, 1994.

Dewey, J. *Democracy and Education*. New York: Macmillan, 1916.

Farstrup, Alan E., and S. Jay Samuels. *What Research Has to Say About Reading Instruction*. 3rd Ed. Newark, DE: International Reading Association, 2002.

Fielding, Linda G., and P. David Pearson. "Reading Comprehension: What Works." *Educational Leadership* 51:5 (1994): 1–11.

Fountas, Irene C. and Gay Su Pinnell. *Leveled Books, K–8: Matching Texts to Readers for Effective Teaching*. Portsmouth, NH: Heinemann, 2006.

———. *Leveled Books for Readers Grade 3–6*. Portsmouth, NH: Heinemann, 2002.

———. *Matching Books to Readers: Using Leveled Books in Guided Reading, K–3*. Portsmouth, NH: Heinemann, 1999.

Gambrell, Linda B., Lesley Mandel Morrow, Susan B. Neuman, and Michael Pressley, eds. *Best Practices in Literacy Instruction*. New York: Guilford Press, 1999.

Hakuta, Kenji, Yoko Goto Butler, and Daria Witt. *How Long Does It Take English Learners to Attain Proficiency?* Santa Barbara, CA: University of California, Linguistic Minority Research Institute, 2000.

Harvey, Stephanie. *Nonfiction Matters: Reading, Writing, and Research in Grades 3–8*. York, ME: Stenhouse Publishers, 1998.

Harvey, Stephanie, and Anne Goudvis. *Strategies That Work: Teaching Comprehension to Enhance Understanding*. York, ME: Stenhouse Publishers, 2000.

Harvey, Stephanie, Sheila McAuliffe, Laura Benson, Wendy Cameron, Sue Kempton, Pat Lusche, Debbie Miller, Joan Schroeder, and Julie Weaver. "Teacher-Researchers Study the Process of Synthesizing in Six Primary Classrooms." *Language Arts* 73 (1996): 564–574.

Herrell, Adrienne L. and Michael L. Jordan. *Fifty Strategies for Teaching English Language Learners*. Upper Saddle River, NJ: Merrill, 2000.

International Reading Association. "What Is Evidence-Based Reading Instruction? A Position Statement of the International Reading Association." Newark, DE: International Reading Association, 2002.

Johnson, David W., Roger T. Johnson, and Edythe Johnson Holubec. *The New Circles of Learning: Cooperation in the Classroom*. Alexandria, VA: Association for Supervision and Curriculum Development, 1994.

Kagan, Spencer. *Cooperative Learning*. San Juan Capistrano, CA: Resources of Teachers, 1992.

Kamil, Michael L., Peter B. Mosenthal, P. David Pearson, and Rebecca Barr, eds. *Handbook of Reading Research, Volume III*. Mahwah, NJ: Lawrence Erlbaum Associates, 2000.

Keene, Ellin O., and Susan Zimmermann. *Mosaic of Thought: Teaching Comprehension in a Reader's Workshop*. Portsmouth, NH: Heinemann, 1997.

Kohlberg, Lawrence. *The Psychology of Moral Development*. New York: Harper and Row, 1984.

Kohn, Alfie. *Beyond Discipline: From Compliance to Community*. Association for Supervision and Curriculum Development, 1996.

———. *Punished by Rewards: The Trouble with Gold Stars, Incentive Plans, A's, Praise, and Other Bribes*. New York: Houghton Mifflin Company, 1999.

Krashen, Stephen D. *Principles and Practice in Second Language Acquisition*. New York: Prentice-Hall, 1982.

Moss, Barbara. "Making a Case and a Place for Effective Content Area Literacy Instruction in the Elementary Grades." *The Reading Teacher* 59:1 (2005): 46–55.

NEA Task Force on Reading. *Report of the NEA Task Force on Reading 2000*.

Neufeld, Paul. "Comprehension Instruction in Content Area Classes." *The Reading Teacher* 59:4 (2005): 302–312.

Nucci, Larry P., ed. *Moral Development and Character Education: A Dialogue*. Berkeley, CA: McCutchan Publishing Corporation, 1989.

Optiz, Michael F., ed. *Literacy Instruction for Culturally and Linguistically Diverse Students*. Newark, DE: International Reading Association, 1998.

Pearson, P. David, J. A. Dole, G. G. Duffy, and L. R. Roehler. "Developing Expertise in Reading Comprehension: What Should Be Taught and How Should It Be Taught?" In *What Research Has to Say to the Teacher of Reading*, J. Farstup and S. J. Samuels (eds.). Newark, DE: International Reading Association, 1992.

Piaget, Jean. *The Child's Conception of the World*. Trans. Joan and Andrew Tomlinson. Lanham, MD: Littlefield Adams, 1969.

———. *The Moral Judgment of the Child*. Trans. Marjorie Gabain. New York: The Free Press, 1965.

Pressley, Michael. *Effective Beginning Reading Instruction: The Rest of the Story from Research*. National Education Association, 2002.

———. *Reading Instruction That Works*. New York: Guilford Press, 1998.

Pressley, Michael, Janice Almasi, Ted Schuder, Janet Bergman, Sheri Hite, Pamela B. El-Dinary, and Rachel Brown. "Transactional Instruction of Comprehension Strategies: The Montgomery County, Maryland, SAIL Program." *Reading and Writing Quarterly: Overcoming Learning Difficulties* 10 (1994): 5–19.

Routman, Regie. *Reading Essentials: The Specifics You Need to Teach Reading Well*. Portsmouth, NH: Heinemann, 2003.

Serafini, Frank. *The Reading Workshop: Creating Space for Readers*. Portsmouth, NH: Heinemann, 2001.

Soalt, Jennifer. "Bringing Together Fictional and Informational Texts to Improve Comprehension." *The Reading Teacher* 58:7 (2005): 680–683.

Taylor, Barbara M., Michael Pressley, and P. David Pearson. *Research-Supported Characteristics of Teachers and Schools That Promote Reading Achievement*. National Education Association, 2002.

Trelease, Jim. *The Read-Aloud Handbook*. New York: Penguin Books, 1995.

Weaver, Brenda M. *Leveling Books K–6: Matching Readers to Text*. Newark, DE: International Reading Association, 2000.

Williams, Joan A. "Classroom Conversations: Opportunities to Learn for ESL Students in Mainstream Classrooms." *The Reading Teacher* 54:8 (2001): 750–757.

Blackline Masters

 Dear Parent or Guardian,

This year I am excited to introduce the *Making Meaning*® program to your child. *Making Meaning* is a new reading program designed to help children build their reading comprehension and social skills. The children hear books read aloud and discuss the stories with partners and as a class. This year your child will learn several comprehension strategies such as retelling, visualizing, and wondering/questioning. The program is helping our class become a community of readers by making everyone feel welcome and safe. In addition, each child in our class reads books that are at his or her reading level for up to 20 minutes every day. This part of the *Making Meaning* program is called Individualized Daily Reading (IDR).

At the end of each unit in the *Making Meaning* program, you will receive a letter telling you about the most recent reading comprehension strategy and social skill your child has learned. Each letter will also include ways to support your child's home reading life.

Our class just finished the first unit of the program, which focuses on the children's reading lives. The children talked about what they like to read, heard stories read aloud, and discussed those stories. The children also learned to make connections between the stories and their own experiences. The program calls this reading comprehension strategy *making connections*. When children make connections between the stories they hear and their own lives, they are able to understand the stories better.

During the first unit, the children also practiced the social skill of listening carefully to others. Listening well to others is a skill that helps students learn and become active members of the reading community.

Here are some ways to build your child's reading life at home:

- Make weekly trips to the local library to borrow books.

- Set aside a time to read together every day.

- Stop every so often while reading aloud to discuss what you both are wondering about the story.

- Model good listening by paying attention to your child when the two of you discuss the story.

Reading and discussing books is one of the most important gifts you can give your child. I hope reading together every day can be an enjoyable time for you and your family.

Sincerely,

Apreciado padre de familia o guardián:

Este año estoy muy entusiasmado en presentarle a su niño el programa "*Making Meaning.®*" Este es un nuevo programa de lectura diseñado para ayudar a los niños a que adquieran destrezas en comprensión de lectura y se desarrollen socialmente. Los niños escuchan libros leídos en voz alta y luego hablan con un compañero y con la clase en grupo acerca de la historia que escucharon. Este año su niño va a aprender varias estrategias de comprensión como el volver a contar la historia, visualizar y el hacer preguntas. El programa está ayudando a que nuestra clase se convierta en una comunidad de lectores al hacer que todos se sientan bienvenidos y seguros. Además durante 20 minutos al día, los niños en la clase leen libros al nivel adecuado para cada uno de ellos. Esta parte del programa "*Making Meaning*" se llama lectura diaria individualizada.

Al final de cada unidad del programa *Making Meaning* usted va a recibir una carta dejándole saber la destreza social y la estrategia de comprensión de lectura que su niño acaba de aprender. Cada carta va a incluir maneras en las que usted puede apoyar en la casa la lectura de su niño.

Nuestra clase acaba de finalizar la primera unidad del programa, cuyo enfoque es la vida de los niños como lectores. Los niños hablaron acerca de lo que les gusta leer, escucharon historias que se les leyeron en voz alta y discutieron esas historias. Los niños también aprendieron a hacer conexiones entre las historias y sus vidas. El programa llama esta estrategia de comprensión *hacer conexiones*. Los niños pueden entender las historias mejor cuando hacen conexiones entre las historias que escuchan y sus propias vidas.

Durante la primera unidad los niños también practicaron la destreza social de escuchar con atención a otros. El escuchar con atención a otros es una destreza que ayuda a que los estudiantes aprendan y que activamente formen parte de la comunidad de lectores.

A continuación hay algunas maneras de fomentar la lectura de su niño en casa:

- Vaya a la biblioteca una vez por semana a sacar libros.

- Tome tiempo todos los días para leer juntos.

- Cuando esté leyendo en alto, pare de vez en cuando para que ambos puedan hablar acerca de lo que están pensando y preguntándose de la historia que leen.

- Sea modelo para su niño y escúchelo con atención cuando ambos estén hablando acerca de la historia.

El leer un libro y charlar acerca de la historia es uno de los mejores regalos que usted le puede dar a su hijo. Yo espero que usted y su familia disfruten del tiempo que pasen leyendo a diario.

Sinceramente,

Dear Parent or Guardian,

Our class just finished the second unit of the Making Meaning® program. The children love the stories we are reading! During this unit, the students continued to practice the comprehension strategy *making connections* by hearing and discussing stories and finding connections between the stories and their own lives. They also answered questions to help them understand the stories they heard.

During this unit, the children also practiced the social skill of talking and listening to one another. Listening well and talking to others are skills that help students learn and become active members of the reading community. One powerful way to build your child's ability to listen and talk is to pay attention to your child when the two of you talk about stories.

You can help your child make personal connections to stories. Before reading, ask your child to listen and think about what in the story is like his or her own life. While reading, stop every so often to ask questions such as:

- How do you think this person or animal feels?

- Have you ever felt that way? Tell me about it.

Another way to help your child think about a story more deeply is to ask questions while reading aloud, such as:

- What has happened in the story so far?

- What do you think will happen next?

Have fun reading, talking, and listening to each other!

Sincerely,

Apreciado padre de familia o guardián:

Nuestra clase acaba de finalizar la segunda unidad del programa *"Making Meaning.®"* ¡A los niños les gustan mucho las historias que estamos leyendo! Durante esta unidad los niños siguieron practicando la estrategia de comprensión de *hacer conexiones* al escuchar y hablar acerca de las historias y al encontrar conexiones entre éstas y sus propias vidas. También, ellos contestaron preguntas que les ayudaron a entender mejor la historia que escucharon.

Durante esta unidad los niños también practicaron la destreza social de hablar entre si y de escucharse unos a otros. El escuchar con atención y el hablar con otros son destrezas que ayudan a los estudiantes a aprender y a que activamente formen parte de la comunidad de lectores. El ponerle atención a su niño cuando los dos hablan acerca de las historias es una manera poderosa de fomentar la habilidad de escuchar y de hablar de su niño.

Usted puede ayudar a que su niño haga conexiones personales con las historias. Antes de empezar a leer la historia, pídale a su niño que escuche y que se ponga a pensar en la historia para ver que parte de la historia es parecida a su vida. Mientras lee, pare de vez en cuando para hacer preguntas de esta clase:

- ¿Cómo crees que esta persona o animal se siente?

- ¿Alguna vez te ha sentido así? Hablemos de eso.

Otra manera de ayudar a que su niño se ponga a pensar en la historia en una forma más profunda es hacer preguntas mientras le está leyendo en voz alta, como:

- Hasta ahora, ¿qué ha pasado en la historia?

- ¿Qué crees que va ha pasar?

Diviértanse al leer, al hablar y al escucharse el uno al otro.

Sinceramente,

 Dear Parent or Guardian,

Our class just finished the third unit of the *Making Meaning®* program. During this unit, the students focused on using *retelling* as a strategy to help them understand what they read. Using the sequence of events to retell a story (remembering what happens first, next, etc.) is a way for readers to make sure the story makes sense to them. Retelling also helps readers talk about stories with other people.

You can help your child practice retelling by stopping from time to time while you read aloud to ask questions such as:

- What happened in the part of the story you just heard?

- What has happened in the story so far?

- What happens at the end of the story?

You can help your child learn how to retell stories by recalling parts of the story together after you read. If your child forgets parts of the story, reread the story and discuss what happened first, next, and how the story ended.

Have fun reading, retelling, and listening to each other!

Sincerely,

Apreciado padre de familia o guardián:

Nuestra clase acaba de finalizar la tercera unidad del programa "*Making Meaning.*®" Durante esta unidad los estudiantes se enfocaron en *volver a contar la historia* como una estrategia para ayudarles a entender lo que leen. El utilizar la secuencia de eventos para volver a contar una historia (recordar lo que sucedió primero, lo siguiente, etc.) es una de las cosas que los lectores pueden hacer para asegurarse que la historia tiene sentido para ellos. El volver a contar una historia también ayuda a los lectores a hablar cerca de las historias con otras personas.

Cuando estén leyendo en voz alta, usted puede ayudar a su niño a practicar a volver a contar la historia si para de vez en cuando y hace preguntas como:

- ¿Qué pasó en la parte de la historia que acabas de escuchar?

- ¿Qué ha pasado hasta ahora?

- ¿Qué pasa al final de la historia?

El recordar partes de la historia con su niño después de haberla leído, es una manera de ayudar a su niño a volver a contar la historia. Si a su niño se le olvida una parte de la historia, vuelva a leerla y hablen acerca de lo que pasa primero, lo que sigue y como acaba la historia.

Diviértanse al leer, al volver a contar la historia y al escucharse el uno al otro.

Sinceramente,

 Dear Parent or Guardian,

Our class finished the fourth unit of the *Making Meaning*® program. The students love the stories and poems we are reading! During this unit, the students visualized to make sense of the stories we read. *Visualizing* means making mental images while reading. Readers might imagine sights, sounds, smells, tastes, sensations, and emotions. *Visualizing* helps readers understand, remember, and enjoy reading.

The children also practiced the social skill of talking and listening to one another. Listening well and talking to others are skills that help students learn and become active members of the reading community. One powerful way to build your child's ability to listen and talk to others is to pay close attention to your child when the two of you talk about stories.

You can help your child practice visualizing by stopping every so often while reading aloud and asking questions such as:

· What did you see in your mind as I read to you?

· What words did you hear in the story that helped you create that picture in your mind?

In addition to stopping and discussing the story with your child, you might:

· Ask your child to close his or her eyes as you read and get a mental picture of the story.

· Give your child the opportunity to draw what he or she visualized, and then talk about the drawing.

Have fun reading, visualizing, talking, and listening to each other!

Sincerely,

Apreciado padre de familia o guardián:

Nuestra clase acaba de finalizar la cuarta unidad del programa *"Making Meaning.®"* ¡A los niños les gustan mucho las historias y poemas que estamos leyendo! Durante esta unidad los estudiantes visualizaron para poder entender las historias que leímos. *El visualizar* quiere decir que hacemos imágenes mentales mientras leemos. Los lectores pueden imaginarse sonidos, imágenes, olores, sabores, sensaciones y sentimientos. El visualizar ayuda a los lectores a entender, recordar y a disfrutar de la lectura.

Los niños también practicaron la destreza social de hablar entre si y de escucharse unos a otros. El escuchar con atención y el hablar con otros son destrezas que ayudan a los estudiantes a aprender y a formar parte activa de la comunidad de lectores. El ponerle atención a su niño cuando los dos hablan acerca de las historias es una manera poderosa de desarrollar su habilidad de escuchar y de hablar.

Cuando estén leyendo en voz alta, usted puede ayudarle a su niño a visualizar al parar de vez en cuando y hacer preguntas como:

- ¿Qué es lo que te viene a la mente cuando leo esto?

- ¿Qué palabras escuchaste en la historia que te ayudaron a crear esa imagen en la mente?

Además de parar y de hablar acerca de la historia con su niño, usted puede:

- Pedirle a su niño que cierre los ojos mientras usted lee y así pueda obtener una imagen mental de la historia.

- Darle a su niño la oportunidad de dibujar lo que ha visualizado y después pueden hablar acerca del dibujo.

Diviértanse al leer, al visualizar, al hablar y al escucharse el uno al otro.

Sinceramente,

Dear Parent or Guardian,

Our class just finished the fifth unit of the *Making Meaning®* program. During this unit, the students continued to use the sequence of events to retell stories they heard. They also used *wondering* to help them understand and enjoy stories. Wondering and asking questions about texts helps readers actively engage with stories and remember what they read. Socially, the students further developed their ability to share ideas with one another.

Before reading aloud to your child, look at the cover of the book together, read the title, and talk about what your child is wondering about the story. You can support your child's understanding by stopping every so often while reading to ask and discuss questions such as:

- What has happened so far in the story?

- What are you wondering about the story right now?

- What do you think might happen next?

Talking about stories after you read together can help deepen your child's understanding. I hope you and your child continue to delight in reading!

Sincerely,

Apreciado padre de familia o guardián:

Nuestra clase acaba de finalizar la quinta unidad del programa *"Making Meaning.®"* Durante esta unidad los estudiantes continuaron utilizando la secuencia de eventos para volver a contar la historia que escucharon. También utilizaron *el hacer preguntas* para entender y disfrutar las historias. El hacer preguntas acerca del texto involucra activamente al lector con la historia y le ayuda a recordar lo que leyó. Socialmente, los estudiantes desarrollaron aún más la habilidad de compartir entre si.

Antes de empezar a leerle a su niño en voz alta, muéstrele la cubierta del libro, léale el título y hablen acerca de las preguntas que se le vienen a la mente a raíz del libro. Usted puede ayudarle a su niño a entender la historia, al parar la lectura de vez en cuando para hablar y hacer preguntas como las siguientes:

- ¿Qué ha pasado en la historia hasta ahora?

- En este momento, ¿qué preguntas tienes acerca de la historia?

- ¿Qué crees que puede suceder después de esto?

El hablar acerca de las historias después de haberlas leído juntos puede ayudarle al niño a entender lo que leyeron más a fondo. Espero que usted y su niño continúen deleitándose con la lectura.

Sinceramente,

 Dear Parent or Guardian,

Our class just finished the sixth unit of the *Making Meaning*® program. During this unit, the students explored differences between fiction and nonfiction texts and used the strategy of *making connections* to their own lives to help them make sense of nonfiction. Nonfiction texts give readers true information about a topic and include not only books, but also other kinds of informational texts, such as magazine articles, recipes, baseball cards, menus, and game directions. The students also explored some of the features often found in nonfiction texts, such as tables of contents, indexes, photos, maps, and diagrams.

You can support your child's reading life at home by:

- Collecting nonfiction materials that are interesting to your child

- Talking about what you both learn from the nonfiction you read together

- Noticing and talking about nonfiction texts you encounter throughout the day, such as street signs, food labels, and park or playground rules

You can help your child make connections to nonfiction texts before reading by talking about what your child already knows about the topic.

While reading, you can help your child make connections by stopping every so often to talk about how what you're reading reminds your child of things he or she has seen or experienced.

I hope you and your child enjoy learning together about topics of interest to both of you. Happy reading!

Sincerely,

Apreciado padre de familia o guardián:

Nuestra clase acaba de finalizar la sexta unidad del programa "*Making Meaning.*®" Durante esta unidad los estudiantes exploraron las diferencias entre los textos de ficción y no ficción y utilizaron la estrategia de *hacer conexiones* con sus propias vidas para que les ayudara a entender el género de no ficción. Los textos del género de no ficción le brindan al lector información veraz acerca de un tema e incluye no solo libros sino también otra clase de textos informativos como: artículos de revistas, recetas, tarjetas para coleccionar, menús y direcciones de un juego. Los estudiantes también exploraron algunos aspectos que frecuentemente se encuentran en los textos de no ficción, como lo son: índices, listas de contenido, fotos, mapas y diagramas.

En casa usted puede apoyar la lectura de su niño al hacer lo siguiente:

- Coleccionar textos de no ficción que sean de interés para su niño.

- Hablar acerca de lo que ambos aprendieron al leer juntos el texto de no ficción.

- Al fijarse y hablar de los textos de no ficción que encuentran durante el día como las señales de calles, los rótulos de las comidas y las reglas de los parques.

Usted puede ayudarle a su niño a hacer conexiones con los textos de no ficción, si antes de empezar a leer hablan acerca de lo que su niño ya sabe acerca del tema.

Cuando estén leyendo juntos usted le puede ayudar a su niño a hacer conexiones al parar de vez en cuando para hablar acerca de lo que están leyendo y como eso le recuerda a su niño cosas que ya ha experimentado.

Espero que el aprender juntos acerca de temas de mutuo interés sea divertido. ¡Feliz lectura!

Sinceramente,

 Dear Parent or Guardian,

Our class just finished the seventh unit of the *Making Meaning®* program. During this unit, the students continued to hear and discuss nonfiction texts. They talked about what they learned from the nonfiction texts, and wondered about the topics they heard about during the read-alouds. *Wondering* about a topic before, during, and after reading helps readers actively engage with the text and make sense of what they are reading.

You can support your child's reading life at home by collecting nonfiction texts that interest your child, and talking about what your child is learning from the nonfiction that you read aloud or that your child reads independently.

Before reading a nonfiction text to your child, it is helpful to ask questions such as:

- What do you think you know about [seals]?

- What do you wonder about [seals]?

Consider stopping every so often during the reading to ask what your child is learning and what he or she is still wondering about.

After reading you might ask questions such as:

- What did you learn about [seals] from this book?

- What did you learn that surprised you?

- What are you still wondering about [seals]?

I hope you and your child continue to enjoy reading together. Happy reading!

Sincerely,

Apreciado padre de familia o guardián:

Nuestra clase acaba de finalizar la séptima unidad del programa "*Making Meaning.®*" Durante esta unidad los estudiantes siguieron escuchando y hablando acerca de textos de no ficción. Ellos hablaron acerca de lo que aprendieron de los textos y artículos de no ficción y formularon preguntas referentes a la materia que escucharon durante la sesión de lectura en voz alta. *El hacer preguntas acerca de un tema, antes, durante y después de la lectura*, ayuda a que los lectores se involucren activamente con el texto y que entiendan lo que están leyendo.

Usted puede apoyar la lectura que su niño hace en la casa al coleccionar textos y libros de no ficción que sean de interés para su niño. También puede ayudar al hablar con su niño acerca de lo que aprende al leer solo y al escucharle a usted cuando le lee en voz alta del género de no ficción.

Es de gran beneficio, si antes de leerle textos de no ficción a su niño le hace preguntas como:

- ¿Qué sabes acerca de (las focas)?

- ¿Qué preguntas tienes acerca de (las focas)?

Considere parar la lectura en voz alta para preguntarle a su niño lo que está aprendiendo y si aún tiene alguna duda.

Después de haber leído hágale a su niño preguntas como:

- ¿En este libro qué aprendiste acerca de (las focas)?

- ¿Qué aprendiste que te sorprendió?

- ¿Qué preguntas tienes todavía acerca de (las focas)?

Espero que continúen disfrutando de la lectura que comparten juntos. ¡Feliz lectura!

Sinceramente,

Dear Parent or Guardian,

Our class just finished the eighth unit of the *Making Meaning*® program. During this unit, the students continued to hear and discuss nonfiction books. They used wondering, making connections, and visualizing to help them make sense of texts. They also *explored text features* often found in nonfiction, such as tables of contents, indexes, chapter headings, and photographs.

You can support your child's reading life at home by collecting nonfiction texts that interest your child and by talking about what you both learn from the nonfiction you read together.

Before reading nonfiction it can be helpful to ask your child:

· What do you think you know about [snow]?

· What do you wonder about [snow]?

Consider stopping every so often during the reading to ask what your child is learning and still wondering about.

After reading nonfiction it can be helpful to ask:

· What did you find out about [snow] from this book?

I hope you and your child enjoy learning together about topics of interest to both of you. Happy reading!

Sincerely,

Apreciado padre de familia o guardián:

Nuestra clase acaba de finalizar la octava unidad del programa *"Making Meaning.®"* Durante esta unidad los estudiantes siguieron escuchando y hablando acerca de textos de no ficción. Para poder entender estos textos ellos utilizaron el hacer preguntas, hacer conexiones y visualización. También exploraron algunos aspectos que frecuentemente se encuentran en el género de no ficción, como: listas de contenido, índices, encabezamientos de los capítulos y fotografías.

Usted puede apoyar a la lectura que su niño hace en la casa al:

- Coleccionar textos y libros de no ficción que sean de interés para su niño.

- Hablar con su niño acerca de lo que ustedes están aprendiendo de los libros y textos de no ficción que leen juntos.

Es de gran ayuda, si antes de leerle textos de no ficción a su niño le hace preguntas como:

- ¿Qué sabes acerca de (la nieve)?

- ¿Qué preguntas tienes acerca de (la nieve)?

Considere parar periódicamente la lectura en voz alta para preguntarle a su niño lo que está aprendiendo y si aún tiene alguna duda.

Puede ayudar si después de haber leído le hace a su niño preguntas como:

- Al leer este libro, ¿qué aprendiste acerca de (la nieve)?

Espero que usted y su niño disfruten el aprender juntos acerca de temas que son de interés para ustedes dos. ¡Feliz lectura!

Sinceramente,

 Dear Parent or Guardian,

We have come to the end of our school year and the end of the *Making Meaning*® grade 1 reading comprehension program. The children have shown great enthusiasm for the variety of texts we read aloud and the conversations we had about reading. They eagerly explored a number of reading comprehension strategies, including: retelling, making connections, visualizing, wondering, and exploring text features. The use of these comprehension strategies strengthened the children's reading comprehension skills and should continue to be a source of support for them for years to come.

In the last unit of the *Making Meaning* program, the students thought about the books and stories they liked this year and considered the strategies that helped them understand the stories.

While reading with your child this summer, you might reflect on the reading comprehension strategies your child used this year. This will help your child continue to use the reading comprehension strategies.

Remember that the more your child reads, the more successful he or she will be as a reader. During the summer, read aloud to your child and encourage your child to read independently every day.

I hope you have a great summer filled with books, fun, and enjoyment.

Sincerely,

Apreciado padre de familia o guardián:

Hemos llegado al final del año escolar y al final del programa de comprensión de lectura para el primer grado de *"Making Meaning®."* Los niños han mostrado mucho entusiasmo por la variedad de textos que leímos en voz alta y por las conversaciones que tuvimos acerca de la lectura. Ellos exploraron afanosamente un número de estrategias de comprensión de lectura, incluyendo: el volver a contar la historia, hacer conexiones, visualizar, el hacer preguntas, y el explorar los aspectos del texto. El uso de estas estrategias de comprensión fortalece las destrezas de comprensión de lectura que los niños tienen y esto será una fuente de apoyo para ellos por muchos años.

En la última unidad del programa *"Making Meaning®"* los estudiantes se pusieron a pensar en los libros y las historias que les gustaron durante el año y consideraron las estrategias que les ayudaron a entender esas historias.

Este verano mientras lee con su niño, puede reflexionar sobre la estrategia de comprensión de lectura que su niño utilizó este año. Esto le ayudará a su niño a continuar utilizando las estrategias de comprensión de lectura que aprendió y será de mucho apoyo cuando su niño entre al segundo grado.

Recuerde que entre más lea su niño, más éxito va a tener como lector. Durante el verano, léale en voz alta y aliéntelo a que lea individualmente a diario.

Espero que tengan un gran verano lleno de libros, diversiones y gozo.

Sinceramente,

Index

from *Raptors!* by Lisa McCourt

Index

Index from *Planet Reader: Raptors!* by Lisa McCourt. Scholastic Inc./Troll Communications. Copyright © 1997 by Lisa McCourt. Reprinted by permission.

Table of Contents

Teacher's Facilitation Bookmark

After photocopying this page, cut along the heavy dotted line and fold along the light dotted line. Laminate if you wish.

Making Meaning
SECOND EDITION

*Strategies That Build
Comprehension and Community*

Prompts

to get students talking to one another

"[Miguel] is going to talk now. Let's all turn and look at him, and get ready to comment on what he says."

"What would you like to add to what [Ann] said?"

"Do you agree or disagree with what [Jeremy] said? Why?"

"What question can we ask [LaToya]?"

Making Meaning
SECOND EDITION

*Strategies That Build
Comprehension and Community*

Tips

for facilitating discussion

Use wait-time. Give the students 5–10 seconds to think before calling on anyone to respond.

Keep the discussion moving. It is not necessary to call on every student who raises his hand.

Use "Turn to Your Partner" when you notice only a few students contributing to a discussion, or when many students want to contribute at the same time.

Avoid repeating or paraphrasing. Encourage the students to listen carefully to one another (not just to you) by not repeating or paraphrasing what you hear them say. If the students can't hear the person speaking, encourage them to ask the speaker to repeat what she said.

Encourage use of prompts. Have the students use "I agree with [Rosa] because…," "I disagree with [Kim] because…," and "In addition to what [Allan] said, I think…."

Resource Sheet for IDR Conferences

General questions you can ask to probe student thinking:

▸ *Why did you choose this book?*

▸ *Why do you like/dislike this book?*

▸ *What kinds of books do you want to read?*

Genre-specific questions you can ask:

Fiction

▸ *What is this story about?*

▸ *What has happened so far?*

▸ *What do you know about the character(s)?*

▸ *What part have you found interesting or surprising? Why?*

▸ *What are you wondering about?*

▸ *What do you visualize (see/hear/feel) as you read these words?*

▸ *What do you think will happen next?*

Nonfiction/Expository

▸ *What is this [book/article] about?*

▸ (Read the information on the back cover.) *What have you found out about that so far?*

▸ (Look at the table of contents.) *What do you think you will find out about* _____ *in this book?*

▸ *What have you learned from reading this article?*

▸ *What's something interesting you've read so far?*

▸ *What are you wondering about?*

▸ *What do you expect to learn about as you continue to read?*

▸ *What information does this [diagram/table/graph/other text feature] give you?*

Poetry

▸ *What is this poem about?*

▸ *What do you visualize (see/hear/feel) as you read these words?*

▸ *What do you think the poet means by* _____ *?*

IDR Conference Notes

Student: _____ Date: _____

Book title: _____

EVIDENCE: _____

1 ▶ **Ask: What is your book about so far?**

Is the student able to describe the book? | YES |
| |

2 ▶ **Have the student read a passage silently, then read it aloud for you.**

Does the student: | YES |

Attend to meaning? | |

Pause / reread if having difficulty? | |

Read most words accurately? | |

Try to make sense of unfamiliar language? | |

Read fluently? | |

3 ▶ **Ask: What is the part you just read about?**

Does the student recall what's important in the passage? | YES |
| |

If the student has difficulty, have him/her reread the passage and repeat Step ▶3.
If the student doesn't understand after the second reading, go to Step ▷4. Otherwise, go to Step ▶4.

4 ▷ **If the student doesn't understand after the second reading, ask yourself:**

Is the difficulty caused by:

Lack of background knowledge? | |

Unfamiliar vocabulary? | |

Too-difficult text (lack of fluency)? | |

Not using an appropriate comprehension strategy? | |

4 ▶ **Ask: What do you think will happen, or what do you think you will learn, as you keep reading?**

5 ▶ **Ask yourself: Is the student using comprehension strategies to make sense of text?**

5 ▷ **Intervene using one or more of the following:**
- Define unfamiliar words.
- Provide necessary background knowledge.
- Suggest an appropriate strategy on the "Reading Comprehension Strategies" chart and have the student reread again, starting at an earlier place in the text.
- Ask clarifying questions about the text.
- Help the student find a more appropriately leveled book.

Next steps:

Making Meaning
SECOND EDITION
Reorder Information

Kindergarten

Complete Classroom Package   MM2-CPK

Contents: Teacher's Manual, Orientation Handbook and DVDs, and 27 trade books

Available separately:

Classroom materials without trade books	MM2-TPK
Teacher's Manual	MM2-TMK
Trade book set (27 books)	MM2-TBSK

Grade 1

Complete Classroom Package   MM2-CP1

Contents: Teacher's Manual, Orientation Handbook and DVDs, Assessment Resource Book, and 28 trade books

Available separately:

Classroom materials without trade books	MM2-TP1
Teacher's Manual	MM2-TM1
Assessment Resource Book	MM2-AB1
Trade book set (28 books)	MM2-TBS1

Grade 2

Complete Classroom Package   MM2-CP2

Contents: Teacher's Manual, Orientation Handbook and DVDs, class set (25 Student Response Books, Assessment Resource Book), and 29 trade books

Available separately:

Classroom materials without trade books	MM2-TP2
Teacher's Manual	MM2-TM2
Replacement class set	MM2-RCS2
CD-ROM Grade 2 Reproducible Materials	MM2-CDR2
Trade book set (29 books)	MM2-TBS2

Grade 3

Complete Classroom Package   MM2-CP3

Contents: Teacher's Manual (2 volumes), Orientation Handbook and DVDs, class set (25 Student Response Books, Assessment Resource Book), and 26 trade books

Available separately:

Classroom materials without trade books	MM2-TP3
Teacher's Manual, vol. 1	MM2-TM3-V1
Teacher's Manual, vol. 2	MM2-TM3-V2
Replacement class set	MM2-RCS3
CD-ROM Grade 3 Reproducible Materials	MM2-CDR3
Trade book set (26 books)	MM2-TBS3

Grade 4

Complete Classroom Package   MM2-CP4

Contents: Teacher's Manual (2 volumes), Orientation Handbook and DVDs, class set (30 Student Response Books, Assessment Resource Book), and 24 trade books

Available separately:

Classroom materials without trade books	MM2-TP4
Teacher's Manual, vol. 1	MM2-TM4-V1
Teacher's Manual, vol. 2	MM2-TM4-V2
Replacement class set	MM2-RCS4
CD-ROM Grade 4 Reproducible Materials	MM2-CDR4
Trade book set (24 books)	MM2-TBS4

Grade 5

Complete Classroom Package   MM2-CP5

Contents: Teacher's Manual (2 volumes), Orientation Handbook and DVDs, class set (30 Student Response Books, Assessment Resource Book), and 19 trade books

Available separately:

Classroom materials without trade books	MM2-TP5
Teacher's Manual, vol. 1	MM2-TM5-V1
Teacher's Manual, vol. 2	MM2-TM5-V2
Replacement class set	MM2-RCS5
CD-ROM Grade 5 Reproducible Materials	MM2-CDR5
Trade book set (19 books)	MM2-TBS5

Grade 6

Complete Classroom Package   MM2-CP6

Contents: Teacher's Manual (2 volumes), Orientation Handbook and DVDs, class set (30 Student Response Books, Assessment Resource Book), and 18 trade books

Available separately:

Classroom materials without trade books	MM2-TP6
Teacher's Manual, vol. 1	MM2-TM6-V1
Teacher's Manual, vol. 2	MM2-TM6-V2
Replacement class set	MM2-RCS5
CD-ROM Grade 6 Reproducible Materials	MM2-CDR6
Trade book set (18 books)	MM2-TBS6

Ordering Information:

To order call 800.666.7270 * fax 510.842.0348
log on to devstu.org * e-mail pubs@devstu.org

Or Mail Your Order to:

Developmental Studies Center * Publications Department
2000 Embarcadero, Suite 305 * Oakland, CA 94606-5300

DEVELOPMENTAL
STUDIES CENTER™